DELIBERATIVE POLITICS IN ACTION

"Deliberative politics" refers to the role of conversation and arguments in politics. Until recently discussion of deliberative politics took place almost exclusively among political philosophers, but many questions raised in this philosophical discussion cry out for empirical investigation. This book provides the first extended empirical study of deliberative politics, addressing in particular questions of the preconditions and consequences of high-level deliberation. Using parliamentary debates in Germany, Switzerland, the United Kingdom, and the United States as an empirical base, the authors measure the level of deliberation by constructing a "Discourse Quality Index." As deliberative politics moves to the forefront of political theory, this book makes an important contribution to deliberative democracy.

JÜRG STEINER is Professor Emeritus of Politial Science at the University of North Carolina at Chapel Hill and at the University of Bern. In the academic year 2003–4 he was also Swiss Chair at the European University Institute, Florence.

ANDRÉ BÄCHTIGER is Swiss Chair Fellow at the European University Institute, Florence.

MARKUS SPÖRNDLI is a researcher at the University of Bern, Switzerland.

MARCO R. STEENBERGEN is Associate Professor of Political Science at the University of North Carolina at Chapel Hill.

D1596311

THEORIES OF INSTITUTIONAL DESIGN

Series Editor
Robert E. Goodin
Research School of Social Sciences
Australian National University

Advisory Editors
Brian Barry, Russell Hardin, Carole Pateman, Barry Weingast
Stephen Elkin, Claus Offe, Susan Rose-Ackerman

Social scientists have rediscovered institutions. They have been increasingly concerned with the myriad ways in which social and political institutions shape the patterns of individual interactions which produce social phenomena. They are equally concerned with the ways in which those institutions emerge from such interactions.

This series is devoted to the exploration of the more normative aspects of these issues. What makes one set of institutions better than another? How, if at all, might we move from the less desirable set of institutions to a more desirable set? Alongside the questions of what institutions we would design, if we were designing them afresh, are pragmatic questions of how we can best get from here to there: from our present institutions to new revitalized ones.

Theories of institutional design is insistently multidisciplinary and interdisciplinary, both in the institutions on which it focuses, and in the methodologies used to study them. There are interesting sociological questions to be asked about legal institutions, interesting legal questions to be asked about economic institutions, and interesting social, economic, and legal questions to be asked about political institutions. By juxtaposing these approaches in print, this series aims to enrich normative discourse surrounding important issues of designing and redesigning, shaping and reshaping the social, political, and economic institutions of contemporary society.

Other books in this series
Robert E. Goodin (editor), *The Theory of Institutional Design*
Brent Fisse and John Braithwaite, *Corporations, Crime, and Accountability*
Itai Sened, *The Political Institution of Private Property*
Bo Rothstein, *Just Institutions Matter*
Jon Elster, Claus Offe, and Ulrich Preuss, *Institutional Design in Post-Communist Societies: Rebuilding the Ship at Sea*
Mark Bovens, *The Quest for Responsibility*
Geoffrey Brennan and Alan Hamlin, *Democratic Devices and Desires*
Adrienne Heritier, *Policy-Making and Diversity in Europe: Escape from Deadlock*
Eric Patashnik, *Putting Trust in the US Budget: Federal Trust Funds and the Politics of Commitment*
Benjamin Reilly, *Democracy in Divided Societies: Electoral Engineering for Conflict Management*
Huib Pellikuan and Robert van der Veen, *Environmental Dilemmas and Policy Design*
John S. Dryzek and Leslie Holmes, *Post-Communist Democratization: Political Discourses across Thirteen Countries*
Jonathan G. S. Koppell, *The Politics of Quasi-Government: Hybrid Organizations and the Dynamics of Bureaucratic Control*

DELIBERATIVE POLITICS IN ACTION

Analyzing Parliamentary Discourse

JÜRG STEINER, ANDRÉ BÄCHTIGER, MARKUS SPÖRNDLI, AND MARCO R. STEENBERGEN

CAMBRIDGE
UNIVERSITY PRESS

PUBLISHED BY THE PRESS SYNDICATE OF THE UNIVERSITY OF CAMBRIDGE
The Pitt Building, Trumpington Street, Cambridge, United Kingdom

CAMBRIDGE UNIVERSITY PRESS
The Edinburgh Building, Cambridge, CB2 2RU, UK
40 West 20th Street, New York, NY 10011–4211, USA
477 Williamstown Road, Port Melbourne, VIC 3207, Australia
Ruiz de Alarcón 13, 28014 Madrid, Spain
Dock House, The Waterfront, Cape Town 8001, South Africa

http://www.cambridge.org

First published 2004

Printed in the United Kingdom at the University Press, Cambridge

Typeface Minion 10.5/12 pt.   *System* LaTeX 2_ε [TB]

A catalogue record for this book is available from the British Library

Library of Congress Cataloguing in Publication data
Deliberative Politics in Action: Analyzing Parliamentary Discourse / Jürg Steiner . . . [et al.].
    p.   cm. – (Theories of institutional design)
Includes bibliographical references and index.
ISBN 0 521 82871 6 – ISBN 0 521 53564 6 (pb.)
1. Communication in politics – Cross-cultural studies.   2. Representative government and
representation – Cross-cultural studies.   3. Discourse analysis – Political aspects.
I. Steiner, Jürg.   II. Series.
JA85.D4   2004
328′01′4 – dc22   2004051891

ISBN 0 521 82871 6 hardback
ISBN 0 521 53564 6 paperback

Contents

Acknowledgments

We acknowledge the generous financial support of the Swiss National Science Foundation. Special thanks go to Wolf Linder and David Lowery who have attentively followed the project from the very beginning to the very end. In various phases of our research, we received helpful suggestions from Rudy Andeweg, Klaus Armingeon, Matthijs Bogaards, Pamela Conover, Rainer Doebert, Robert Goodin, Jürgen Habermas, Adrienne Heritier, Liesbet Hooghe, Katja Kleinberg, Hanspeter Kriesi, Arend Lijphart, Gary Marks, Donald Searing, and Philippe Schmitter. We are grateful for the stimulating discussions in seminars on deliberation at the University of Bern, the University of North Carolina at Chapel Hill, the European University Institute in Florence, and the Oslo Summer School in Comparative Social Science Studies.

Introduction

The research questions

This book is about deliberation in parliamentary institutions. It presents data on the institutional antecedents as well as the consequences of legislative deliberation in four countries: Germany, Switzerland, the United Kingdom, and the United States. Our goal is to connect the literature on deliberation, which has developed almost exclusively within the field of political philosophy, to a theoretical and empirical understanding of political institutions. Our main argument will be that talk matters: the nature of speech acts inside legislatures is a function of institutional rules and mechanisms, and bears an influence on political outcomes that transcends those rules and mechanisms. Our main vehicle of analysis is a Discourse Quality Index (DQI), which measures the quality of deliberation.

To give a feeling for the empirical data to be presented in the main body of the book, we open with two illustrations, one of a high quality of deliberation and one of a low quality of deliberation. The former example comes from a debate in the Swiss Council of States on amending the constitution with a language article. In the committee stage German-speaking René Rhinow made the proposal to establish in the amendment the abstract principle of freedom of language. He withdrew his proposal in the plenary session in deference to the opposition of many French speakers, referring to the importance of peaceful relations among the language groups. From a deliberative perspective it is important that Rhinow was willing to listen with respect to the arguments of the French speakers and that he did not withdraw his proposal as part of a bargaining deal in exchange for the votes of the French speakers in other matters important to him. Rather, he based the withdrawal of his proposal on his concern for language peace. An extreme example of a low quality of deliberation occurred in an abortion debate in the German Bundestag when Claus Jäger interrupted another member of parliament, saying: "You deserve a slap in the face for that!" With this rude remark Jäger lacked any respect for other arguments; in this way he signaled that he was unwilling to yield to the force of the better argument. He denied that other arguments had any merits at all so that it was not worth his while to consider them in any serious way. The speech acts of Rhinow and Jäger are at the extreme ends of our Discourse Quality Index with most speech acts being somewhere in between.

At the beginning of the book we put forward two concrete illustrations in order to make clear at the outset that we are addressing the issue of deliberative politics in an empirical way. We wish to investigate the level of discourse quality in the parliamentary debates of several countries and to see how variation in discourse quality can be systematically explained by its preconditions and consequences. Until very recently, the discussion on deliberative politics took place almost entirely among political philosophers. Within this philosophical discussion the following questions are at the center: (1) How is the deliberative model of democracy to be defined and how is it different from other models of democracy? (2) Is deliberation a good thing in itself? (3) Has deliberation beneficial consequences, in particular for social justice? (4) What are the favorable conditions for deliberation? The last two questions cry out for empirical investigation, and it is precisely our intention to tackle them in this book.

We address several audiences in this book. First, we address political philosophers by formulating our DQI in a theoretically justifiable way, linking it in particular to the ideas of Jürgen Habermas. Because of this theoretical foundation, empirical data generated using the DQI should be of interest to political philosophers. They can inform future philosophical debates about the preconditions for and merits of deliberation.

Our second audience consists of the scholars of political institutions. Much of the theoretical understanding of institutions is based on two traditions – rational choice theory and psycho-sociological models of norms. The former tradition typically views legislators' preferences as fixed and generally focuses on the way in which institutional rules translate those preferences into formal outcomes (e.g. votes). The latter tradition focuses on the manner in which legislators adopt behavioral norms and how those norms influence behavior. In both traditions, strong emphasis is given to voting. Of course, voting is an important aspect of legislative behavior, and part of this book is concerned with that topic. But much (if not most) of what legislators do is talk. Is such talk cheap, as some have argued? Perhaps, but we believe this cannot be determined in the absence of empirical data. This book takes political talk in legislatures seriously, asking if and when such talk is politically consequential. In this manner, we seek to introduce a neglected aspect of legislative institutions – deliberation.

Our third audience consists of those interested in comparative politics. We believe that the institutional antecedents of deliberation are best studied from a comparative perspective, which provides better leverage over the key predictors. One institutional aspect is particularly strongly related to the comparative literature, namely our distinction between consensus and competitive systems, which relates back to the literature on consociationalism. Thus consociational scholars should have a particular interest in our findings.

The senior author has himself a longstanding interest in consociational theory going back to the creation of the theory in the 1960s. Until now, deliberative and consociational theories have hardly been linked at all. We will argue that the two theories can be linked in a fruitful way. The consociational model stands in contrast to the competitive model, well illustrated by the Westminster model. The latter is characterized by the winner-takes-all system for parliamentary elections, the winning party forming the cabinet, weak veto power for minority groups, and a strong centralization of the state. The consociational model, by contrast, uses proportionality for parliamentary elections, grand coalitions for cabinet formation, strong veto power for minorities, and federalism. The consociational model is often recommended for deeply divided societies which are encouraged to use its institutional features. Such recommendations, however, are too mechanical and even somewhat naïve since they neglect the *cultural* aspect of how political actors interact and speak with each other in these consociational institutions. To be sure, this cultural aspect was part of consociational theorizing from the beginning, but merely in the vague expression "spirit of accommodation." The *intellectual history* of the current project is that the initial impetus was to come to terms in a theoretically grounded way with the phenomenon of a "spirit of accommodation." What exactly does this concept involve? As we read the consociational literature, a "spirit of accommodation" means to a large extent prudent leaders bargaining for compromises with prudent leaders of other societal groups. But there is more to a "spirit of accommodation," namely, something captured in the philosophical literature by the concept of deliberation.

Theoretically, we make the causal linkages differently than is traditionally done by consociational scholars. Their key dependent variable is democratic stability, their independent variables, on the one hand, institutions and, on the other hand, the talk culture[1] known as the spirit of accommodation. Graphically depicted it looks like this:

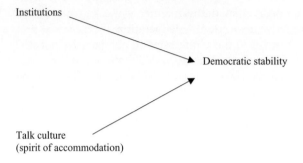

Institutions

Democratic stability

Talk culture
(spirit of accommodation)

For our current project, the ultimate dependent variable is political outcome, in particular with regard to the aspect of social justice. We then investigate how these outcomes depend on the talk culture of deliberation and how the level of deliberation in turn depends on institutional settings. In addition to institutional features, we also investigate to what extent the polarization of the issues under discussion influences the level of deliberation (for this aspect see figure 4.1).

Institutions   →   Talk culture (deliberation)   →   Political outcomes

In chapter 1 we will elaborate how, starting with consociational literature, we arrived at the current project on deliberation. In chapter 2, we summarize the philosophical literature on deliberation. The concept of deliberation is so broad that it can be usefully applied to any political system. Thus, although the starting point of the current project is consociational theory, our immersion in the philosophical literature on deliberation has allowed us to greatly broaden our research interest beyond consociational theory. We are now squarely involved in this broad literature on deliberation, and our research questions have to be seen in this broader context. We still wish to make a contribution to consociational theory, but our ambition is to a make a contribution to the discussion of the deliberative model at large. At the core of the deliberative model is the idea that all arguments in a political discussion are respected and that the force of the better argument in terms of the common good prevails. Deliberative politics contrasts with bargaining where arguments are used in a strategic sense to realize the personal interests of the individual political actors. Instruments to attain a bargain are threats

---

[1] In German there is the word "Gesprächskultur" that captures nicely how people talk to each other. Talk culture is a somewhat clumsy translation.

of punishment and promises of reward, and the actors make cost-benefit analyses in order to determine whether they should enter into a bargain.

In chapter 3, as already mentioned, we develop our Discourse Quality Index (DQI) to measure the level of deliberation. There is disagreement among political philosophers on what exactly constitutes deliberation. For the construction of our index, we follow closely the deliberative model developed by Habermas that has inspired much of the interest in and debate about deliberative politics. The success of our research, however, should not be judged on whether we defend Habermas's model in a compelling way. This is not our intention at all. We are not philosophers, but empirically oriented political scientists, and our research interest is not to defend the Habermasian model but rather to establish in an empirical way the preconditions of a high-quality discourse and its consequences for policy outcomes. Our first task was to get an empirical handle on the Habermasian model. We broke down the model into its key elements, such as broad participation, justification of arguments, references to the common good, respect for the arguments of others, and willingness to change one's preferences. To code these various elements of the deliberative model needs a sophisticated interpretation of the entire decision situation and its context. It was not simply a matter of making a list, for example, of respectful terms and to count the number of these terms in the various speeches. One and the same term, depending on the context, may indicate quite different levels of respect, so that each coding decision has to take account of the context in which a term is uttered. The same is true for the coding of the other elements of the deliberative model. Despite this interpretative nature of the coding procedures, we attained high inter-coder reliability. To our knowledge, ours is the first effort to submit coding decisions on the deliberative model to reliability tests.

In chapter 4, we develop the hypotheses about our two main research topics: (1) the favorable conditions for a high-quality discourse, and (2) the influence of a high-quality discourse on the policy outcome. To address these two topics, we take as our units of analysis debates in plenary sessions and committee meetings of parliaments. Why debates in parliament? First, parliament is the place where, according to democratic theory, the representatives of the people are supposed to debate the crucial issues of their country. We will ask to what extent reality corresponds to this normative idea. Second, there is much cross-national institutional variation between parliaments, and there is also much institutional variation within individual parliaments; such variation allows the investigation of the impact of different institutional settings on discourse quality. Third, parliaments usually have good records of their debates, which is a great practical help for doing the actual research. We acknowledge, however, that in a later phase of our research it will also be necessary to investigate debates in the wider public sphere, which is so important for deliberative theorists. For them, opinion formation among friends, neighbors, at the workplace, in voluntary associations, on the internet, and elsewhere in the public sphere is crucial for the democratic quality of a society.

With regard to the first research topic, the favorable conditions for high-quality discourse, we unpack the consociational model into its key elements: for example, whether cabinet formation is by grand coalition or by a majority-opposition pattern. Another variable unpacked from the consociational model is the number and strength of veto points for minorities. We also include variables that are less central to the consociational model but are quite important for the comparative study of institutions: for example, the difference between a presidential and a parliamentary system and the corresponding difference in party discipline. We also look at the differences between first and second chambers of parliament and between plenary sessions and committee meetings. With regard to the issues under discussion, we ask to what extent they polarize members of parliament. In order to relate such variables to the quality of the discourse of a parliamentary debate, we anchor our hypotheses in the broad literature of new institutionalism, taking our insights from a combination of rational institutionalism, sociological institutionalism, and historical institutionalism. We expect that members of parliament pursue their individual preferences to a large extent but that they are also sensitive to the prevailing social norms in parliamentary settings so that they follow rules of appropriateness. What the individual preferences and the prevailing norms are in specific parliamentary situations has to be seen in a historical perspective with an emphasis on the path dependency of parliamentary behavior. Our approach is actor-centered, with the assumption that behavior is always constrained to some extent, but not completely determined so that there is always some room for choice. With this theoretical approach to the explanation of variation in the discourse quality of parliamentary debates, we cast the net for our first research topic very broadly in investigating the potential explanatory power of new institutionalism for the behavior of political actors. In this sense, investigating the first research question should also be seen as a contribution to the general literature on new institutionalism.

With regard to the second research topic, the influence of a high-quality discourse on the policy outcome, we distinguish a procedural and a substantive aspect. For the procedural aspect, we examine whether a high-quality discourse increases the probability of unanimous decisions. For the substantive aspect, we investigate whether a high-quality discourse increases the level of social justice in the sense that the most disadvantaged in society are particularly helped.

In chapter 5 we test the hypotheses for the first research topic, for which we need enough variation in the independent variables. We attain this goal in investigating parliamentary debates in Germany, Switzerland, the United Kingdom, and the United States. Chapter 6 presents the results for the second research topic. Here the discourse quality becomes the independent variable, and for the research design it is important to have debates with enough variation in the discourse quality with all other variables being kept as constant as possible, so that the effect of discourse quality on the policy outcome can be established. Debates from the German Conference Committee fulfill these criteria in an optimal way; this committee has the task of mediating between the two parliamentary chambers. We try to present the results in chapters 5 and 6 as much as possible in a non-technical sense so that they are also accessible to readers without much statistical background.[2]

---

[2] For the more technical aspects of the analyses we refer readers to the website of our research project: www.ipw.unibe.ch/discourse.

1

Institutions and behavior: the example of consociational theory

In its intellectual history, this book evolved from an interest in consociational theory and an increasing dissatisfaction with the integration of the behavior aspect into the theory. As consociational theory moved from studies of single countries like the Netherlands, Belgium, Switzerland, and Austria to the analysis of a large number of countries all over the world, the emphasis shifted increasingly to the institutional aspect. How political actors interact and speak with each other in consociational institutions was more and more neglected. In this opening chapter we use consociational theory as an illustration to show how the *culture* of how politicians interact and speak with each other is an important element that must be integrated into any institutional theory. Our basic argument is that speech is not cheap but may very well matter in many important theoretical ways (Noel 1990).

While we illustrate this argument for consociational theory, it also applies to other institutional theories. As we discuss in greater detail in chapter 4, much institutional research to date draws on two intellectual traditions. On the one hand, rational choice theories typically focus on a logic of consequentialism, which assumes that political actors seek the most efficient means to desired ends (Risse 2000). Institutional rules and structures are formulated to aid in this process. On the other hand, sociological theories frequently postulate a logic of appropriateness. In this view, institutions create behavioral norms that guide the actions of politicians (Risse 2000). We do not deny the importance of the insights that these perspectives offer, but we believe that both underestimate the importance of speech acts.[1] That is,

---

[1] There is an important exception to this within the rational choice literature. Over the past decade, Austen-Smith (1995) and others have made a concerted effort to unite rational

we believe that there is a "logic of arguing" (Risse 2000) that contributes to political outcomes independently of the logics of consequentialism and appropriateness, and cannot be reduced to those two logics. A fuller understanding of political institutions requires that we understand how the members of those institutions engage in deliberation. What happens during political debate? What role do argumentation and respect play during parliamentary deliberations? How constructive is the political dialogue? We maintain that these questions should be answered if we want to obtain a complete understanding of institutions.

The creation of the concept of a spirit of accommodation

Let us elaborate on this broad argument by considering one particular institutional theory, consociational theory, which has played a central role in comparative politics for almost forty years. Consociational theory tries to explain the conditions for democratic stability in culturally fragmented political systems. The hypothesis is that the probability of democratic stability in culturally fragmented political systems increases if these systems are characterized by the following four institutions: (1) parliamentary election systems of proportionality, (2) cabinet formation by grand coalition, (3) federalism, (4) many strong veto points. Besides these four institutional elements, consociational theory already contained in its initial formulation a cultural element called the *spirit of accommodation*. This cultural element was the starting point for the current book. We will argue in this chapter that the concept of the spirit of accommodation is conceptually ambiguous and theoretically not sufficiently grounded, and we will replace it with the concept of deliberation.

Initially, consociational theory was developed on the basis of a few country case studies, in particular studies of the Netherlands, Belgium, Switzerland, and Austria. The most influential country study at the beginning of the development of consociational theory was Arend Lijphart's (1968) *The Politics of Accommodation. Pluralism and Democracy in the Netherlands*. In a chapter entitled "A Divided Nation," Lijphart argues that the Netherlands was for a long time culturally fragmented into Roman Catholic, orthodox Calvinist and secular subcultures. Lijphart then asks whether the Netherlands was at the time a stable democracy. Based on a number of indicators, he answers this question in a positive way: "Democratic government has proved both legitimate and effective . . . Dutch politics appears to be . . . healthy and stable" (p. 77).

institutionalism with deliberative theory. This work has come to view deliberation as more than cheap talk. Instead, deliberation is depicted as an essential vehicle of information transmission without which decision making in institutions would be severely hampered.

In the political science literature at the time, there was the puzzle of how a divided nation could manage to be democratically stable. Lijphart's explanation refers to the practice of the "politics of accommodation." According to Lijphart, it was of particular importance that the principle of *proportionality* was not only applied to the parliamentary election system, but to the political system at large. Besides proportionality, *grand coalitions* in cabinet formation are a second important institutional device of consociationalism. The Netherlands never had grand coalitions in the fullest sense, but coalitions were usually oversized and political parties not represented in the cabinet had nevertheless some influence. With regard to *federalism*, the Netherlands never practiced federalism on a territorial basis, but they had federalism on a sectoral basis. With the institutional features of proportionality, oversized cabinet coalitions and sectoral federalism, the Dutch political system also had *strong veto points* built into the decision making process.

With the establishment of the four consociational institutional features, Lijphart was not yet at the end of his explanation of democratic stability in the Netherlands. He did not limit himself to the institutional argument that proportionality, oversized cabinet coalitions, sectoral federalism, and strong veto points were sufficient conditions for the culturally fragmented country to achieve democratic stability. Lijphart rather argued that these four institutional features were necessary, but not sufficient conditions for the achievement of democratic stability. For a full explanation, Lijphart added what he called a spirit of accommodation. Indeed, he had an entire chapter entitled "The Spirit of Accommodation." This spirit is considered to be at a high level when politicians are "willing and capable of bridging the gaps between the mutually isolated blocs and of resolving serious disputes in a largely nonconsensual context" (p. 104). Thus, according to Lijphart, it is not only important what kind of political institutions the Netherlands had established, but also in what spirit the politicians interacted in these institutions. This is not only an academic argument, but also an argument that one finds among insightful politicians. When on November 16, 2001, the parliament in Macedonia changed its constitution in a consociational direction, Arben Xhaferi of the Albanian Democratic Party exclaimed: "We have improved the constitution to reduce ethnic conflicts, now we must improve the mentality that has caused these ethnic conflicts."[2] Reinforcing this point, Matthijs Bogaards correctly points out, "ultimately, consociationalism is not about getting the institutions right, but about changing elite behavior."[3]

[2] *Neue Zürcher Zeitung*, November 16, 2001.
[3] Personal communication, December 13, 2003.

To what extent does the spirit of accommodation correspond to the deliberative model in the sense that the force of the better argument prevails? As Rudy Andeweg commented on an earlier version of this chapter: "The 'spirit of accommodation' to which you refer is in my reading much less of a positive attitude towards opponents but a 'prudent' attitude of elites who realize that the alternative to compromise is, in the long run, too detrimental."[4] We agree that the spirit of accommodation is not simply a synonym for deliberation but also contains strong bargaining elements. The problem is, however, that both bargaining and deliberative elements are packed into the same concept and should be distinguished in the interests of conceptual clarity. The conceptual ambiguity of a spirit of accommodation had the consequence that there was never an attempt to put the concept into operational terms. Lijphart did not try to measure in a systematic way the spirit of accommodation in undertaking, for example, interviews with a sample of Dutch political elites. Lijphart rather offers a wealth of anecdotal evidence to support his claim that there was a high level of spirit of accommodation among Dutch politicians.

At about the same time, and, independently of Lijphart, the same argument was made on the basis of case studies of Belgium, Austria, and Switzerland (Huyse 1971; Lehmbruch 1967; Steiner 1970, 1974). In these case studies too, the emphasis was not only on consociational institutions but also on a culture of consociational behavior. But, here again, consociational behavior was not measured in a systematic way, for example with interviews, but inferred from anecdotal evidence of specific decision making situations.

The concept of a spirit of accommodation in the testing phase

In the foreword to Steiner (1970, 1974), Stein Rokkan expressed the wish that the consociational study on Switzerland (and by implication the consociational studies on Austria, Belgium, and the Netherlands) would lead to "direct cross-national comparisons." This challenge has indeed been taken up in the last thirty years. The task was to systematically test the hypotheses generated from the four classical consociational countries. Could other fragmented countries also achieve democratic stability in establishing consociational institutions and a spirit of accommodation? To answer this question, it was no longer sufficient to offer anecdotal evidence on these two sets of explanatory variables; it was rather necessary to develop reliable and valid measurements of the two variables. For the institutional aspect, this

---

[4] Personal communication, December 30, 2003.

was relatively easy to accomplish. For the parliamentary election system, for example, one had to determine to what extent it fulfilled the criterion of proportional representation. It is non-controversial to say that the Netherlands has the purest form of proportional representation. With regard to cabinet formation, it is also relatively easy to determine to what extent a cabinet is oversized up to becoming a grand coalition. One can also measure quite easily to what extent a country is centralized or decentralized in the sense of having a federalist structure. Good indicators are, for example, the amount of public money spent by the central government or the number of public officials working for the central government. The most difficult institutional aspect to measure is the existence of strong veto points in a political system. But, even here, the measurement problem seems quite manageable. One can determine, for example, without too many difficulties, to what extent the supreme court, the central bank, or various advisory commissions have factual veto power over important policy issues or whether there is a second parliamentary chamber with veto power.

To measure the spirit of accommodation turned out to be much more difficult and was never actually accomplished in a systematic way (Bogaards 2000). No consociational scholar has ever attempted to operationalize the concept of a politics of accommodation. As a consequence, tests of consociational theory were never quite satisfactory, and there was more criticism raised against the theory than when it was initially generated in the 1960s (Steiner and Ertman 2002). Tests of consociational theory also occurred outside Europe, in example in South Africa (Lijphart 1985) and India (Lijphart 1996). We limit ourselves to a discussion of tests within Europe, beginning with Northern Ireland and then moving to former Czechoslovakia and former Yugoslavia. The focus of our discussion will be on how to conceptualize the spirit of accommodation and how this concept is related to the concept of deliberation.

When the Republic of Ireland attained independence in 1921, Northern Ireland remained part of the United Kingdom. There were two antagonistic groups confronting each other in Northern Ireland: a larger group of Protestants of Anglo-Saxon descent and a smaller group of Roman Catholics of Irish descent. Within the United Kingdom, Northern Ireland had a fair amount of autonomy with its own local parliament at Stormont. The Northern Irish institutions were not at all consociational since elections to Stormont were by winner-takes-all, the cabinet was formed by the winning party, no federalism existed, and there were no strong veto points for the Catholic minority. Given the uneven numerical strength of the two groups, Protestants won one election after another and always formed the cabinet, while Catholics remained politically impotent. Exactly as predicted by consociational theory, the absence of consociational institutions led to instability, with widespread violence beginning in 1968. A turning point came with the Good Friday accord in 1998. This accord stipulated that important consociational institutions should be introduced in Northern Ireland, in particular a proportional parliamentary election system and a grand coalition in the cabinet. To explain this outcome, we have to deal with the potential role of a spirit of accommodation. Was the Good Friday accord only possible because it was preceded by a surge in the spirit of accommodation? Did the Good Friday accord, in turn, lead in its aftermath to a surge in the spirit of accommodation? Why is it taking so long to implement the Good Friday accord and why have there been so many setbacks? Is the cause still a lack in the spirit of accommodation? Is the spirit of accommodation even declining again? These questions make clear that a compelling explanation would depend on good measurements of the spirit of accommodation. In the literature, one finds anecdotal evidence of some spirit of accommodation, in particular at the time of the Good Friday accord between the Catholic leader Gerry Adams and the Protestant leader David Trimble (McGarry 2001). But there was no spirit of accommodation from other actors, in particular from Ian Paisley on the Protestant side. In the testing phase of consociational theory, it is no longer sufficient to rely merely on anecdotal evidence; what is needed are reliable and valid measurements of the key explanatory variables, including the spirit of accommodation. For the latter variable, one would have to differentiate between a bargaining and a deliberative aspect. If there was any spirit of accommodation at all, were the key actors merely willing to bargain with each other to their mutual self-interest or were they also willing, at least to some extent, to show respect for the arguments of the other side and to yield to the force of the better argument? None of the literature on Northern Ireland addresses these questions in a systematic way.

The case of former Czechoslovakia helps to illustrate further that the spirit of accommodation needs to be measured for a good test of consociational theory. Of critical importance here is a compelling explanation for the breakup of former Czechoslovakia at the end of 1992. To what extent does this breakup validate or invalidate consociational theory? When the Communist regime was overthrown at the end of 1989, consociational institutions were quickly established. The first free elections in June 1990 were held according to party list proportionality. The cabinet formed after the elections was oversized since Civic Forum[5] had the absolute majority in parliament but nevertheless formed a coalition with the Christian Democrats. Even more importantly, there was power sharing between Czechs and Slovaks in the cabinet, with the rule that if a minister was Czech the deputy minister

[5] And its sister organization in Slovakia, Public Against Violence.

had to be Slovak and vice versa. Another power sharing arrangement was that when Václav Havel, a Czech, was made head of state, great care was taken to ensure that the important position of president of the parliament was filled by a Slovak, Alexander Dubcek. This link between the two positions was made very explicitly and publicly. There was also a fair amount of autonomy for the Czech and the Slovak parts, and the political system contained many strong veto points for the Slovak minority. In addition to consociational institutions, there seems to have been a high degree of spirit of accommodation, even in a deliberative sense, especially between the two key leaders Havel and Dubcek.

Czechoslovakia appeared as a positive test for consociational theory. What happened then, after the second parliamentary elections in June 1992, to cause the country to break apart six months later? Nothing had changed in the consociational institutions. Thus, the suspicion is that something must have changed in the spirit of accommodation. Two strong new leaders had emerged: Václav Klaus from the Czech part, and Vladimir Meciar from the Slovak part, and there seems to have been very little spirit of accommodation between these two emerging leaders, either in a bargaining or in a deliberative sense. Klaus headed a coalition that was market-oriented and libertarian-cosmopolitan, Meciar a coalition that was economically redistributive and authoritarian-particularistic (Kitschelt 1992). The lesson from Czechoslovakia is that if we want to get an empirical handle on the spirit of accommodation, we cannot simply speak of it in a general way, but we must be able to determine exactly among whom such a spirit exists and among whom it does not. For a compelling explanation of the breakup of Czechoslovakia it is important that we make clear to whose spirit of accommodation we refer. Czechoslovakia shows how challenging it is to develop a reliable and valid measure for the spirit of accommodation in a country. One has to take account of the possibility that different members of the political elites have different levels in their spirit of accommodation and give different emphasis to the bargaining and the deliberative parts. No systematic research has been done on this aspect of the breakup of Czechoslovakia.

When communism was swept away in former Yugoslavia, one can say without refined measurements that there was very little spirit of accommodation among the various ethnic groups, not even in a bargaining sense. As a consequence no effort at all was made to establish consociational institutions linking the individual republics of the country. But the question remains whether this lack of a spirit of accommodation existed already under the Communist regime or whether it was caused by short-term factors like some of the policies of the Serb leader Slobodan Milosevic, for example, with regard to Kosovo. In order to get an answer to this question, we would need to measure the spirit of accommodation over time. When former

Yugoslavia broke apart, the worst fighting with many atrocities happened in Bosnia-Herzegovina. At this smaller scale, there was also clearly no spirit of accommodation among the ethnic groups so that here, too, no consociational institutions were established. Such institutions, however, were finally imposed from outside with the help of NATO peacekeeping forces by the Dayton accord of 1995. Parliamentary elections were held according to proportionality, the three major groups of Muslims, Serbs and Croats had to share power in the executive branch, there was a strongly federalist structure, and many strong veto points for each group were built into the political system. These were almost ideal typical consociational institutions. Did they cause an increased spirit of accommodation in the years afterwards? There is some anecdotal evidence to this effect, but here again it would be desirable to have measurements for the development of the spirit of accommodation for both the bargaining and the deliberative aspects.

This overview of the testing problems with regard to consociational theory should have demonstrated that the key unresolved problem concerns the variable of the spirit of accommodation. As we have seen earlier in the chapter, the standard definition stated by Lijphart (1968) is that politicians are "willing and capable of bridging the gaps between the mutually isolated blocs and of resolving serious disputes in a largely nonconsensual context." The problem with this definition is that it contains elements of both bargaining and deliberation. For conceptual clarity the two elements should be distinguished. Our interest in the current project is in the deliberative element. Consociational theory has taught us that politics does not only consist of bargaining with the emphasis on power but also in deliberation with the emphasis on the force of the better argument. This lesson has taken us way beyond consociational theory to broader questions of democratic theory in general.

2

The philosophical literature on deliberative politics

The previous chapter left us with the challenge of how to conceptualize in a systematic way what consociational scholars call the spirit of accommodation. We have demonstrated on the basis of several empirical cases that the concept of the spirit of accommodation is too vague to be used in cross-national empirical research. We need a concept that goes beyond everyday language and is grounded systematically in a theoretical literature. We found such an anchor in the philosophical literature on deliberative politics. In this literature, a high deliberative quality has a very specific meaning. Of course, this meaning is somewhat differently defined from author to author. We base our project on the rationalistic argumentative version of authors such as Jürgen Habermas. This version corresponds best with the emphasis on rationality in most theories of institutionalism; we will develop this argument fully in chapter 4, where we will present the theoretical framework of how the quality of political deliberation can play a role in theories of institutionalism. Immersing ourselves in the literature on deliberation, our research interest has broadened from the narrower perspective of consociational theory to the larger questions of deliberative politics. In our thinking, consociational theory has become just one of many applications of the deliberative model.

Normative theories of deliberative politics

Instead of deliberative politics, one may also speak of discursive politics. We use the two terms as synonyms. The key for both terms is the dialogical aspect. This aspect is perhaps a little less contained in the term deliberative, since one may also deliberate in a monological way with oneself, whereas the term discursive can hardly be used in a monological way. But in the way the term deliberative is used in the literature, the dialogical aspect is so central that the two terms can easily be used as synonyms. Correspondingly, we speak both of a high-quality discourse and high-quality deliberation. Deliberative or discourse theories are normative in orientation and make the claim that high levels of deliberation or discourse are good for democracy. Dryzek and Braithwaite (2000: 241–2) put in a nutshell what the core of these theories is:

> The theory (and, to a lesser extent the practice) of democracy has in the last ten years or so taken a "deliberative turn." That is, the idea that democratic legitimacy rests on authentic deliberation – rather than say, voting or interest aggregation – is increasingly stressed by democratic theorists. Deliberative democrats pin their hopes on the transformative power of deliberation. They argue that if it proceeds in suitably unconstrained and egalitarian circumstances, deliberation induces individuals to think through their interests and reflect upon their preferences, becoming amenable to changing the latter in light of persuasion from other participants . . . deliberative democrats believe that to the extent effective deliberation occurs, political outcomes will secure broader support, respond more effectively to the reflectively held interests of participants, and generally prove more rational.

For Habermas (1996a: 296), "the central element of the democratic process resides in the procedure of deliberative politics." Our purpose in this book is not to engage ourselves in this normative debate. We are not political philosophers but empirically oriented political scientists. Accordingly, we use the concept of deliberative politics not in normative but in descriptive terms. Our research question is not whether a good democracy should have much deliberation. We rather ask how the concept of deliberative politics can be measured for debates in real-world politics and what the causes and consequences are of a high degree of deliberation. We hope that such an empirical project will throw some light on the normative questions raised by political philosophers.

If we wish to understand the philosophical theory of deliberative politics, we must understand that the concept is usually used in ideal typical terms. Habermas (1996a: 296, 326) stresses that discourse theory uses the "concept of an ideal procedure for deliberation and decision making."[1] He acknowledges that "[e]ven under favorable conditions, no complex society could ever correspond to the model of purely communicative social relations." Cohen (1989: 22) speaks of the "ideal deliberative procedure." Real political debates are usually far away from the ideal type. As Habermas (1996b: 323)

---

[1] In his earlier writings, Habermas used the term "ideal speech situation." More recently, he has not used the term although he has never refuted it. Whatever concept is used, the important point is that in the philosophical literature deliberative politics is usually described in ideal typical terms.

puts it, "rational discourses have an improbable character and are like islands in the ocean in everyday praxis."[2] In the same vein, Dryzek (1990: 36–7) acknowledges that the "the ideal speech situation does not exist, and clearly cannot exist in this world of variety in opinions and traditions. Its canons are always and unavoidably violated in the real world." A frequently articulated criticism is that the ideal deliberative situation is far away from reality. We agree with Pellizzoni (2002: 69) that "this is a weak objection, which can be countered by pointing out that the theory represents a regulatory ideal, a benchmark against which the existing institutions or the reformist projects can be measured." Thus, it is a weak objection to the deliberative enterprise when Mendelberg (2002: 180) concludes from a review of the social psychology literature:

> The research reviewed here sounds a cautionary note about deliberation. When groups engage in discussion, we cannot count on them to generate empathy and diminish narrow self-interest, to afford equal opportunities for participation and influence even to the powerless, to approach the discussion with a mind open to change, and to be influenced not by social pressures, unthinking commitments to social identities, or power, but by the exchange of relevant and sound reasons.

Rosenberg (2003: 6–7) expresses the same cautionary note on the feasibility of deliberation in the real world:

> In sum, there is a great deal of social psychological research that suggests that individuals generally do not think in the logical, rational or reasonable way and do not evidence the communicative competence assumed by deliberative democratic theory . . . several different strands of cognitive development research indicates that not only some, but perhaps most people lack the requisite capacity of reason . . . Failing to adequately consider the perspective of the listener, most people do not present their views in a sufficiently elaborated manner so that others can fully understand them. In addition, most people tend to view the different views that others express not as a constructive input, but rather as an obstruction or simply incorrect. Overall, the opportunity for discussion and argument is not viewed as a cooperative exercise leading to greater insight and mutual benefit, but rather it is understood as a zero-sum game that ends in some participants winning and others losing.

Such cautionary notes are certainly empirically correct, but they miss the point that deliberative theorists do not in reality expect to find the ideal type of deliberation. In order to study empirically deliberative politics, the ideal type of deliberation must be seen as the end point of a continuum that will never be fully reached. The empirical question then is how far away specific political debates are from the ideal type of deliberation. As Dryzek (1990: 87)

---

[2] "Rationale Diskurse haben einen unwahrscheinlichen Charakter und heben sich wie Inseln im Meer der alltäglichen Praxis heraus."

puts it, "the fact that an ideal is unattainable does not preclude its use for evaluative purposes . . . the precepts of communicative rationality can be used as critical standards to distinguish degrees of departure from the ideal." In chapter 3, we will show how we measure the distance from the ideal type of deliberation in constructing a Discourse Quality Index (DQI). In order to be able to construct this DQI, we first had to understand precisely what is meant by the ideal type of deliberative politics. We reconstruct its key elements in the following paragraphs.

A first characteristic of the ideal type of deliberative politics is *participation* by all citizens at an equal level and without constraints in a publicly open political process. Thereby, the political process is conceptualized in a very broad sense, encompassing not only formal political institutions but also the public sphere at large. For Dryzek (2000: 171), a "vital public sphere is essential for the continued health of democracy." Habermas (1996a: 299) hopes that the deliberation in the public sphere at large will have an influence on elections, legislation and administrative power since "[t]he flow of communication between public opinion formation, institutionalized elections, and legislative decisions is meant to guarantee that influence and communicative power are transformed through legislation into administrative power." In this way, citizens should be a strong countervailing force against the two traditional influences in politics, "money and administrative power" (Habermas 1996a: 299). Given the assumption that citizens have potentially great political influence, they should discuss political issues with neighbors, at the workplace, in leisure time associations, and so on. In doing so, ordinary citizens are participants in a broad-based process of opinion and will formation. No one with the competency to speak and act may be excluded from the discourse. All have the same chances to question and to introduce any assertion and to express their attitudes, desires, and needs. No one may be prevented, by internal or external coercion, from expressing these rights; all have the right to question the assigned topic of conversation; and all have the right to initiate reflexive arguments about the very rules of the discourse procedures and the way in which they are applied and carried out (Cohen 1989: 23; Benhabib 1996: 70; Chambers 1995: 233). This first characteristic of the ideal type of deliberative politics illustrates well that reality will never correspond to the ideal type. There will always be some constraints limiting the full and equal participation of all citizens. In the real world, political deliberation can never be completely free of domination (*herrschaftsfrei* in the sense of Habermas). It is always only a question of how close reality comes to the ideal type of deliberative politics.

A second characteristic of the ideal type of deliberative politics is that everyone participating in a political discourse expresses his or her views in a *truthful* way.[3] According to Habermas (1983: 98), "each speaker may only assert what he believes himself."[4] This criterion of truthfulness (*Wahrhaftigkeit*) means that all participants are open about their true preferences and do not try to deceive and mislead others about their true intentions. Put in other terms, participants in the discourse really mean what they say. When they refer to particular values such as justice for all, they truly believe in these values and do not utter them merely for tactical reasons in order to strengthen an argument. Thus, talk can be taken at face value. Here again, reality will often not even come close to this ideal. As Baccaro (2001: 257) argues, there is usually great skepticism about whether political actors indeed mean what they say; "in real as opposed to ideal debates people pursuing strategic goals might try to present themselves as animated by communicative intents to increase their persuasiveness." In order to be credible with regard to their truthfulness, according to Baccaro (2001: 263),

> Speakers need to pass a preliminary "consistency test" and provide evidence that they do not use arguments in a purely rhetorical fashion to "dupe" the audience but really "mean what they say." This test involves not only consistency between past and present words but also, and more important, between words and actions.

As an example of such consistency between words and actions, Baccaro (2001: 261) mentions a union leader working in a southern Italian Fiat factory who supported a pension reform scheme although he had personally to make the sacrifice to postpone his own retirement by two years. In gaining credibility in this way, other union members were willing to take at face value his arguments that the new pension scheme was for the common good of the union.

A third characteristic of the ideal type of deliberative politics requires the *logical justification* of assertions and validity claims. That is, assertions should be introduced and critically assessed through "the orderly exchange of information and reasons between parties" (Habermas 1992: 370).[5] The arguments must have intrinsic characteristics that make them compelling to others (Habermas 1983: 97).[6] Dryzek (1990: 218) expresses the same idea when he writes that political choices should be "based on good cognitive reasons." In the following quote, Habermas (1996a, 322–3) stresses that these reasons should have universal appeal:

---

[3] Good synonyms for truthful are sincere, genuine, and authentic.
[4] "Jeder Sprecher darf nur behaupten, was er selbst glaubt."
[5] "den geregelten Austausch von Informationen und Gründen zwischen Parteien."
[6] "Argumentationen sind zunächst darauf angelegt, triftige, aufgrund intrinsischer Eigenschaften überzeugende Argumente, mit denen Geltungsansprüche eingelöst oder zurückgewiesen werden können, zu produzieren."

> Communicative action refers to a process of argumentation in which those taking part justify their validity claims before an ideally expanded audience. Participants in argumentation proceed on the idealized assumption of a communicative community without limits in social space and historical time . . . The[se] counterfactual presuppositions assumed by participants in argumentation indeed open up a perspective allowing them to go beyond local practices of justification and to transcend the provinciality of their spatiotemporal contexts.

From semiotics we know that argumentation is a process in which "someone tries to convince someone of something by citing evidence and drawing, or suggesting, inferences from the evidence and from other beliefs and assumptions (hypotheses)" (Sebeok 1986: 50–1). An inference means a "semiotic process in which from something given (the premises), something else (the conclusion) is derived on the basis of certain relations between premises and conclusion" (Sebeok 1986: 51). The tighter the connection between premises and conclusions, the more coherent the justification is and the more useful it will be for deliberation. However, the connections between premises and conclusions do not always have to be stated explicitly, using terms such as "since," "for," "so," "therefore," and "because." Indeed, "economies of speech" may cause individuals to leave out entire parts of their arguments since they may be so obvious it is unnecessary to state them (Angell 1964). Whatever the exact form of the justification, the key point is that the participants present their arguments in a logically coherent way so that the other participants can understand what the arguments are. As Gutmann and Thompson (2002: 156) put it, "citizens owe one another justifications for the mutually binding laws and public policies they collectively make." If the participants in a political debate are inarticulate in the presentation of their arguments, nobody knows where anyone stands, so that the merits of the various arguments cannot truly be debated. In this sense, logical coherence is the basis for true deliberation. Thus, only actors who can argue in a rational way are expected to participate in the ideal type of deliberation, which reveals a tension with the first criterion of the ideal type, namely the participation of all. To overcome this tension, it would be necessary to take measures such as improved education so that all citizens are able to argue in a logical and rational way. Again, reality will never even come close to the ideal type.

A fourth characteristic of the ideal type of deliberation is that the merits of the arguments should be expressed in terms of the *common good*. That is, there should be a sense of empathy or solidarity that allows the participants to consider the well-being of others and of the community at large. This does not mean, however, that self-interest should be excluded as an argument. But someone using it as an argument must demonstrate that his or her self-interest is compatible with the common good or even contributes to the common good. Appeals to the common good can take several forms. On the one hand, the common good may be stated in utilitarian terms, i.e. as the best solution for the greatest number of people (Mill 1998). The common good may also be expressed through the difference principle in the sense that the common good is best served if the least advantaged in a society are helped (Rawls 1971). This fourth characteristic must be seen in connection with the second, namely that all participants express their arguments in a truthful way. This must also hold for arguments regarding the common good. In real political life, it often happens, of course, that someone expresses for strategic gains a selfish argument in terms of the common good. In the ideal type of deliberative politics such behavior would never occur, which emphasizes once again that the ideal type is a construct far removed from ordinary politics. With regard to the necessity in politics to express arguments in terms of the common good, Ackermann and Fishkin (2002: 143) distinguish between politics and the economic marketplace. In the latter it is appropriate exclusively to pursue one's self-interest, but not in the former:

> When entering a marketplace, it is generally acceptable for the consumer to limit herself to a single question when choosing amongst competing products – and that is "Which product do I find most pleasing?" . . . But this is not true of citizenship. When you and I get together to choose a new set of leaders, we are not engaged in a private act of consumption, but a collective act of power – one that will profoundly shape the fate of millions of our fellow citizens, and billions more throughout the world. With the stakes this high, it is morally irresponsible to choose the politician with the biggest smile or the biggest handout. Rather than asking the question, "What's good for me?" the good citizen asks "What's good for *the country?*" Undoubtedly, there may be many occasions when what is good for the country is also good for me personally. But the good citizen recognizes, as the good consumer does not, that this convergence is by no means preordained, and that the task of citizenship is to rise above self-interest and take seriously the nature of the common good.

A fifth characteristic of the ideal type of deliberative politics is that the participants are willing to truly listen to the arguments of others and to treat them with genuine *respect* (Macedo 1999; Müller 1999). This criterion necessitates empathy: the capacity and the willingness to put oneself in the shoes of others and to consider a situation from their perspective. Of crucial importance in this respect are the capacity and the willingness to listen to others, which is easier said than done, since it is always difficult to imagine being in someone else's situation. As Orlie (1994), based on Hannah Arendt, points out, each of us has his or her own social location different from the locations of all others, so that we can never fully understand the perspective of others. But we should always make an effort to do so in listening carefully to the arguments of others (Koch 2002). Several dimensions of respect play a role in discourse. One of these dimensions is respect toward *groups* whose needs and rights are under discussion. Another dimension is respect toward the *demands* under discussion, at least as long as they can inter-subjectively be seen as justified. A third dimension is respect toward *counterarguments*, i.e. arguments raised by opponents that contradict one's own conclusion with regard to the demand (Gutmann and Thompson 1990). These last two dimensions pertain to the treatment of other participants in the debate and are especially important for deliberation. In particular, respect toward counterarguments is a necessary condition and an indication for the weighing of alternatives (Chambers 1999; Luskin and Fishkin 2002). "At the core of any notion of deliberation is the idea that reasons for and against various options are to be weighed on their merits" (Fishkin and Laslett 2002b: 125). The idea that one should consider the counterarguments against one's own position was already articulated in a classical way by the German writer and philosopher Lessing in a 1778 pamphlet against the pastor Goez whom he criticized for constantly repeating his own arguments rather than addressing the counterarguments of Lessing.[7]

Sixth, there should be a willingness on the part of all participants to yield to the force of the better argument, which means that the preferences of the participants should not be fixed, but be open to change. Habermas (1996a: 305) speaks in this context of "the unforced force of the better argument." What the better argument is, is not a priori given, but must be searched for in the common deliberation. It is precisely through deliberation that the participants find out what counts as a good argument. Elaborating on the concept of a good argument, Dryzek (1990: 41) points out that "no individuals may possess authority on the basis of anything other than a good argument." This criterion, which we call constructive politics, is at the very core of the ideal type of deliberative politics. To yield to the better argument should not be mixed up with the quid pro quo occurring in ordinary bargaining. As Keohane (2001: 10) correctly points out, "in a bargaining situation, actors know their interests and interact reciprocally to seek to realize them." Instruments to attain a bargain are threats of punishment and promises of reward. Actors make cost-benefit analyses in order to determine whether they should participate in a bargain. Pellizzoni (2002: 60) succinctly puts the difference between bargaining and deliberation in the following way: "According to the strategic perspective each party appraises

---

[7] "mit was für Gründen kann der Mann streiten, der sich auf meine Gegengründe noch mit keinem Worte eingelassen hat? der, anstatt zu antworten, nur immer seine alten Beschuldigungen wörtlich wiederholt?" (Lessing 1853: 275).

the arguments of the others in terms of exchange, and relates them to personal advantage. According to the deliberative perspective the arguments of each party are compared, in consideration of the interests of everyone." Adam Smith (1991: 13) formulated the bargaining model in a classical way:

> Man has almost constant occasion for the help of his brethren, and it is in vain for him to expect it from their benevolence only. Man will be more likely to prevail if he can interest their self-love in his favour, and show them that it is for their own advantage to do for him what he requires of them. Whoever offers to another a bargain of any kind, proposes to do this. Give me that which I want, and you shall have this which you want, is the meaning of any offer; and it is in this manner that we obtain from another the far greater part of those good offices which we stand in need of. It is not from the benevolence of the butcher, the brewer, or the baker that we expect our dinner, but from their regard to their own interest. We address ourselves, not to their humanity but to their self-love, and never talk to them of our own necessities but of their advantages.

By contrast, in the ideal type of deliberative politics what counts is the quality of the arguments. Actors are willing to be persuaded by better arguments. According to Keohane (2001: 10), "persuasion must appeal to norms, principles, and values that are shared by participants in a conversation. Persuasion requires giving reasons for actions, reasons that go beyond assertions about power, interests, and resolve." Habermas (1983: 68) makes the same distinction as Keohane between bargaining and deliberation, with the former being based on the threats of sanctions and the prospects of rewards, the latter on rational reasons.[8]

What is a good argument? Is it enough that in the words of Keohane it appeals to the shared norms, principles, and values of the participants? What if these norms, principles, and values do not correspond to criteria of social justice? This is the worry of Gutmann and Thompson (2002: 161), who as political philosophers insist on their right to criticize political outcomes as unjust even if the process leading to the outcomes corresponds to criteria of deliberation. To illustrate their point, they give the example where a political body, "following perfectly deliberative procedures, decides to institute a practice of compulsory organ donation. On a purely procedural conception of deliberative democracy, this law would be justified." But Gutmann and Thompson allude to the possibility that from a philosophical perspective one may criticize this law with the argument that it violates the "bodily integrity" of the people involved. They emphasize that such philosophical

---

[8] "Während im strategischen Handeln einer auf den anderen empirisch, mit der Androhung von Sanktionen oder der Aussicht auf Gratifikationen einwirkt, um die erwünschte Fortsetzung einer Interaktion zu veranlassen, wird im kommunikativen Handeln einer vom anderen zu einer Anschlusshandlung rational motiviert."

critiques should not be put in absolute terms, but merely "be understood as normative hypotheses about political morality . . . because their confirmation, refutation, or revision calls for public deliberation in the democratic process" (p. 173). If we read Gutmann and Thompson correctly, they become themselves participants in the deliberative process, articulating values from general philosophical principles such as "liberty and opportunity" (p. 159). For political philosophers this is a legitimate enterprise that we applaud. For our own research project, however, as we state at the beginning of this chapter, we take an empirical approach in investigating in the sense of Keohane the norms, principles, and values that have persuasive force in a particular political context. An interesting further empirical question is why there is variation in this regard among different political contexts. Why, for example, is a particular argument considered as persuasive in the United States Congress but not in the Swedish parliament?

On another issue, Gutmann and Thompson (2002: 162, 166) rightly point out that the procedural rules of deliberative politics should also be open to deliberation:

> Procedural principles may also be rejected by a deliberative democracy (and so may a purely procedural conception of deliberative democracy). Pure proceduralists do not have access to some moral basis, which our conception lacks, on which to claim that the procedural constraints that they recommend for a constitutional deliberative democracy are correct or authoritative . . . Deliberative democracy supports the means for fundamental change in the content of the theory itself. Deliberative democracy subjects its own principles, as well as other moral principles, to scrutiny over time . . . It is . . . possible to question, from within deliberative theory, whether deliberation is justifiable.

The emphasis of Gutmann and Thompson that the principle of deliberation should also apply to the rules of deliberation is an important one that we will consider in our empirical investigation.

Must deliberation necessarily lead to unanimous decisions? In the words of Cohen (1989: 23), "ideal deliberation aims to arrive at a rationally motivated consensus." It should be noted in this quote that consensus is merely an aim and not an absolute necessity. More important than actually reaching consensus is that all arguments are duly considered and seriously debated and that all participants are honestly willing to yield to the better arguments. If this is accomplished, "the results enjoy the presumption of being reasonable" (Habermas 1996a: 301). But since at a later time still more convincing arguments may come up, every political outcome should be treated as provisional and fallible (Habermas 1996a: 301). As Gutmann and Thompson (2000: 171–2) put it, any claims "can be challenged and changed over time in response to new philosophical insights, empirical evidence, or interpretations of both the insights and evidence." Given that all decisions may be revised later on, a temporary closure with a majority vote is compatible with the ideal type of deliberation. As Müller (1993: 70–1) writes, those actors who lose in a particular vote are treated with respect and can come back with their arguments at a later time, when they may win.

We are now at the end of our reconstruction of the ideal type of deliberative politics. It is on this basis that in chapter 3 we will build our Discourse Quality Index (DQI). Not all deliberative theorists may agree on all the nuances of our reconstruction of the deliberative model. There is, however, general agreement on the key aspect that the political process should be based on a "talk-centric" style of decision making rather than on a "voting-centric" style; outcomes should be determined by reasons rather than numbers (Bohman and Rehg: 1997: xiii; Chambers 1999: 1). According to the broad definition of Cohen (1989: 17, 21), deliberative democracy is "an association whose affairs are governed by public deliberation of its members," an association whose members "share a commitment to the resolution of problems of collective choice through public reasoning." Or, as Keohane (2001: 2) puts it, deliberative politics allows "changing others' minds on the basis of reason, not coercion, manipulation, or material sanctions." Another good summary definition is by Pelletier et al. (1999: 104) for whom deliberative democracy is "founded on the premise that citizens can collectively and self-consciously reflect on goals and purposes, think critically and make value judgements." In a recent review article, Chambers (2003: 309) summarizes deliberative politics as follows:

> Generally speaking, we can say that deliberation is debate and discussion aimed at producing reasonable, well-informed opinion in which participants are willing to revise their preferences in light of discussion, new information, and claims made by fellow participants. Although consensus need not be the ultimate aim of deliberation, and participants are expected to pursue their interests, an overarching interest in the legitimacy of outcomes (understood as justification to all affected) ideally characterize deliberation.

Where does the deliberative model stand with regard to other prominent models in modern philosophy? It can best be located somewhere between republicanism and liberalism. According to Habermas (1996a: 296), "it differs both from the liberal conception of the state as guardian of an economic society[9] and from the republican concept of an ethical community

---

[9] Habermas (1996a: 298): "The liberal model hinges not on democratic self-determination of deliberating citizens but on the constitutional framework for an economic society that is supposed to guarantee an essentially nonpolitical common good by satisfying personal life plans and private expectations of happiness."

institutionalized in the state."[10] The deliberative model shares with republicanism the vision of an active, talk-centric participation of citizens. However, in accordance with liberalism, deliberative theorists believe in the pluralistic character of modern societies and thus reject as unrealistic and not even desirable the republican premise of a shared community ethos and of a citizenry united and actively motivated by a shared conception of the good life. But, in turn, deliberative theorists reject liberalism's interpretation of the political process as being primarily the competition between, and aggregation of, private and fixed preferences. "Discourse theory invests the democratic process with normative connotations stronger than those found in the liberal model but weaker than those found in the republican model" (Habermas 1996a: 298).

Taking a middle position between liberalism and republicanism, the deliberative concept of democracy "no longer has to operate with the notion of a social whole centred in the state and imagined as a goal-oriented subject writ large. Nor does it represent the whole in a system of constitutional norms mechanically regulating the balance of power and interests in accordance with a market model" (Habermas 1996a: 298). Generally speaking, deliberative politics means that the actions of the participating actors are not coordinated via egocentric calculations of success, but through acts of common understanding and agreement. Actors pursue their individual goals with the expectation that they are able to share the definition of the situation and thus can coordinate their actions. This process may need much time, and ideally deliberation should have no fixed end point but should be allowed to continue for as long as it takes to find agreement. Furthermore, when agreement is found it has to be considered as fallible and can therefore always be put in question by new and better arguments.

Historical roots of the deliberative model

Earlier in this chapter, we quoted Dryzek who speaks of a deliberative turn in political philosophy. This is also our impression; the empirical evidence is revealed when we search on our computer for the term "deliberation" and hundreds of recent books and articles are found. We should not forget, however, that the deliberative model has deep roots in the history of philosophy. They go as far back as Ancient Greece. Socrates was already arguing against

---

[10] Habermas (1996a: 297): "According to the republican view, the citizens' opinion and will-formation forms the medium through which society constitutes itself as a political whole. Society is, from the very start, political society – *societas civilis* – for in the citizens' practice of political self-determination the community becomes conscious of itself, as it were, and acts upon itself through the citizens' collective will. Hence democracy becomes equivalent to the political self-organization of society as a whole."

the sophists that they used rhetoric too much for egotistical purposes, to get their own way without considering the common good. Socrates postulated that real human dialogues help to reach higher truth and justice. For these dialogues he stressed, as deliberative theorists do today, that careful listening and mutual respect are important. Socrates put to Gorgias the question: "Of what sort of persuasion is oratory a craft, and what is this persuasion about?" (Plato 1997: §799). Socrates gives himself the answer that unfortunately orators are often "eager to win instead of investigating the subject under discussion" (Plato 1997: §802). The negative result will be that such orators are "disputing some points and one maintains that the other isn't right or isn't clear, they get irritated, each thinking the other is speaking out of spite" (Plato 1997: §802). Socrates calls such bad oratory the attempt to use "conviction without knowledge." For him true oratory should lead to "persuasion that comes from teaching, concerning what's just and unjust" (Plato 1997: §800). But what is just and unjust for Socrates? He articulates explicitly a key theme of the deliberative model of Habermas, namely that actors in a good deliberation should be willing to correct their views in yielding to better arguments (Plato 1997: §802):

> And what kind of man am I? One of those who would be pleased to be refuted if I say anything untrue, and who would be pleased to refute anyone who says something untrue; one who, however, wouldn't be any less pleased to be refuted than to refute. For I count being refuted a greater good, insofar as it is a greater good for oneself to be delivered from the worst thing there is than to deliver someone else from it.

This quote shows that Socrates, and Plato speaking through him, made the clear distinction between a teaching function and a convicting function of oratory. In the latter case the orators have fixed preferences that they try to impose with clever rhetoric. In the former case, by contrast, deliberation is a teaching tool to reach higher levels of truth and justice. More so than Socrates and Plato, Aristotle stressed the political aspect of deliberation and put it in political praxis; as Terchek and Moore (2000: 905, 907) state,

> Aristotle is concerned with the constitution of the polis and the formation of crucial institutions and practices that support deliberative citizens and the public sphere ... participation in deliberative politics not only helps citizens develop the skills to apply the law well to particular cases but also helps ensure that the laws that habituate us are good laws. It is through deliberation that belief and narrow interest are at least potentially exposed to reasoned examination in a democracy.

This interpretation of Aristotle already contains crucial aspects of the deliberative model, in particular the expectation that deliberation leads to good laws and that narrow interests are exposed in reasoned deliberation.

Among modern philosophers, one may expect that Rousseau (1966) had the most to say about the deliberative model since for him the concept of deliberation is so important for the formation of the general will. But a closer reading of Rousseau reveals that this is for the most part not the case. To be sure, in accordance with the deliberative model Rousseau puts great emphasis on the participation of all citizens, although he still excludes women. He stresses that for the will of the people to be general it is necessary that all voices be counted.[11] But when the citizens are assembled to express the general will, there should be no communication between them, and each citizen should only express his own view without being influenced by others.[12] Rousseau came to this view because he feared that if citizens communicated with each other in the assembly they would be corrupted by special interests, and, according to Rousseau, nothing is as dangerous for public affairs as private interests organized into subgroups of the assembly.[13] Thus, deliberation for Rousseau does not mean that various groups in the assembly listen to each other's claims and demands and try to reach a mutual accommodation of their interests and preferences. Rousseau feared that such deliberation would be too lengthy, divisive and tumultuous and would lead to the prevailing of special interests and the decline of the state.[14]

For Rousseau the general will should not emerge from the deliberation in the assembly but rather from each citizen expressing individually his vote on what he considers best for the common good. Since citizens, if well educated as described by Rousseau in *Emile*, are assumed to be good, they will always strive for the common good if they are only left alone to make up their minds. They are not asked if they personally support a new law but whether in their view the new law corresponds best to the general will.[15] Rousseau acknowledges that some citizens, although they try to cast their vote in the spirit of the general will, occasionally may make an error of judgment. Rousseau expects such errors to be minor and to cancel each other out. Thus, unanimity in the assembly will not always occur, but the

---

[11] "Pour qu'une volonté soit générale . . . il est nécessaire que toutes les voix soient comptées" (Rousseau 1966: 64).

[12] "[L]es citoyens n'avaient aucune communication entre eux . . . chaque citoyen n'opine que d'après lui" (Rousseau 1966: 66–7).

[13] "Rien n'est plus dangereux que l'influence des intérêts privés dans les affaires publiques . . . Il importe donc pour avoir bien l'énoncé de la volonté générale qu'il n'y a pas de société partielle dans l'Etat" (Rousseau 1966: 67).

[14] "Les long débats, les dissensions, le tumulte annoncent l'ascendant des intérêts particuliers et le déclin de l'Etat" (Rousseau 1966: 150).

[15] "Quand on propose une loi dans l'assemblée du peuple, ce qu'on leur demande n'est pas précisément s'ils approuvent la proposition ou s'ils la rejettent, mais si elle est conforme ou non à la volonté générale qui est la leur; chacun en donnant son suffrage dit son avis là-dessus, et du calcul des voix se tire la déclaration de la volonté générale" (Rousseau 1966: 149).

vote will in most cases be close to unanimity. If a citizen finds himself in the minority this proves that he has made an error of judgment in evaluating what is best for the common good.[16]

Although unanimity is not required for ordinary laws, it is necessary for the founding law on the social contract itself. But, once again, such unanimity is not reached by deliberation among all participants, but through the non-inclusion of the dissenters into the social contract; they are henceforth considered as foreigners and do not have citizen status. Only those who gave it their support are bound by the social contract.[17] This procedure to establish a political community is virtually the opposite of the deliberative model that we presented earlier in the chapter. Instead of continuing the discussion with the minority dissenters, with the expectation that ultimately what will count is not the number of votes but the strength of the better arguments, Rousseau simply wants to consider as foreigners those who see the substance of the social contract in a different light than the majority.

Generally speaking, it is easy to misread Rousseau with regard to what happens in the assembly of citizens because he indeed uses the term "deliberation" and furthermore puts great emphasis on the participation of all citizens and on unanimity or near unanimity in support of the decision outcome. But when the assembly meets there is no debate on the merits of the various arguments. In fact, the assembly as postulated by Rousseau is quite a silent affair. The general will emerges from each citizen voting according to what he considers as best for the common good. It is strange and puzzling that Rousseau uses for this procedure the term deliberation – *délibération* in French. It is certainly not deliberation in the sense of the deliberative model. Thus, although Rousseau stresses the importance of the participation of all citizens and the importance of unanimity or near unanimity, he can hardly be seen as a pathbreaker for the deliberative model.

The deliberative model can be traced back much more to Kant than to Rousseau, at least for the Habermasian version of the model (Lind 2000). At first sight, this may be surprising since the concept of deliberation has no prominent place in the philosophy of Kant. His categorical imperative

---

[16] Pour qu'une volonté soit générale il n'est pas toujours nécessaire qu'elle soit unanime . . . Il s'ensuit de ce qui précède que la volonté générale est toujours droite et tend toujours à l'utilité publique; mais il ne s'ensuit pas que les délibérations du peuple aient toujours la même rectitude. On veut toujours son bien, mais on ne le voit pas toujours . . . du grand nombre de petites différences résulterait toujours la volonté générale . . . Quand donc l'avis contraire au mien l'emporte, cela ne prouve autre chose sinon que je m'étais trompé, et que ce que j'estimais être la volonté générale ne l'était pas" (Rousseau 1966: 64, 66–7, 149).

[17] "Il n'y a qu'une seule loi qui par sa nature exige un consentement unanime. C'est le pacte social . . . Si donc lors du pacte social il s'y trouve des opposants, leur opposition n'invalide pas le contrat, elle empêche seulement qu'ils n'y soient compris; ce sont des étrangers parmi les citoyens" (Rousseau 1966: 148).

is not submitted to a deliberation with others. When Kant postulates in his categorical imperative that the maxim of one's actions should always be able to serve as a principle for the law of the entire community,[18] this maxim is not deliberated with others. It is rather the individual who deliberates in a monological sense what the maxim should be. Habermas is strongly influenced by the categorical imperative. When he develops his discourse ethics, he states that the process of moral deliberation takes for him the place of the categorical imperative.[19] This change in perspective from a monological to a dialogical orientation is certainly of great importance and sets Habermas apart from Kant. But this difference between the two philosophers should not obscure the fact that Habermas's deliberative model has also much in common with Kant's categorical imperative. Both the categorical imperative and the deliberative model put great emphasis on reason (*Vernunft*) to the detriment of emotion (Varga 2001). When Kant writes that reason is in itself sufficient to give human beings a general moral law,[20] this is echoed in the writings of Habermas. Both Kant and Habermas also share a deontological orientation in their philosophies, which means that they do not set specific moral goals but merely rules of how to reach moral goals. With his categorical imperative Kant does not say in a specific way how one should act, he only gives the rule on how to make moral decisions, namely that the maxim of one's actions should be able to serve as guidance for societal laws and that therefore other human beings should always be treated as ends and never as means. In the same way, Habermas does not tell us what the substance of the decision outcome should be; he merely tells us what rules should be applied in a decision process so that the outcome has a high moral quality. Furthermore, Kant and Habermas both have a universalistic approach in the sense that the categorical imperative and the deliberative model should apply to all human situations, without regard to time and space. Finally, it was Kant who already stressed the importance of publicity in public life, an aspect that became so crucial for the work of Habermas. Kant argued that lack of publicity prevents the progress of a people to improve itself.[21] In the same vein, for Habermas a broad and open public sphere is of crucial importance in his deliberative model.

---

[18] "Handle so, dass die Maxime deines Willens jederzeit zugleich als Prinzip einer allgemeinen Gesetzgebung gelten könnte" (Kant 1994: 54).

[19] "In der Diskursethik tritt an die Stelle des kategorischen Imperativs das Verfahren der moralischen Argumentation" (Habermas 1984: 12).

[20] "Reine Venunft ist für sich allein practisch und giebt [dem Menschen] ein allgemeines Gesetz, welches wir das Sittengesetz nennen" (Kant 1994: 56).

[21] "So verhindert das Verbot der Publizität den Fortschritt eines Volkes zum Besseren" (Kant: 1975: 363).

Besides Kant, it was also Hegel and Marx, with their dialectical thinking, who had considerable influence on Habermas. As for Hegel and Marx, there is an element of progress in the philosophy of Habermas in the sense that the deliberative process in a dialectical way will lead to progress. There will always be twists and turns, delays and setbacks, but basically Habermas expects that ultimately progress through deliberation is possible if only human beings are willing to use their reason, which is harking back to Kant who encourages human beings to use their reason, warning them that they would only reach human maturity (*Mündigkeit*) if they did so.[22] This is also the key message of Habermas who hopes in a Kantian sense that citizens will use their reason in the political process and thereby become *mündig*, an expression that is insufficiently translated by terms such as coming of age or mature. *Mündig* means to have the courage to use one's reason, or as Kant puts it, *sapere aude*, have the courage to know.

Habermas had several modern predecessors who had already developed key elements of the deliberative model in their democratic thinking. Bryce (1921: 160), in particular, stressed that democracy should not only be based on the voting of the citizens but also on public debates between votes. For Bryce,

> voting is serviceable just in proportion as it has been preceded and prepared by the action of public opinion. This discussion which forms opinion by securing the due expression of each view or set of views so that the sounder may prevail enables the citizens who wish to find the truth and follow it to deliver a considered vote. It is an educative process constantly in progress . . . The clash and conflict of argument bring out the strength and weakness of every case, and that which is sound tends to prevail.

Criticism of the deliberative model

There is much criticism in the philosophical literature of the deliberative model. *The fact that the model is controversial makes it not less but rather more interesting to study in an empirical way, which is the project of this book.* In the present chapter, we outline the main criticisms of the deliberative model, without taking a position ourselves. At a personal level, we have, of course, our subjective views on the merits of the deliberative model. We find some of the criticism of the deliberative model quite compelling, but we do not consider it our task to argue in a normative way for or against

---

[22] "Aufklärung ist der Ausgang des Menschen aus seiner selbstverschuldeten Unmündigkeit. Unmündigkeit ist das Unvermögen, sich seines Verstandes ohne Leitung eines anderen zu bedienen. Selbstverschuldet ist diese Unmündigkeit, wenn die Ursache derselben nicht am Mangel des Verstandes liegt, sich seiner ohne Leitung eines anderen zu bedienen. Sapere aude! Habe Mut, dich deines eigenen Verstandes zu bedienen" (Kant 1975: 53).

the model. As already stated earlier in the chapter, we want to investigate deliberative politics with regard to its empirical causes and consequences. We hope that such an investigation will throw some light on the philosophical controversies surrounding the model.

The most severe criticism of the deliberative model is that it is detrimental to social justice. This criticism is particularly severe because the supporters of the deliberative model make exactly the opposite claim, namely that deliberation helps to attain social justice, since all points of view – including those of the socially most disadvantaged – are considered in a good deliberation. What is the basis of the criticism that deliberative politics is detrimental to social justice? Young (2001) makes the argument most forcefully in an essay entitled "Activist Challenges to Deliberative Democracy," where she constructs a dialogue between two persons, a deliberative democrat and an activist:

> the purpose of the dialectic is not to recommend one side over the other because I think that both approaches are valuable and necessary to demonstrate practice that aims to promote justice. Bringing the approaches into critical relation with one another in this way, however, helps sound a caution about trying to put ideals of deliberative democracy into practice in societies with structural inequalities (p. 671).

According to this quote, it is an open question for Young whether deliberative politics indeed helps or hurts social justice. Her goal is to caution us that there are good arguments why deliberative politics can also be negative for social justice. In using her dialectic approach, Young is able to present in a coherent way what an activist would criticize in the deliberative model. An activist is someone "who filled the streets of Seattle in December 1999" to disrupt the meeting of the World Trade Organization (p. 677). The tactics of the activist are: "picketing, leafleting, guerrilla theater, large and loud street demonstrations, sit-ins, and other forms of direct action, such as boycotts" (p. 673). The key argument of the activist against the deliberative model is that "the deliberative democrat who thinks that power can be bracketed by the soft tones of the seminar room is naive" (p. 675).

> The activist is suspicious of exhortations to deliberate because he believes that in the real world of politics, where structural inequalities influence both procedures and outcomes, democratic processes that appear to conform to norms of deliberation are usually biased toward more powerful agents. The activist thus recommends that those who care about promoting greater justice should engage primarily in critical oppositional activity, rather than attempt to come to agreement with those who support or benefit from existing power structures (p. 671).

The activist does not believe that full and equal participation of all citizens in the political process will ever be possible. The deliberative democrat does not believe this either, but he hopes that steps can be made in the direction of the ideal type of deliberative politics. The activist does not share this hope.

> In a society structured by deep social and economic inequalities, [the activist] believes that formally inclusive deliberative processes nevertheless enact structural biases in which more powerful and socially advantaged actors have greater access to the deliberative process and therefore are able to dominate the proceedings with their interests and perspectives. Under conditions of structural inequality, normal processes of deliberation often in practice restrict access to agents with greater resources, knowledge, or connections to those with greater control over the forum. We are familiar with the many manifestations of this effective exclusion from deliberation. Where radio and television are major fora for further deliberation, for example, citizens either need the money or connections to get air time. Even when a series of public hearings are announced for an issue, people who might wish to speak at them need to know about them, be able to arrange their work and child care schedule to be able to attend, to be able to get to them, and have enough understanding of the hearing process to participate. Each of these abilities is unevenly present among members of a society (p. 680).

At an even more basic level the activist makes the argument that the language used in a deliberation is of a hegemonic nature favoring the powerful in society.

> The phenomenon of hegemony or systematically distorted communication is more subtle . . . It refers to how the conceptual and normative framework of the members of a society is deeply influenced by premises and terms of discourse that make it difficult to think critically about aspects of their social relations or alternative possibilities of institutionalization and action. The theory and practice of deliberative democracy have no tools for raising the possibility that deliberations may be closed and distorted in this way. It lacks a theory of, shall we call it, ideology, as well as an account of the genealogy of discourses and their manner of helping to constitute the way individuals see themselves and their social world. For most deliberative democrats, discourse seems to be more "innocent" . . . This level of the influence of structural inequality over public discussion is the most insidious because it is the least apparent to all participants. It concerns the conceptual and imagistic frame for discussion, which often contains falsifications, biases, misunderstandings, and even contradictions that go unnoticed and uncriticized largely because they coincide with hegemonic interests or reflect existing realities as though they are unalterable (pp. 685–6).

In the final analysis, the activist fears that deliberative politics rather than helping to attain greater social justice helps to cement the existing inequalities in society. He therefore prefers direct actions to attain more social justice.

> Because [the activist] suspects some agreements of masking unjust power re-
> lations, the activist believes it is important to continue to challenge these dis-
> courses, and the deliberative processes that rely on them, and often he must do
> so by nondiscursive means – pictures, song, poetic imagery, and expressions of
> mockery and longing performed in rowdy and even playful ways aimed not at
> commanding assent but disturbing complacency. One of the activist's goals is to
> make us *wonder* about what we are doing, to rupture a stream of thought, rather
> than to weave an agreement (p. 687).

Although Young does not fully agree with her constructed activist, in her
summary statement she has much sympathy for him.

> Screen and song celebrate social justice movements that protested in the streets
> when they were convinced that existing institutions and their normal procedures
> only reinforced the status quo. Many rights have been won in democratic societies
> by means of courageous activism – the eight-hour day, votes for women, the right
> to sit at any lunch counter. Yet contemporary democratic theory rarely reflects
> on the role of demonstration and direct action (p. 670).

Young also acknowledges that the deliberative democrat, too, has good arguments why his model may contribute to social justice, and she concludes
that "both are important for democratic theory and practice" (p. 688).

There are other political philosophers who are even more skeptical than
Young about the positive influence of deliberative politics on social justice. Prominent among these critics is Sanders (1997), who gives her essay
the provocative short title "Against Deliberation." She complains that there
is too much consensus among political philosophers about the merits of
deliberative politics.

> One might simply be suspicious of the near consensus among democratic the-
> orists on its (deliberative politics) behalf. It isn't clear, after all, that this wide
> endorsement has itself emerged through a genuinely deliberative process: demo-
> cratic theorists are a select group who cannot and do not claim in any way to
> represent the perspectives of ordinary citizens (p. 349).

Ordinary citizens, especially those who are "materially disadvantaged,
namely women, racial minorities, especially Blacks, and poorer people" may
not necessarily like the deliberative model to redress their grievances. For
Sanders, the deliberative model is popular among academic philosophers
because they are accustomed to deliberate in their seminars, but the model
is far removed from the everyday struggles of the disadvantaged groups in
society. If these disadvantaged groups want to attain more social justice,
Sanders recommends that they use the strategy of giving public *testimony*
of their lives.

What is fundamental about giving testimony is telling one's own story, not seeking communal dialogue ... There's no assumption in testimony of finding a common aim, no expectation of a discussion oriented to the resolution of a community problem. Testimony is also radically egalitarian: the standard for whether a view is worthy of public attention is simply that everyone should have a voice, a chance to tell her story. What might recommend testimony right now to democrats is the need to bring more perspectives into democratic discussions and to figure out a way not to close off the views of any because they are different, not common. Unlike deliberation, the standard of testimony does not exclude positions if they are voiced in an immoderate or emotionally laden way. Testimony encourages the democratic consideration of the worthiness of perspectives not obviously rooted in common ground and not necessarily voiced in a calmly rational way (p. 372).

As illustrations of effective testimonies Sanders mentions the African American culture, particularly their churches, where it is common for ordinary citizens to stand up in public and to tell others about the tragedies in their life stories. Testimonies do not necessarily have to be expressed in verbal form. Sanders alludes to rap music that "began as a form of 'testimony' for the underclass. It has enabled underclass black youth to develop a critical voice . . . Rap projects a critical voice, explaining, demanding, urging" (p. 371).

For Sanders, the biggest problem of the deliberative model is that it postulates that all participants should have equal status and respect but does not say how this equality is to be achieved. According to Sanders, it will not do to say that deliberation will contribute to equality since equality is a precondition for deliberation. Therefore, the argument would become circular in the following form: if we want deliberation, we need equality, but if we want equality, we need deliberation. For Sanders, the articulation of the standards for good deliberation "is a far cry from assessment of the probability of meeting them. In the absence of such an assessment, appeals to deliberation do nothing to challenge an undesirable status quo" (p. 348). Sanders concludes that she is not in principle against deliberation, but "that we [should] forget deliberation for the time being, and try to imagine a model for democratic politics that more plausibly encourages mutual respect" (p. 350). In a nutshell, Sanders argues that equality as a precondition for deliberation cannot be achieved through deliberation itself, so that other means for more equality and thus more justice have to be tried, for example more testimonies of life stories of ordinary citizens, especially of disadvantaged citizens.

On a more optimistic note than Sanders, Rosenberg (2003: 22) hopes that the practice of deliberation may indeed improve deliberative skills: "This suggests a shift in deliberative democratic theory in a direction that is more explicitly pedagogical. Deliberative settings must not only be seen as the stage for realizing a more democratic practice, they must also be seen as the training ground where the skills required to engage in that practice can be developed."

Sanders is also challenged by Dryzek (2000: 67–9), who, although sympathetic to the notion of storytelling, warns that with this method other kinds of hierarchy may develop, since not everyone is a good storyteller, "[g]raduates of creative writing programs and those with lots of accumulated experience might be the best storytellers." In addition, there may be oppression with regard to what stories can be told: for example, "in fundamentalist religions, where the newcomer to the group must offer a story based on past sin leading to realization of god's mercy and the hope for redemption; and the bigger the sin, the better the story."

Hauptmann (2001: 420–1) is still another political philosopher who is critical of whether deliberative politics really helps to redress social injustice. She criticizes the cautiousness of the deliberative model, which "dulls the theory's critical edge . . . deliberative democrats have fashioned a theory of democracy lacking critical perspective . . . deliberative theorists of democracy are not able to tell us much about what is wrong with the political world and, consequently, can tell us little about how we might make it better." When Hauptmann refers to a better world, she means a socially more just world, and in this respect she expects little from the deliberative model.

Gabardi (2001: 556) is the last voice we want to quote who also argues along the lines of Young, Sanders, and Hauptmann that deliberative politics discriminates against the less educated[23] and therefore does little to redress social injustice:

> [The norms of deliberative politics] privilege a type of speech that is formal and argumentative, articulate and dispassionate, that abstracts from ascriptive characteristics of race, class, gender, lifestyle, and religion, and that is oriented toward the greater public good. Speech that is dramatic and expressive, rhetorical, testimonial, that involves storytelling, humor, and figures of speech, and discussion settings that focus on cultural difference, on listening, and on protest and performative resistance are accorded second-class status . . . the diversity of civic associations and public voices which constitute our civil society would be effectively streamlined into the homogeneous thematic voice of an abstract, postconventional moralism . . . the deliberative model of democracy is too demanding, too narrow, and too coercive.

We find these critical voices against the deliberative model intriguing, and we take them seriously. Our response is that there are good arguments on

---

[23] Dryzek (2000: 172) cautions, however, that we should "be wary of the implicit condescension involved in claiming that materially disadvantaged people are necessarily the poorest communicators."

both sides of the debate and that we should attempt to find out which
arguments correspond better to the empirical reality. Put in other terms, we
consider the conflicting arguments as conflicting hypotheses that cry out
for empirical testing. This is exactly what we try to do in chapter 6, where
we investigate whether the discourse quality in a debate has an influence on
the social justice dimension of the political outcome.

Besides the critique that deliberative politics does not help but may even
hurt social justice, there are other criticisms in the philosophical literature.
Another particularly severe criticism is that deliberative politics as conceived by deliberative theorists is an impossibility because politics is always
a power game and will remain so. Mouffe (1999) urges us "to acknowledge
the dimension of power and antagonism and their ineradicable character,"
and from this premise she postulates "the impossibility of the ideal speech
situation" (p. 752).[24] If this statement merely meant that the ideal type of
deliberation could never be attained, deliberative theorists would agree. As
we remember from earlier in the chapter, Habermas compares rational discourses to islands in the ocean. Deliberative theorists, however, hope that
important steps can be made in the direction of the ideal type of deliberative politics. It is precisely this hope that political philosophers like Mouffe
consider as illusion.

> To deny that there ever could be a free and unconstrained public deliberation of all
> matters of common concern is therefore crucial for democratic politics . . . This is
> why an approach that reveals the impossibility of establishing consensus without
> exclusion is of fundamental importance . . . There is absolutely no justification
> for attributing a special privilege in this respect to a so-called "moral point of
> view" governed by impartiality and where an impartial assessment of what is in
> the general interest could be reached (pp. 752, 756–7).

Mouffe bases her impossibility statement of deliberative politics mainly on
her reading of Ludwig Wittgenstein, which leads her "to challenge the very
idea of a neutral or rational dialogue" (p. 749).

> For Wittgenstein to have agreement in opinions there must first be agreement
> on the language used and this, as he points out, implies agreement in forms of
> life. According to him, procedure only exists as a complex ensemble of practices.
> Those practices constitute specific forms of individuality and identity that make
> possible the allegiance to the procedures. It is because they are inscribed in shared

[24] In a similar vein, Morris (2001: 787, 790) argues against the notion "of a master code or
a universalism that governs acceptable speech." For him there should be an awareness of
historically based "unique perspectives in language and speech." Based on this premise,
"it does not follow that agreement must then be the telos of all political communication."
In his criticism of the deliberative model, Morris draws heavily from the deconstructivist
ideas of Derrida (1995).

forms of life and agreements in judgments that procedures can be accepted and followed. They cannot be seen as rules that are created on the basis of principles and then applied to practices, they are inseparable of [sic] specific forms of life. Therefore, distinctions between "procedural" and "substantial" . . . central to the Habermasian approach cannot be maintained and one must acknowledge that procedures always involve substantial ethical commitments (p. 749).

If the procedures postulated by deliberative theorists for good deliberation are never neutral and if all politics is a power game, then, according to Mouffe, deliberative politics is a power game like any other form of politics and has no special status for morality and legitimacy.[25] Besides Wittgenstein, Mouffe also refers to the philosopher Jacques Lacan, whose "approach reveals how discourse itself in its fundamental structure is authoritarian since out of the free-floating dispersion of signifiers, it is only through the intervention of a master signifier that a consistent field of meaning can emerge" (p. 751). For Mouffe, "Lacan undermines in that way the very basis of [the]Habermasian view, according to which the inherent pragmatic presuppositions of discourse are non-authoritarian" (p. 751). In contrast to the deliberative model, Mouffe offers a model of agonistic pluralism that starts with the premise that politics consists of antagonism, power, and passion. Under these conditions, the purpose of democracy is

> that the "other" is no longer seen as an enemy to be destroyed, but as an "adversary," i.e., somebody with whose ideas we are going to struggle but whose right to defend those ideas we will not put into question . . . An adversary is a legitimate enemy, an enemy with whom we have in common a shared adhesion to the ethico-political principles of democracy. But our disagreement concerning their meaning and implementation is not one that could be resolved through deliberation and rational discussion, hence the antagonistic element in the relation (p. 755).

Contrary to the deliberative model, Mouffe "asserts that the prime task of democratic politics is not to eliminate passions nor to relegate them to the private sphere in order to render rational consensus possible, but to mobilise those passions towards the promotion of democratic designs. Far from jeopardizing democracy, agonistic confrontation is in fact its very condition of existence" (pp. 755–6).

Whether it is really impossible to have any degree of deliberative politics, as Mouffe claims, is ultimately an empirical question. One would have to put the concept of deliberative politics *in operational terms so that it becomes*

---

[25] For a discourse analysis based on the linguistic approach of Wittgenstein, see also the research symposium "Discourse Analysis and Political Science" with contributions from Terrell Carver, Jacob Torfing, Véronique Mottier, and Maarten Hajer in *European Political Science* 2 (autumn 2002): 48–67.

measurable. We will address this question of operationalization in chapter 3. To operationalize a concept means to establish procedural rules of how to classify events in the real world. Following the teaching of Wittgenstein, one may object to such an enterprise with the argument that procedures are never derived from general principles and then applied to practices; they are rather inseparable from specific forms of life. Therefore, procedures are only accepted if they are inscribed in shared forms of life. We accept this criticism, and we will not claim to measure the degree of deliberative politics in any objective way. Of course, the shared forms of life in our research group have influenced how we operationalize deliberative politics. Because they belong to other forms of life, scholars such as Mouffe may operationalize the concept of deliberative politics quite differently and consequently arrive at different results. It is then a question of who has more convincing arguments in the scholarly community at large. We acknowledge that the position that is ahead in this scholarly competition is not necessarily closer to objective truth. The scholars who are ahead may simply belong to larger and more powerful forms of life with greater resources of grant money, journals, publishing houses, and so on. Acknowledging that the power dimension is not absent in scholarly competition does not imply that it is the only factor. Sometimes, at least this is our hope, the force of the better argument may still prevail in scholarly debates. If we give up this hope, scholarship becomes nothing but a crude power game and the universities lose their privileged position as places for the search of truth.

Besides the two fundamental criticisms of the deliberative model discussed so far – the potentially negative impact of deliberative politics on social justice and the impossibility of having any deliberative politics at all – there are some more specific criticisms. One such criticism deals with the question of how exactly deliberative politics should be defined. Here, we find interesting the criticism of Basu (1999) that the Habermasian definition of deliberative politics leaves out the aspect of humor. Basu quotes Habermas as writing that "jokes, fictional representations, irony, games, and so on, rest on intentionally using categorical confusions" (p. 398). In contrast to this negative view of Habermas on the role of humor in deliberation, Basu sees "humor as a virtue" (p. 385):

> The liberal-democratic polity may be uniquely friendly to humorous citizens ... Humor contributes openness, playfulness, and pleasure to epistemological practices ... Humor provisionally suspends decorum, putting the mind at liberty to hear all sides. It allows one to temporarily suspend one's cherished beliefs and contemplate the implications without treachery ... Humor finds ambiguities, contradictions and parables in what is otherwise taken literally ... Humor keeps the process of reasoning open-ended ... If humor facilitates cognition, it also prompts dispositional finesse, that is, ease, modesty and tolerance ... it makes one available for convivial relations with others and otherness ... humor can

be a social lubricant. It breaks the ice and fills the awkward silences . . . Comedy permits frankness to be less threatening . . . comedy can make palatable what is otherwise hard to swallow . . . humor is more civil and productive than the vicious triangle of dogmatism, disputatiousness and deadlock . . . humor can gain entry into a closed mind . . . A well-placed joke may, then, act like a firm prod or provocation to another to reconsider what she holds dear in herself and dire in others (pp. 385, 387–92).

Basu concludes that "although Habermas regards humor as aberrant and dubious linguistic behavior, the ability to joke is actually a measure of the mastery of a given language and its limits. In short, 'communicative competence' ought to include a humorous awareness of the incompetence of communication" (pp. 398–9). These different approaches of Basu and Habermas towards the role of humor in good deliberation is an excellent illustration of the argument of Wittgenstein – mentioned above – that language depends on "agreement in forms of life." It is obvious that Habermas as a German professor and Basu as a professor in the northwest of the United States do not share the same forms of life and therefore have different views of what communicative competence is. Who is right? How one defines a concept is not a question of right or wrong but of useful or not useful. Empirical studies would have to show whether the explanatory power of communicative competence is increased if the element of humor is included in its definition. For the time being, we have excluded the element of humor in our definition of deliberation, but we may very well include it in later research phases.

Another more specific criticism of deliberative politics is that the act of deliberation, instead of reducing disagreements, may rather increase them. Sunstein (2002: 187) argues that deliberation may increase polarization, so that "the results of deliberative judgments may be far worse than the results of simply taking the median of predeliberative judgments." According to Shapiro (1999) "deliberation can bring differences to the surface, widening the political divisions rather than narrowing them" (p. 31). His point is "that there is no particular reason to think deliberation will bring people together, even if they hope it will" (p. 31). Shapiro postulates that in order to know

> how effective . . . [the] deliberative model would be, either at reducing moral disagreements or at promoting accommodation of irresolvable differences in American politics, one would have to see it in action in debates among pro-lifers and pro-choicers . . . or protagonists in debates over redistricting, affirmative action, welfare reform, child support (p. 28).

Shapiro is right that it is not enough to speculate about the effects of deliberation. What is needed are systematic empirical investigations on whether deliberation increases or reduces political tensions. According to a review of the social psychology literature, Mendelberg (2002: 161) hypothesizes that deliberation reduces tensions when factual questions of truth are involved, whereas the opposite effect occurs when values are at the center of the discussion. He concludes that "[a]dvocates of deliberation would do well to promote deliberation on issues of fact but to advance alternatives to deliberation on issues of value."

Our overall conclusion of this review of the criticisms of the deliberative model is that the scholarly debate on the model may be helped if the model is submitted to systematic and wide-ranging empirical investigations. In the same vein, Fishkin and Laslett (2002b: 126) argue that we should empirically investigate "[w]hat goes on in a deliberative process . . . we are to envisage real people under realistic conditions making actual policy choices." Sunstein (2002: 176) notes that, for the most part, the literature on deliberation "has not been empirically informed. It has not dealt much with the real-world consequences of deliberation, and with whether generalizations hold in actual deliberative settings, with groups of different predispositions and compositions." For Lascher (1996: 502–3, 516) "it is important that researchers not shirk from a more thorough assessment of how deliberation works in real-world legislatures." He emphasizes that "measures of deliberation and related concepts need to be developed, tested, and refined." Dryzek and Braithwaite (2000: 242) complain that "the defenders and various critics of deliberation share one belief: that matters can be resolved at the level of theoretical stipulation, with little recourse to empirical evidence beyond illustrative anecdotes."

We agree with Dryzek and Braithwaite that the controversies surrounding the deliberative model cannot be resolved at the level of theoretical speculations and that research needs to go beyond illustrative anecdotes. In chapter 3, we address the issue of how real-life deliberation can be empirically investigated in a systematic way. Having done empirical investigations of deliberative politics, what will then be the relationship between normative-philosophical theories and empirical research into deliberation? We agree with the following assessment of Chambers (2003: 320): "Empirical research can be invaluable in keeping normative theorists on their toes and in zeroing in on some specific institutional design questions. Empirical research cannot be either the last or the leading word in deliberative democratic theory, however."

Chambers is correct in pointing out that empirical research cannot determine whether deliberation is a good thing in itself and whether we should value the policy outcomes resulting from a high level of deliberation. These will remain questions that must be evaluated at a normative-philosophical level. Thus, empirical research can merely be a helping hand in the big controversies of democratic theory. But, as a helping hand, empirical research has its place.

3

Measuring deliberation:
a Discourse Quality Index

As we have seen in chapter 2, up to now the scholarly debate on the deliberative model has mainly taken place at a philosophical level. But we have also seen that there are important voices asking that the philosophical debate on deliberation should be supplemented with empirical investigations of real-life deliberations. In the present chapter, we take up this challenge.

Empirical studies on deliberation

There are already some studies in this direction. Some of them limit themselves to the formulation of hypotheses without testing them. Lascher (1996: 501) acknowledges explicitly in the title of his study that his is only a "Preface to Empirical Analysis." With the focus on legislatures, he offers some indicators of how the quality of deliberation might be measured: for example, "whether arguments are framed in terms of some conception of the public good," or whether "participants are able to critique each other's arguments and respond to such criticism." Lascher then looks at factors promoting deliberation, hypothesizing, for example, that "legislative decisions will better meet deliberative standards when an issue is salient to constituents," or "when there is greater uncertainty about the effects of different policy alternatives." Lascher also presents hypotheses about possible consequences of deliberation: for example, "deliberation increases the legitimacy of legislators' decisions," or "deliberation has cognitive benefits for participants, such as reducing erroneous judgments related to the policy issue in question." Alluding to later empirical tests of his hypotheses, Lascher warns that "the required work will not be easy."

Another study limiting itself to the formulation of hypotheses to be tested later on is by Dryzek and Braithwaite (2000). Based on Australian data, they distinguish four dominant political orientations among the public, which they call political discourses. They are "inclusive republicanism," "right-minded democracy," "anxious egalitarianism," and "resigned acceptance." Inclusive republicanism is a discourse that "refers to the affirmation of previously excluded groups or categories and their acceptance into full political membership in Australian society. The discourse is republican in both its rejection of monarchy and its sense of invigorated citizenship" (p. 249). According to anxious egalitarianism, "we need to protect democratic procedures against loud minorities in politics . . . Affirmative action is fine, but we shouldn't give special political rights to anyone" (pp. 250–1). According to the hypotheses of Dryzek and Braithwaite, deliberation between inclusive republicanism and anxious egalitarianism is particularly difficult, and it is to be expected that this particular "encounter of discourses produces only the dogmatic reassertion of identity . . . and it is hard to see any deliberative process changing matters" (pp. 259–60). Dryzek and Braithwaite see the greatest potential for deliberation between inclusive republicanism and right-minded democracy. For the latter, "government's main task is to maintain peace and justice, and otherwise not to interfere in people's lives . . . What we need is strong, honest, realistic leadership, putting into practice tried and trusted principles like those found in the Bible" (p. 250). For Dryzek and Braithwaite, it is important for their hypothesis that inclusive republicanism and right-minded democracy "are both engaged in the political process, and there is plenty of opportunity for positive-sum outcomes in the interactions of these two discourses, precisely because they are committed to different kinds of values" (p. 261). Dryzek and Braithwaite end their paper by saying that, if their "analysis holds true . . . the prospects for deliberative democracy are rosy to the extent that conflicts are between inclusive republicanism and right-minded democracy and dim to the extent that they are between inclusive republicanism and anxious egalitarianism." They acknowledge that the answer to these hypotheses is ultimately "an empirical matter, which we cannot begin to resolve here" (p. 262). Investigations such as the ones by Lascher and Dryzek/Braithwaite that limit themselves to the formulation of hypotheses are still useful in stimulating actual empirical work on deliberation.

Among actual empirical work on deliberation, there are some studies that use the concept of deliberation more or less as a synonym for *public talk*. Roberts (1997), for example, investigated two decision processes in Minnesota, one about reducing a school district's budget, the other about crafting state educational policy. In both case studies she finds it remarkable how the decision process is broad-based in expanding to ordinary citizens. With regard to the school budget cuts, for example,

> the board of education held workshops to study budget issues. The 13,000 students in the district met in quality circles to offer suggestions on how they could save money . . . citizens' meetings were held in 10 elementary schools in the district. More than 2,000 people came to speak, listen, and react to the recommendations that had been developed at that point, and to provide their own recommendations for budget reductions (p. 126).

Roberts sees many advantages in such broad-based decision processes:

> they invite others' viewpoints and trust that some new solutions will surface and learning will take place. Public deliberation requires some humility in dealing with the many tensions of public management . . . Deliberation can help people examine the premises and values on which their actions are based and can stimulate the discovery of alternative visions of society . . . [deliberation] asks for patience, trust in self and others, respect for those whose ideas are different, ability to see a whole system and its interdependent parts, and suspension of self-interest for the common good (p. 130).

These characteristics correspond very much to the philosophical concept of deliberation as presented in chapter 2. Roberts hopes that broad-based public talk will contribute to deliberation thus defined, but she does not systematically study to what extent this indeed happens in her two case studies. She limits herself to showing how broadly the decision processes were expanded to ordinary citizens and how these citizens actually took part in the public talk about the budget cuts and the state educational policy. But Roberts does not show us, for example, to what extent the participants in this public talk had indeed "respect for those whose ideas are different." She only postulates that such respect is necessary for a good deliberation.

Another study where deliberation is more or less a synonym for public talk is by Baccaro (2001), who investigated workers' decision making in two southern Italian Fiat factories. The issue in both places was whether the workers should accept a tradeoff offered by the management to expand the factories and to create more jobs in return for more work flexibility, with Saturday, for example, becoming a regular working day. In both factories the trade union leaders supported this tradeoff. The difference between the two places was that in one place workers voted without discussion, whereas in the other place the vote was preceded by what Baccaro calls deliberation. It was, however, not deliberation in the specific sense defined in chapter 2, but simply public talk. The outcome was very different in the two factories, with the tradeoff being rejected in the factory without public talk but being accepted in the other factory. Thus, public talk in itself seems to have had an effect. It would be interesting to compare factories that all have public talk but with different levels in the quality of deliberation.

Still another study comparing two cases of decision making, one with talk and the other without talk, is by Sulkin and Simon (2001). Theirs is an experimental study using the well-known *ultimatum game.* It is a two-player game, with one player having the role of proposer, the other of acceptor. The players have the task of dividing $100. The proposer offers a percentage to the acceptor who accepts or rejects the offer. If accepted, the money is allocated according to the proposal. If rejected, neither player receives any money. Sulkin and Simon use undergraduate students to do the experiment. The players do not meet face to face, but sit at computers. Three situations are distinguished: (1) they communicate with each other *before* the proposer makes an offer; (2) they communicate with each other *after* the proposer makes an offer but before the offer is accepted or rejected; (3) no communication is allowed. The instruction for the nature of the communication reads as follows: "sometimes you will be allowed to communicate with the other player, either before or after the proposal is made. All communication is strictly anonymous and completely confidential" (p. 823). For each game, communication is limited for both players together to a maximum of 180 seconds. The result was that communication before the offer had the effect that the offer was more generous to the acceptor. When communication was permitted only after the offer or when no communication was permitted, the offer was less generous with no significant difference between the two latter situations. Sulkin and Simon conclude that talk before an offer is made leads to a fairer outcome. This is an interesting result, but we doubt that they really test "Habermas in the Lab" as the title of their paper implies. As in the study of Baccaro, here too the concept of deliberation is used in a loose way, meaning only that the two players communicated with each other. Whether this communication was purely strategic or had some features of deliberation in the sense of Habermas is not investigated. Sulkin and Simon acknowledge this critique, when they write that "a potential critique of such an approach is that our manipulations of deliberation do not approximate the ideals envisioned by democratic theorists . . . Whether the deliberation that does take place is of high quality is an open question" (p. 815). They claim "that it is impossible to experimentally manipulate the presence or absence of successful deliberation" (p. 815). We are not so pessimistic. What is needed is a measurement instrument that allows us to assess the quality of deliberation, either in the real world or in experiments. Later in this chapter we will show that this task is not beyond reach.

The critique that they study merely talk and not deliberation in a more specific sense also applies to the well-known "deliberative polling" of Fishkin (1997) and his collaborators. The basic research design is that randomly selected groups of citizens talk with each other, and polls before and after these talks establish whether any changes in opinion occurred:

> A random sample (of citizens) is first given a survey of the conventional sort. Then, it is invited to come to a single place, at the expense of the project, to engage in a weekend of small group discussions and larger plenary sessions in which it is given extensive opportunities to get good information, exchange competing points of views and come to a considered judgment. At the end of the weekend, it is given the same questionnaire as on first contact. The resulting changes of opinion are often dramatic (Ackermann and Fishkin 2002: 156).

Such changes in opinion are, for example, that citizens become more informed, interested, trusting, participatory, and supportive of democracy (Luskin and Fishkin, 2002). As for the research of Baccaro and Sulkin/Simon, here too it is impressive how much difference talk makes. These results certainly go a long way towards testing the deliberative model. Already mere talking seems to make a difference.[1] But, as outlined in chapter 2, there is much more to the deliberative model than mere talking. In the above quote by Ackermann and Fishkin it is stated that participants in the deliberative polling were given "opportunities" to "exchange competing points of views and come to a considered judgment." But it is not systematically investigated to what extent these opportunities were actually used. Here again, an instrument to measure the quality of the deliberation would be necessary. Only on such a basis would it be possible to treat deliberation as a variable and to study its preconditions and consequences. When it is stated in the above quote that "changes of opinion are often dramatic," it would be interesting to know when they are dramatic and when not, and how this depends on the quality of the deliberation.

From the review of the empirical literature on deliberation up to now it should have become clear that it is not only a question of whether talk takes place or not, but at what quality of deliberation such talks occurs. The challenge to distinguish different qualities of deliberation is taken up in several *qualitative* studies. One of these studies is by Chambers (1999) who in the fall of 1992 investigated the decision making process leading up to a referendum in Canada on the question of Quebec. In the summer of 1992, a number of conferences were set up across Canada to discuss possible solutions to the various constitutional impasses facing the nation. Conference participation represented a relatively broad cross-section of Canadians. According to the

---

[1] For another study investigating the influence of talk, see Pelletier et al. (1999); they looked at planning conferences on local food systems in six rural counties in northern New York state. Comparing viewpoints before and after these conferences, they found significant changes, in particular "a more thoughtful consideration of public issues . . . akin to what Dahl has called enlightened understanding" (p. 121).

investigation by Chambers, these conferences corresponded to a large extent to the model of deliberative politics:

> Advocates even of quite extreme positions were willing to sign on to "consensual" documents that reflected the general tenor of the weekend-long debates. The procedures adopted within the conferences conformed to ideals of deliberation in that there was a conscious attempt to guarantee dialogical equality so that everyone could speak and be heard and to exclude influences, such as money and power, that might distort the conversation. But even more interesting was the fact that no votes were taken. The mornings were taken up by workshops, which came together in afternoon plenary sessions to work out position papers. These papers reflected a conference wide "consensus" in that they recorded what people were able to agree on as well as those issues upon which no agreement was reached (p. 4).

The hope of many Canadians was that the positive experience of the conferences could be recreated in the referendum campaign. But according to Chambers it did not "pan out."

> The great disappointment was focused on the caliber and tenor of the debate. Lacking was the openness and flexibility of the conference participants, that is, the willingness to revise claims, to make them fit with other, now perceived as equally legitimate, claims. Instead, the referendum campaign appeared to harden positions. Furthermore, leaders and spokespersons began to talk in zero sum terms, to the effect that any concession to other interests would be a loss for their side. Rather than reasonable argument, fear of being a loser in the deal was played up. All in all, the referendum debate had an effect opposite to what deliberation is supposed to have: it moved participants further apart, heightened distrust, exacerbated misunderstandings and left Canadians in a worse place than when they started (pp. 4–5).

From her investigation, Chambers derives the hypothesis that the discourse quality decreases as the date of decision making approaches:

> I want to single out one difference that offers an interesting perspective on the dynamics that can account for the different types of deliberation. This difference has to do with the relationship between deliberation and decision making. Not only did participants at the conferences not take any votes or make any internal decisions but their role in the larger constitutional debate was left vague. They had no clear mandate. The outcomes of these conferences did not bind in any authoritative way. The end of the conferences did not represent any kind of closure or decision. It is not quite right to say that nothing was at stake, for it was not an academic conference discussing constitutional options for ancient Athens but rather citizen participants who were aware of the seriousness and urgency of the issues and knew that they had the ear of the public as well as the political elite. Nevertheless, it is correct to say that a binding or authoritative decision was not at stake and this freed participants from the fear of premature or disadvantageous

closure. Participants could "afford" to be flexible, open, and cooperative. This in turn led to real movement of positions and convergence on issues. It was impossible to recreate that flexibility during the referendum campaign because the referendum put a whole new procedural dynamic in motion. Now participants were confronted with a deadline at which point the proposal, if passed, would be authoritative and very difficult if not impossible to revise. The fear of being the loser overwhelmed any principled desire to reach cooperative agreement. This quite natural fear, raised with any prospect of closure on a disputed issue, was played on and exacerbated by competing political elites (pp. 5–6).

The investigation of Chambers clearly goes beyond studying mere talk. She tries to assess different qualities of discourse in two phases leading up to a political decision. She derives from her investigation a testable hypothesis, namely that the discourse quality decreases as the decision date approaches. Whereas Chambers tries to get an empirical handle on different levels of deliberative politics in a national context,[2] Risse (2000) attempts to do the same at the international level. He investigates

the international negotiations ending the Cold War in Europe and settling the international issues concerning German unification. At the end, the Soviet Union under President Mikhail Gorbachev agreed to German unification within NATO in exchange for limits on Germany's and NATO's military posture in the former East Germany, on the one hand, and the transformation of NATO from an anti-Soviet alliance to a cooperative security institution, on the other hand (p. 23).

Risse acknowledges that "traditional distributive bargaining played a significant role in the negotiations settling the Cold War in Europe," and he also claims that "the Soviet Union still had some bargaining leverage" (pp. 24–5). But he also insists that some persuasion according to the deliberative model went on. Instead of deliberation, he speaks of arguing, which he defines pretty much according to our own criteria of the deliberative model:

Arguing implies that actors try to challenge the validity claims inherent in any causal or normative statement and to seek a communicative consensus about their understanding of a situation as well as justifications for the principles and norms guiding their actions. Argumentative rationality also implies that the participants in a discourse are open to being persuaded by the better argument and that relationships of power and social hierarchies recede in the background. Argumentative and deliberative behavior is as goal oriented as strategic interaction, but the goal is not to attain one's fixed preferences, but to seek a reasoned consensus (p. 7).

---

[2] Another study looking at different levels of deliberation in a national context is by Button and Mattson (1999) who investigated several public forums in the United States. In a similar way, Ryfe (2002) investigated sixteen organizations in the United States that claim deliberation as their goal: for example, "Citizen Juries" and "Americans Discuss Social Security."

Arguing, according to Risse's analysis, must play an important part if one wishes to explain the outcome of his case study. He claims "that this particular outcome largely resulted from a successful effort on both sides at arguing out the differences in a true dialogue of mutual persuasion . . . the outcome of these negotiations went well beyond a simple compromise" (p. 23). Risse states that the groundwork for true deliberation was laid from the mid-1980s when the key actors in the negotiations began to develop a common outlook on the world:

> Both sides had been interacting since the mid-1980s when Gorbachev and his foreign minister Shavardnadze came into power; they had created a common life-world establishing mutual trust. In this case, arguing was about problem solving to establish which norms should guide the post-Cold War security architecture in Europe. It entailed a practical discourse on the "right thing to do" in this peculiar situation (p. 24).

In order to make his point, Risse gives several illustrations of phases in the negotiations where true deliberation is supposed to have occurred. In one particularly dramatic incident "Gorbachev changed his mind right at the table," being persuaded by an argument from Bush: "The two leaders were engaged in a discourse about norms. Bush apparently persuaded Gorbachev by reframing the NATO issue from realist terms linked to Soviet security and stability in Europe to a liberal argument emphasizing democracy and self-determination" (p. 27). Generally speaking, it was important according to Risse, that "Western leaders treated their Soviet counterpart as an equal and serious negotiating partner, even though the power relationship between them was increasingly asymmetrical . . . Avoiding aggravating language in a tense negotiation serves a communicative purpose. It acknowledges empathy for the bargaining partner's concerns and communicates that the partner's demands are legitimate even if disagreed with" (p. 25). In his conclusion, Risse does not claim that the international negotiations he studied represent "the 'ideal speech situation' in the strict sense of the concept." But he claims "that we cannot explain the cooperative outcome of these negotiations without acknowledging that argumentative rather than instrumental rationality prevailed during crucial phases" (p. 28). One may or may not agree with this conclusion, but one must give credit to Risse that he makes a valuable effort to get an empirical grip on the concept of deliberative politics for international negotiations. Whoever disagrees with his conclusion is challenged to explain the outcome of these crucial international negotiations in a more convincing way.

On the role of arguments about norms in international negotiations, there is also an interesting study by Schimmelfennig (2001: 49, 62), who investigates why the European Union opened the accession process with

Central and Eastern European countries. He concludes that the decision to begin these accession negotiations cannot be explained only as a result of egoistic cost-benefit calculations and patterns of state preferences and power: "some sort of moral appeal was needed to change the uncooperative strategy of the dominant actors."

On still another level of analysis, della Porta (2003) looked at the level of deliberation in global social movements, in particular the European Social Movement meeting in Florence on November 6–9, 2002. The methods of investigation were semi-structured interviews with participants and six focus groups. Della Porta comes up with the conclusion that there was a great ambition among participants to conduct the meetings in a deliberative way, and there were also some instances of high-quality discourse. As one participant put it, "this encounter was really something great for me, the possibility of a way of doing politics which is immediately a building of public spaces, building the *polis*, not organizing in order to get votes" (p. 22). But there were also critical voices concerning the level of deliberation: for example, the complaint that "it's always the same ones that talk" (p. 14).

There are also quite a few studies of deliberation at the local level. A particularly interesting one is by Bobbio (2002) on waste management in the Turin region in Italy. He comes to the conclusion that thanks to deliberative efforts a consensus could be reached on where to locate two new waste management plants. The study is particularly interesting because Bobbio was himself the organizer of these deliberative efforts, showing a linkage between theory and praxis. Such linkages for local projects can also be seen in other places and occur more and more frequently. From a research perspective such linkages are not unproblematic because if the scholarly observer is at the time a key participant the effects of deliberation may be presented in terms that are too positive. Nevertheless, such praxis-oriented research has some value and should not be neglected by the scholarly community. Within the general deliberative literature it should be noted that there seems to be a growing interest in using the deliberative model for practical purposes. It would be interesting to do some meta-research about such praxis-oriented research and to investigate what exactly happens when a scholar of deliberation also becomes an organizer of deliberation.

The efforts of scholars such as Chambers, Risse, Schimmelfennig, della Porta, and Bobbio to study different levels of deliberative politics in a qualitative way must be applauded. In our own view, such qualitative studies have much merit since they get at the subtleties of the deliberative model. But some scholars may not be convinced by such qualitative studies. Thus, Voigt (2001: 17), an economist, who is interested in deliberative politics, states that "qualitative data [on discourse quality] will not convince many economists. They would prefer quantitative instead of qualitative analyses."

Such quantitative analyses are very rare – almost nonexistent. The first such attempt that we are aware of stems from Gerhards (1997), who investigates the discourse quality in two German newspapers[3] on abortion. A first indicator of discourse quality is the degree of respect expressed towards other participants in the debate on the abortion issue. As an illustration of a low level of respect, Gerhards mentions a newspaper article in which a member of the federal cabinet is called the "minister of propaganda." A second indicator of discourse quality concerns the question of whether a statement in a newspaper is justified or not. Gerhards gives as an example the fact that some articles justify the statement that the fetus is a living being whereas other articles make this statement without any justification. The level of rationality is a third indicator for the discourse quality of a newspaper article. The more an article refers not only to a single value but deals with conflicting values the higher the rationality. Based on these indicators, Gerhards concludes that the discourse quality in the two newspapers is "far away"[4] from the ideal speech situation of Habermas. A weakness of Gerhards' investigation is that no reliability tests of the coding procedures are made.

The lack of reliability tests is also a problem in the quantitative analysis of deliberative politics by Holzinger (2001). She investigates a mediation process in the German district of Neuss. The issue at hand is the construction of a plant to burn household garbage. The mediation takes place at nine meetings from March to August 1992. Participants are representatives of local administrative bodies, political parties, and various interest groups. Holzinger distinguishes between bargaining and arguing. The latter concept she uses as a synonym for deliberation, as Risse does. To determine whether a speech is characterized by arguing, bargaining, or a mixture of the two, Holzinger uses the so-called speech act theory (*Sprechakttheorie*). Thereby, she classifies individual words and groups of words as indicating bargaining or arguing. The same word can fall in either category depending on the context. Holzinger emphasizes that the coding was very time consuming and demanding. She reports in a footnote that the coding was done by three coders working independently of each other, but she does not tell us how often the three coders agreed with each other and what the procedure was if they did not (p. 429). Thus we have no information about the reliability of her measurement instrument.

The construction of a Discourse Quality Index (DQI)

We conclude from our review of the empirical investigations into deliberative politics that in the past few years a good beginning has been made. What

---

[3] *Frankfurter Allgemeine Zeitung* and *Süddeutsche Zeitung*.
[4] "weit entfernt" (p. 27).

is still lacking are *quantitative* investigations with *reliability* tests. To develop such a measurement instrument is the task that we address in the remainder of this chapter. Such a measure can serve as a bridge between political theory and empirical scholarship only if it does justice to the former and provides guidance to the latter. We believe, therefore, that such a measure should meet four different criteria: (1) it should be theoretically grounded, (2) it should tap into observable phenomena, (3) it should be general, and (4) it should be reliable. The first criterion is essential because it concerns the validity of the discourse measure. An improperly grounded measure lacks construct validity, would be of little practical use, and would fail to convince theorists. The complication here is the lack of agreement between political theorists about what exactly constitutes deliberation. As Chambers (2003: 307–8) states in her recent review article,

> the number of scholars working with a model of deliberative democracy or writing about this model is enormous . . . The problem is that nearly everybody these days endorses deliberation in some form or another (it would be hard not to). And more and more people understand constitutional democracy as entailing deliberation in some fundamental way. The language and concepts of deliberative democratic theory have filtered into many discourses and debates.

One could attempt to develop a measure that captures all of the different nuances of these concepts, but this would result in an instrument that is too complex to be of practical value and one that lacks internal consistency (since the different theories are not necessarily compatible). Our approach is different; we have selected a particular theory of deliberation – one that is most closely associated with Habermas's discourse ethics (see chapter 2) – and have used this as the foundation of the Discourse Quality Index (DQI) that we are about to present. This ensures internal consistency, as well as greater simplicity in the resulting measure. Moreover, Habermas's ideas have inspired much of the interest in and debate over deliberative politics, which makes them a good starting point for the development of a measurement instrument.

The second through fourth criteria speak to the empirical power of a discourse measure. Most importantly, the measurement instrument should tap into observable discourse behavior. This is essential if the measurement instrument is to produce reliable data and if it is to convince empirical scholars. In addition, an ideal measure of discourse quality should be general, so that it can be transported from one research domain to another. Finally, such a measure should be reliable. This requires not only that it is based on observable behavior, but also that its coding instructions are specific, and that its coding categories are sufficiently clear that different coders can agree on the classification of the same discourse. Of course, reliable measurement is never guaranteed, so that reliability assessments should be a standard practice in discourse analysis.

As we know from chapter 2, the aspect of deliberation is important both in formal political institutions and the broader public sphere. Ideally, we would investigate both aspects. For pragmatic reasons, we limit the current project to deliberations in formal political institutions, leaving the investigation of the public sphere to a later research phase (see our concluding chapter). We are aware that this later extension will be of crucial importance, but for the time being it is beyond our research means. To study deliberations in families, among neighbors, in the workplace, in leisure associations, and other places of the public sphere will require a very extensive research effort.

What research methods should we use to investigate deliberation in formal political institutions? One possibility would be to interview the participants. One could ask them, for example, whether they are willing to truly listen to the arguments of their political opponents. We decided against using interview methods for the present project because we feared that the responses would be strongly influenced by what is socially desirable. Probably very few interviewees would acknowledge that they were unwilling to listen to the arguments of their political opponents. We decided to base our research on what is actually said in a political discourse, which presupposes that we have access to transcripts of the debates. This is the case for parliamentary debates, certainly for plenary sessions, in many countries, as well as for parliamentary committees. For other formal political institutions, in particular cabinets, there are often either no transcripts or they are not open to researchers. In the Netherlands transcripts of cabinet meetings become available after twenty years, which will give us the opportunity to expand on our research to the cabinet level later, at least for countries such as the Netherlands.

Choosing parliaments for our current research cannot only be justified by the pragmatic reason that transcripts are available, but also by the argument that according to democratic theory parliaments should be the place where the representatives of the people come together to talk about the key issues of a country. Thus, from the point of view of democratic theory, it should be of particular interest to investigate to what extent parliamentary debates in full sessions and in committee meetings correspond to the standards of deliberation. John Stuart Mill (1991: 116) argued that parliament is a particularly important deliberative institution, a "Congress of Opinions,"

> where every person in the country may count upon finding somebody who speaks his mind as well or better than he could speak it himself – not to friends and partisans exclusively, but in the face of opponents, to be tested by adverse controversy; where those whose opinion is over-ruled feel satisfied that it is heard, and set aside not by a mere act of will, but for what are thought superior reasons.

Present-day parliaments may or may not correspond to this description by Mill, which makes it all the more necessary to study the question empirically. It would, of course, also be interesting to know the level of deliberation when members of parliament come together informally, for example over lunch or coffee. In an earlier project on consociationalism, the senior author had the opportunity to investigate such informal meetings with the method of participant observation (Steiner 1974). Perhaps, in a later research phase on deliberative politics, we can make an attempt to use this method as well.

On the basis of all these considerations, we constructed a measurement instrument to study parliamentary debates at a cross-national level both in plenary sessions and in committees. In chapters 5 and 6, we will explicate which parliaments and what debates within each parliament we have studied. For the moment, we will present the measurement instrument which we expect can be applied to any parliament. We call this instrument the Discourse Quality Index (DQI). The starting point for this instrument is the idea that real acts of deliberation can be placed on a continuum that runs from no deliberation, at one extreme, to ideal deliberation, at the other extreme. Thus, while philosophers may view deliberation as an all-or-nothing affair, we view it as a continuum. Real speech acts can fall anywhere on this continuum. The question is how closely they approximate to the ideal speech act.

The unit of analysis of the DQI is a *speech*, i.e. the public discourse by a particular individual delivered at a particular point in a debate. Thus, the entire discourse is broken down into smaller speech units. If an individual delivers multiple speeches, each is coded separately, even if the codes are the same as those for an earlier speech. If an individual is interrupted, then the interruption itself is also considered a speech. For each speech, including interruptions, we distinguish between relevant and irrelevant parts, and only the relevant parts are coded. A relevant part is one that contains a *demand*, i.e. a proposal on what a decision should or should not be made.[5] Irrelevant parts make no demands; these could be clarifying questions or remarks unrelated to the debate.[6] Our emphasis on demands stems from the fact that they constitute the heart of the deliberation. That is, demands stipulate what ought to be done and what ought not to be done, and this normative character puts them at the center of discourse ethics.

If a speech contains relevant parts, then the demands are noted and the speech is coded for its discourse quality. We rely on seven coding categories, which closely follow the principles of Habermas's discourse ethics discussed

---

[5] A series of related demands constitute an issue. A discourse may consider more than one issue. In this case, each issue is coded separately.

[6] While we do not code irrelevant parts, we make note of them, in particular if they contain friendly or unfriendly remarks towards other participants.

in chapter 2. Taken together, these categories reflect how well a discourse corresponds to the principles outlined by Habermas. In this sense, the DQI is a measure of discourse *quality*. The DQI in its entirety, with illustrations for each coding category, is in the appendix. The only criterion that we did not include in the index is the truthfulness of a speech. Habermas's (1981: 149) discourse ethics requires truthfulness, which is the absence of deception in expressing intentions. In political terms, the stated preferences should be sincere rather than strategic, so that the discourse can develop in an open and honest manner. While we acknowledge the importance of truthfulness for deliberative theory, it causes the greatest difficulties from a measurement perspective. To judge if a speech act is truthful is to make a judgment about a person's true versus their stated preferences. This is exceedingly difficult, since true preferences are not directly observable. We considered using indirect measures. Gutmann and Thompson (1996: 81–4) mention as a possible indirect indicator for truthfulness consistency of speech. We think that this indicator would be very problematic, and may sometimes measure the opposite of what it is supposed to measure, namely the lack of deliberative quality. It is at the very core of the concept of deliberation that preferences are not fixed but are open to be changed by the force of the better argument. Therefore, consistency of speech may at times indicate that an actor is stubborn and unwilling to yield to the force of the better argument. Another indirect indicator of truthfulness mentioned by Gutmann and Thompson is the coherence of speech, with a lack of coherence indicating a lack of truthfulness. As we will see below, we capture this aspect with the level of justification. It is indeed crucial for a high-quality discourse that arguments are justified in a coherent way with reasons, conclusions, and linkages between the reasons and conclusions clearly stated. But this is altogether a different dimension from truthfulness. Someone with a low level of intelligence and education may not be capable of articulating an argument in a coherent way, but may still be truthful in what he or she says. These considerations lead us to the conclusion that indirect measures of truthfulness do not fare much better, so with regret we shall not consider this dimension. All other elements of Habermas's discourse ethics, however, find a place in our DQI.

Participation

This refers to a speaker's ability to participate freely in a debate. In the larger public sphere there are often so many inequalities that such participation is often lacking (see the criticism of the deliberative model in chapter 2). It would not be easy to find good indicators for such a lack of free participation. How would we measure, for example, to what extent citizens concerned with environmental issues are able to participate in an effective way in the various environmental groups?[7] For parliamentary debates, however, this dimension is not very problematic since members of parliament have formally established rights of participation. This makes our research task for this dimension relatively easy in the sense that we can limit ourselves to two straightforward categories:

(0) *Interruption of a speaker*
(1) *Normal participation is possible*

The first code is reserved for situations in which a speaker explicitly states that he or she is disturbed by an interruption and for situations in which the interruption occurs through a formal decision, which does not include, however, situations in which speakers are interrupted because their speaking time is up. If no interruption thus defined occurs, normal participation is possible.

Level of justification

This refers to the nature of the justification for demands. Here we judge to what extent a speech gives complete justifications for demands. The completeness of the justifications is judged in terms of the inferences that are made. We should point out that the completeness of a justification does not depend on whether it is explicit. Implicit inferences can qualify as complete inferences. However, it must be beyond a reasonable doubt for the coder that the meaning of the implicit linkage is well understood by all of the participants in the debate. There are four levels of justification:

(0) *No justification:* A speaker only says that X should or should not be done, but no reason is given.
(1) *Inferior justification:* Here a reason Y is given why X should or should not be done, but no linkage is made between X and Y – the inference is incomplete. This code also applies if a conclusion is merely supported with illustrations.
(2) *Qualified justification:* A linkage is made why one should expect that X contributes to or detracts from Y. A single such complete inference already qualifies for code 2. If a speech contains other conclusions, but these are embedded in incomplete inferences, then code 2 still applies.
(3) *Sophisticated justification:* Here at least two complete justifications are given, either for the same demand or for two different demands.

[7] Patrizia Nanz of the University of Bremen is engaged in an ambitious large-scale project on deliberation in which she investigates, among other aspects, the level of participation in the public sphere.

Content of justifications

This coding category captures whether appeals are made in terms of narrow group interests, in terms of the common good, or in terms of both. We employ four codes:

(0) *Explicit statement concerning group interests:* If one or more groups or constituencies are mentioned in a speech, then code 0 is assigned.

(1) *Neutral statement:* There are no explicit references to constituency/ group interests or to the common good.

(2a) *Explicit statement of the common good in utilitarian terms:* There is an explicit mention of the common good and this is conceived in utilitarian terms, i.e. with reference to the "greatest good for the greatest number" (Mill 1998).

(2b) *Explicit statement of the common good in terms of the difference principle:* There is an explicit mention of the common good and this is conceived in terms of the difference principle, i.e. with reference to helping the least advantaged in society (Rawls 1971).

Note that codes 0, 2a, and 2b are not mutually exclusive. In many cases, one will find references to group interests as well as the common good and a speech is coded for all of these. The balance in such appeals is often of particular interest, since it suggests the relative emphasis that is placed on the common good versus more narrowly defined interests.

Respect

The DQI contains three indicators of respect. First, there is respect for the *groups* that are to be helped through particular policies. Here we use three different codes:

(0) *No respect:* This code is reserved for speeches in which there are only negative statements about the groups.

(1) *Neutral:* We use this code if there are neither explicitly negative nor explicitly positive statements about the groups.

(2) *Explicit respect:* This code is assigned if there is at least one explicitly positive statement about the groups, regardless of the presence of negative statements.[8]

---

[8] A more precise measure would consider the balance between positive and negative statements, perhaps using a five-point scale like Gerhards (1997) has developed. However, we have found that the reliability of such an indicator can be problematic, especially if there are subtle differences between the positive and negative statements.

The next indicator is respect toward the *demands* of others. This indicator uses the same codes as the group respect indicator.[9] Explicit respect for the demands of other actors differentiates a deliberative situation from a mere bargaining situation. If mere bargaining is involved there is no reason to express respect for the demands of other actor; if you get something in return, you simply accept the demands of other actors and there is no need to make any further positive or negative comments. If, on the other hand, you express explicit respect for the demands of other actors, you signal the willingness to enter a deliberative process.

Our final indicator of respect concerns *counterarguments*. This type of respect is coded only if there are one or more counterarguments on the table or if a speaker anticipates such arguments. We employ four codes to measure respect toward counterarguments:

  (0) *Counterarguments ignored:* There are one or more counterarguments but the speaker ignores them all.
  (1) *Counterarguments included but degraded:* This code applies when a speaker acknowledges counterarguments but explicitly degrades at least one of them and makes no positive statements about any of them. A degradation also includes negative statements about the individuals and groups making counterarguments.
  (2) *Counterarguments included – neutral:* We use this code if counterarguments are acknowledged but there are neither explicitly negative nor explicitly positive statements about them.
  (3) *Counterarguments included and valued:* This code applies if counterarguments are acknowledged and at least one of them is explicitly valued. We assign this code even if there are also negative statements about one or more of the counterarguments.

Constructive politics

Our final indicator concerns consensus building, or what we call constructive politics. We capture this via three codes:

  (0) *Positional Politics:* Speakers sit on their positions. There is no attempt at compromise, reconciliation, or consensus building.
  (1) *Alternative proposal:* A speaker makes a mediating proposal that does not fit the current agenda but belongs to another agenda. In such

---

[9] However, respect toward demands is not always coded. It is not coded when there is only one demand on the agenda and the speaker supports it. In this case, the speaker obviously respects the demand and we do not explicitly code respect.

cases, the proposal is really not relevant to the current debate, although it may be taken up in a different debate.

(2) *Mediating proposal:* A speaker makes a mediating proposal that fits the current agenda.

The codes contained in our DQI can be refined where this is useful. Indeed, chapters 5 and 6 contain such refinements. However, we can always return from these more fine-grained codes to the categories of the DQI.

For the DQI at large, our assumption is that its seven components are, at least in principle, scalable. That is, we expect the coding categories to hang together reasonably well so that a subset (or perhaps all) of them can be combined to form a scale that can serve as an overall measure of discourse quality. We do not require all of the components to be combined all of the time, since much depends on the specific circumstances of the discourse. For instance, there may be no variation on one or more components, so there is no value in adding them into a composite scale. Alternatively, in the context of a particular debate, one of the components may be negatively associated with the other components. Methods for creating the composite will be discussed in the empirical chapters 5 and 6, where we will deal with the debates relevant to our project.

Before we discuss the measurement properties of the DQI, it should be pointed out that coding with this instrument is not a mechanical exercise, based on counting words and phrases, which is now routinely handled by computer software.[10] While this approach works well in many contexts, we do not believe that political discourse analysis is one of them. Assessing the quality of discourse requires interpretation. One needs to know the culture of the political institution, the context of the debate, and the nature of the issue under debate, to get a true understanding of how actors in the institution use and interpret language. Not even computerized natural language processors are advanced enough at this stage to perform these tasks. Our project requires careful human judgment. Thus, while the DQI is a quantitative instrument, its construction is not dissimilar to the more qualitative approaches to discourse analysis discussed at the beginning of this chapter. Both the qualitative and our approach require extensive contextualized interpretation. However, instead of using nouns to discuss attributes of discourse quality, we use numeric codes. Moreover, the DQI incorporates coding guidelines that should help coders arrive at similar interpretations of a discourse. This allows for a certain degree of inter-subjectivity, although it does not impose it because different coders can have legitimate differences in interpretation. This emphasis on inter-subjectivity or reliability is

---

[10] For a discussion of this approach, see Holsti (1969).

consistent with the tradition of content analysis. It is to this topic that we turn next.

A reliability test of the DQI

For the remainder of the chapter we shall address the question of the reliability of our measurement instrument. In the academic years 1998–9, 1999–2000, and 2000–1 we developed the DQI in research seminars at the University of Bern and the University of North Carolina at Chapel Hill. Participants in these seminars applied the DQI to parliamentary debates in the United States, the United Kingdom, France, Germany, Italy, Switzerland, Austria, and the European Union. Based on these applications, the DQI was revised and refined after each seminar. Finally, in the fall of 2001, we submitted the index to a first rigid reliability test. Two of us, Marco Steenbergen and Jürg Steiner, coded independently of each other the debate in the House of Commons of February 27, 1998, on government priorities with regard to women's issues. The objective of the debate was to discuss ways to improve the lives of British women. Women's issues had been one of Labour's main themes during the 1997 election campaign and had become an important priority in the Labour government of Tony Blair after the election. The February 27, 1998, debate was one of the first opportunities for the government to discuss its ideas and for the Conservatives – in the opposition for the first time since 1979 – to react. The Secretary of State for Social Security and Minister for Women, Harriet Harman, started the debate, which lasted approximately five hours.[11]

Coding proceeded in two steps. First, each coder read through the debate individually and coded the relevant speeches. These independent codings will serve as the basis for the reliability statistics reported later in the chapter. Next, the coders came together to compare codes. In cases where there was a disagreement, the coders read through the speech again and discussed the merits of the rival codes. At the end of this deliberative process, they settled on a particular code, but not until each coder had been convinced of the accuracy of that code. In the debate on women's issues, the two coders identified a total of fifty-six relevant speeches ($N = 56$), i.e. speeches that made a demand. There was no disagreement between the coders on the identification of these speeches. In addition to coding the speeches, the coders also wrote down comments that justified the codes. These comments were also used to resolve disagreements between the coders. We shall now

[11] The text of the debate can be downloaded from the online edition of the House of Commons Hansard (http://www.parliament.the-stationery-office.co.uk/pa/cm199798/cmhansrd/vo980227/debindx/80227-x.htm). We shall refer to passages of this debate via the column numbers in this electronic edition.

illustrate how we used the coding categories for this debate. Before doing this, let us emphasize that the reliability tests are based on the first step of the coding procedure, i.e. before the two coders had deliberated about their disagreements.

Participation

No abnormal interruptions of the speakers occurred during the entire debate. This is not to say there were no interruptions, only that none of the speakers complained about them. Thus, all fifty-six speeches received code 1 – normal participation was possible. An illustration of a disturbing interruption can be found in the June 25, 1998, debate in the House of Commons concerning social welfare. John Sweeney (Scottish National Party) was interrupted several times, which clearly annoyed him. Finally, he exclaimed: "I shall not take any more interventions."

Level of justification

The debate contained instances of each of the categories of our level of justification indicator. The lowest level of this indicator is 0 – no justification. An example is the following demand made by Cheryl Gillan (Conservative, Chesham and Amersham):

> I am pleased that the hon. Lady [Julie Morgan, Labour, Cardiff North] praises the work of Chwarae Teg, on which the fair play for women exercise was built by the previous Conservative Government. Does she share my hope that the Government will continue to support fair play for women in Wales and the rest of the country? We want a firm commitment from the Minister to back that (col. 666).[12]

Gillan demands continued support for the "fair play" program, but she does not justify why this is desirable. Since we doubt the rationale would have been obvious to other MPs, we coded the statement as a 0 on the level of justification. An example of inferior justification can be found in a statement made by Jacqui Lait (Conservative, Beckenham):

> Does my hon. Friend [Eleanor Laing, Conservative, Epping Forest] agree that, if the rumours are true that people will not need receipts to claim the child care allowance, they could indeed spend the money on washing machines? (col. 660).

The implicit demand here is that people should have receipts in order to claim childcare allowance. However, the justification is incomplete. The suggestion

---

[12] Chwarae Teg is a Welsh organization promoting equal opportunities for women in the workforce. The name translates as "fair play."

is that, without receipts, people will spend their allowances frivolously, but this is not backed up by an argument or evidence. Thus, it is doubtful that this argument could serve as the foundation for serious deliberation, as would be required by discourse ethics. An example of a qualified justification comes from David Rendel (Liberal Democrat, Newbury):

> Does the hon. Lady [Caroline Spelman, Conservative, Meriden] agree that there is a further point on the separate taxation of men and women? Women who are abused in the household sometimes find it difficult to get away from the home. Separate taxation helps women to have the courage to move out of an abusive household (cols. 624–5).

The demand is that there should be separate taxation of men and women. A complete justification is provided: such a policy would give women the courage to escape from an abusive household. Finally, let us consider an example of a sophisticated justification. For this, we turn to Beverly Hughes (Labour, Stretford and Urmston), who demands family-friendly employ-ment policies, which should extend to fathers. She goes on to provide three complete justifications for this demand:

> There are several reasons why that is important. First, some parents want to look after their own children. Secondly, it is not so bad looking after one child, but when there are two or three children, the difficulty of getting them to different arrangements at different times and juggling child care with work increases exponentially. Thirdly, and I believe this to be the most important reason, for many children there are advantages in experiencing daily daytime care from their father. Although in practice it is a women's issue, we must try to redefine the issue of who cares for children as an issue for men and women. In demanding an end to the segregation between work and mothering, we must extend the argument to ending the segregation between work and fathering (col. 652).

Content of justification

There were no instances of neutral statements. All of the speeches made explicit reference to group or constituency interests. In addition, quite a few speeches also appealed to the common good, stated either in utilitarian terms or in terms of the difference principle. As one would expect in a debate of this sort, most of the group interest references pertained to women in gen-eral or particular groups of women (e.g. poor women or abused women). To count as an appeal to the common good in utilitarian terms we looked for explicit references to such terms as "the good of the country," "the best for society," "best for the most people," or any other macro-level statement about benefits or costs. To count as an appeal to the common good stated in terms of the difference principle, we focused on explicit references to the most disadvantaged. These references did not have to say "most disadvantaged" or something similar; if it was clear that a particular group was among the least advantaged (e.g. poor women), then a reference to that group would be sufficient. As an example, consider the speech made by Jackie Ballard (Liberal Democrat, Taunton). She raises questions about the Labour government's welfare reform policies, in particular the decision to cut the single-parent benefit. Ballard begins by focusing on the least advantaged of society. Citing the situation of a constituent on income support who was negatively affected by the cut, she makes a broader statement: "I hope that the Government will consider back-to-work benefits for *the many people in that situation.* Those of us who have been single parents on income support know that people do not have savings to fall back on in such situations" (col. 629 – italics are ours). This focus on the least advantaged qualifies as an appeal to the common good stated in terms of the difference principle. Ballard then focuses on the implications of welfare reform for society as a whole: "Any welfare system with paid work as its primary goal has serious implications for women and for society. I do not believe that it is in our best interests as a society to force carers out to work" (col. 629). This focus on the best interests of society qualifies as an appeal to the common good stated in utilitarian terms. Thus Ballard is coded for both common good aspects.

Respect toward groups

In this debate there were no explicitly disrespectful statements about groups. However, an example of a disrespectful statement can be found in the March 10, 1997, House of Commons debate concerning "public responsibility for social justice." In this debate, Labour MP Brian Wilson (Cunninghame) makes the following statement about the Scots and the Welsh: "I wonder why we should be less concerned about people in England who are homeless than about those in Scotland and Wales. A proportionate number of people are homeless in England, many of whom are Scottish or Welsh in origin. Does that upset the primary nationalist argument that England is somehow a land flowing with milk and honey at Scotland's expense?" With the rhetorical question at the end, Wilson implies that the Scots unduly play the nationalistic card to receive more aid. In the debate on women's issues, quite a few of the statements showed explicit respect for women. Consider, for example, the following speech delivered by Lorna Fitzsimons (Labour, Rochdale):

> I warmly welcome the announcements made by my right hon. Friend the Secretary of State in the first momentous debate under our Government celebrating the achievements of women, both inside and outside the House (col. 619) . . . I pay tribute to the women's organisations, the unsung heroes of our communities; we should be better off if we listened to them (col. 622).

Clearly, this speech contains a great deal of explicit respect for women and women's organizations and was 2 on our respect toward groups indicator.

Respect toward demands

Respect toward the demands of other speakers in the debate spanned the entire range of our indicators. First, let us consider some examples of disrespectful statements. Early in the debate, Labour MP Margaret Hodge (Barking) complained that the previous Conservative government had a man representing women's issues. The demand implicit in the complaint was that female politicians should be responsible for women's issues. This demand elicited the following negative reaction of Bernard Jenkin (Conservative, North Essex): "Would we not be going backwards if, while we were trying to abolish woman-free zones in public life, we started to create man-free zones?" (col. 617). The sarcasm of Jenkin's remark is a clear example of disrespect toward a demand from others. Jenkin tries to depict Hodge as a segregationalist advocating spatial areas reserved for women as there are spatial areas like private clubs reserved for men. Such disrespect can also manifest itself through negative statements about the person or groups making the demand. Consider, for example, a speech made by Debra Shipley (Labour, Stourbridge), which contains the following statements: "How far out of touch the Opposition are with the 40-nation Council [of Europe] was clearly demonstrated when the British Conservative delegates blocked the establishment of a full standing committee on equality . . . The Tories are as out of touch in Europe as they are in Britain" (col. 626).

Some of the speeches showed explicit respect for the demands of others. Consider, for example, a speech made by Robert Syms (Conservative, Poole): "All issues affect women, and it is important that we tackle those issues across Government. The previous Government recognised that fact by ensuring that a range of Ministers understood the needs of women, and I believe that this Government are doing the same. I think that that is a *positive step forward*" (col. 668 – italics are ours).

Respect toward counterarguments

This dimension of respect was coded only if a counterargument was on the table or if a speaker anticipated one. Thus the first coding decision was to identify the presence of a counterargument. The second decision was to determine if a speaker was ignoring a counterargument. An example of this occurred in the speech by Jane Griffiths (Labour, Reading East). She describes how a whole generation of women had grown up under Conservative governments, "who treated whole groups in society with contempt, effectively excluding them" (col. 657). This evokes an interruption by Robert Syms (Conservative, Poole) and a response by Griffiths:

> *Syms*: Does the hon. Lady not consider that the position of women in society today is better than it ever has been, and is improving? It has certainly improved over the past 20 years, especially under Conservative Governments.
>
> *Griffiths*: If the hon. Gentleman believes that there is reason for complacency about the position of women, I do not agree with him (col. 657).

While it may appear that Griffiths responds to the counterargument, she does not actually address its claim, stating only that one should not be complacent. Once it is established that a counterargument is acknowledged, the next step is to code for the tone of the reaction to the argument. In this debate, many of the reactions were negative. Consider, for example, the following exchange between Michael Fabricant (Conservative, Lichfield) and Barbara Follett (Labour, Stevenage):

> *Fabricant*: The point I was making is that I support – as I believe we all support – equal opportunities. What we do not support is positive discrimination and quotas, which tend to lower standards.
>
> *Follett*: Positive discrimination is illegal in this country. Positive action is legal, and quotas come under positive action. I would point out to the hon. Gentleman, whom I thank for his courtesy in giving way, that positive discrimination and positive action have acted in favour of men for centuries, and I agree with him that it has lowered standards.

The counterargument of Follett is clearly meant in a sarcastic way, showing no respect at all for the argument of Fabricant. Not all counterarguments are expressed in such a negative way. Consider, for example, the speech by Teresa Gorman (Billericay), a fellow Conservative of Fabricant's. When Gorman criticizes the House of Commons because it "often gives the impression that young women are an underclass or an underdog group" (col. 642), Laura Moffatt (Labour, Crawley) interrupts:

> Does the hon. Lady agree that there has been no suggestion of painting women as victims, as the debate has been wide-ranging – about all sorts of women and the contributions that they make? Does she also agree that many of the women she met were of postgraduate age and that it is a little later, when one has to face child care issues and all that those bring to bear, that women start to run into trouble? (col. 642).

Gorman acknowledges Moffatt's argument in a neutral manner, simply by stating "I hear what the hon. Lady says" (col. 642). Thus Gorman's speech was coded 2 – "counterarguments included – neutral." The opening speech by Secretary Harriet Harman (Labour) serves as an example of a positive appraisal of counterarguments. After Conservative MP Jacqui Lait

(Beckenham) raises a concern about the equal funding of pensions for men and women, which serves as a counterargument to the Secretary's proposal of a second pension to be added to the state pension, Harman responds: "The hon. Lady raises an important issue, about which the pensions review is liaising with actuaries" (col. 608). This speech received a code of 3 – "counterarguments included and valued."

Constructive politics

This debate showed no variation on our constructive politics indicator. All of the speakers stood by their initial positions. Even at the end of the debate there were no attempts at reconciliation. Thus all speeches received a code of 0 – "positional politics." For an example of an alternative proposal (code 1), we turn to America. During the 1996 debate in the House of Representatives on an increase in the minimum wage, Representative Campbell (Republican) opposed the increase but advocated an alternative proposal consisting of an increase in the earned income tax credit. Since the tax code was not under debate, this proposal did not fit the agenda and received a code of 2. For a mediating proposal (code 2), consider the November 28, 1997, debate in the House of Commons concerning the Wild Mammals Bill whose goal was to outlaw the hunting of wild mammals with dogs. Labour MP Michael Foster (Worcester) expressed his strong wish to "vote to ban hunting with dogs." Despite this strong view, he offered a mediating proposal that took account of the grievances of sheep farmers in Wales. Thus he proposed to make an exemption "that dogs could be used to flush foxes out of cover, where they could be quickly and humanely shot."

These illustrations of the individual coding categories show how discursive parliamentary texts can be quantified using the indicators of the DQI. But there remains an important question: can two different coders, both familiar with the context of the debate, agree on the codes that should be given to the text? Put differently, is the DQI a reliable measurement instrument? The reliability of the DQI hinges on two types of judgment. First, do coders agree in their judgment that a particular indicator is applicable? Second, if the indicator is deemed applicable, do coders agree on the code that a speech should receive? Agreement on both of these judgments is essential for obtaining a reliable measure. The following analysis shows that the DQI is indeed a reliable measure.[13]

To assess the inter-coder reliability we rely on several standard indicators. First, we used the ratio of coding agreement (RCA), which is simply the ratio

---

[13] A complete discussion of these reliability statistics can be found on our project website: www.ipw.unibe.ch/discourse.

Table 3.1 *Inter-coder reliability for the UK House of Commons debate on women (coded by Steenbergen and Steiner)*

Category	RCA	κ	Rank correlation	α
N = 56				
Participation	1.000			
Level of justification	0.732	0.615**	0.716**	0.834
1st content of justification	1.000			
2nd content of justification	0.875	0.775**		
3rd content of justification	0.964	0.837**		
Respect toward groups	0.875	0.746**	0.747**	0.855
Respect toward demands	0.893	0.844**	0.855**	0.922
Respect toward counterarguments	0.893	0.559**	0.791	0.883
Constructive politics	1.000			
Overall	0.915			

Notes: Rank correlation and α computed only for level of justification and respect and only for speeches for which coders agreed that the category was applicable. κ computed only if RCA < 1.000. **$p < 0.01$.

of the number of identical codes given by two coders and the total number of codes (Holsti 1969). Second, we used Cohen's (1960) κ ("kappa"), which judges inter-coder reliability relative to the agreement in coding decisions that one would expect by chance. For ordinal indicators of the DQI (level of justification and respect) we also report the Spearman rank correlation between the codes offered by two coders. This indicates how far apart these codes are (Siegel 1956). Finally, where the rank correlation was computed, we also report Cronbach's α ("alpha"), which is a commonly used reliability statistic (Holsti 1969).

In total, the two coders rendered 504 judgments for the debate.[14] They agreed on 461 of these judgments. This included agreements on specific codes, as well as on judgments of whether a particular indicator was applicable. Thus, RCA = 0.915; the coders agreed 91.5 percent of the time, which is an excellent reliability score. Table 3.1 shows the reliability statistics for specific coding categories.

[14] They made fifty-six coding decisions for each of the following indicators: participation, level of justification, respect toward groups, respect toward demands, respect toward counterarguments, and constructive politics. Since there were no neutral codes for the content of the justification, the coders also rendered separate judgments of whether the codes 0, 2a, and 2b applied for this indicator. (Remember that these codes are not mutually exclusive, so that a speech could receive up to three codes for the content of justification.)

First, consider participation. Both coders agreed that normal participation was possible for all of the speakers. Thus, RCA = 1.00, a perfect score.[15] Considering the level of justification, RCA = 0.732, which is respectable. Taking into consideration that the coders may have agreed by chance alone, we also computed Cohen's κ, which equals 0.615. This is both significant and indicative of substantial agreement (Landis and Koch 1977). Since the level of justification is an ordinal indicator, it is also useful to consider Spearman's rank correlation, which takes into consideration the difference in the rank orderings of speeches between coders. For this debate, Spearman's $r = 0.716$, which produces a standardized item α of 0.834. This may be considered a very good reliability.

For the content of justification, we performed three reliability analyses, since up to three codes could be given. All speeches contained references to group or constituent interests, and the coders were in perfect agreement about this; RCA = 1.00. In addition, some speeches also contained one or more references to the common good. The coders had to judge first if this was the case, and next what kind of reference to the common good was being made (utilitarian or difference principle). For the utilitarian justification, the coders agreed 87.5 percent of the time (RCA = 0.875).[16] Taking chance agreement into account, $\kappa = 0.775$; this is statistically significant and indicates substantial agreement. For the difference principle justification, RCA = 0.964 and $\kappa = 0.837$, indicating excellent reliability.[17]

The reliability of the indicators for respect was also excellent. The coders agreed 87.5 percent of the time (RCA = 0.875) in their judgment of a speech's respect toward groups. Further, $\kappa = 0.746$, which is again significant and indicative of substantial agreement. Since the indicator for respect toward groups is ordinal, we also computed Spearman's rank correlation, $r = 0.747$, which results in an impressive α of 0.855. The results for respect toward demands are even better. Here RCA = 0.893 and $\kappa = 0.844$, which is significant and indicative of near-perfect agreement (Landis and Koch 1977).[18] The respect toward demands category was deemed applicable by both coders

---

[15] Since there was no variation in the codes, Cohen's κ and Spearman's r cannot be computed.

[16] There were seven disagreements. In four cases, the first coder believed there to be an appeal to the difference principle while the second coder did not. In two cases, the reverse pattern occurred. Finally, in one instance the two coders disagreed over whether the appeal was stated in utilitarian terms or in terms of the difference principle.

[17] The only disagreement that could occur on the third coding concerned the presence of a second appeal to the common good. The way the coding was set up, if a second appeal was present it had to be in terms of the difference principle. In just two cases did the first coder believe that there was a second appeal to the common good, while the second coder believed there was not.

[18] There were six disagreements. In one case, the first coder believed that the category was applicable, while the second coder believed it was not. In three cases, this pattern was

for twenty-nine speeches. For those speeches, Spearman's r is an impressive 0.855, which implies $\alpha = 0.922$. The last dimension of respect concerns counterarguments. Here RCA = 0.893, which again reflects excellent agreement.[19] Since this level of agreement does not differ much from that expected by chance, κ is only 0.559. While this is the lowest reliability in table 3.1, it still corresponds to "moderate agreement" (Landis and Koch 1977). Since counterarguments were rare in the debate, there are only five cases in which both coders deemed this indicator applicable. Focusing on those cases, the rank correlation between the codes was 0.791, producing $\alpha = 0.883$, which is again outstanding. Our final coding category is constructive politics. Here both coders agreed that all speeches reflected positional politics. Hence, RCA = 1.00, which is perfect.

The overall results indicate that reliable measurement of discourse through the DQI is possible. Even the worst reliability scores are still respectable, suggesting that different coders looking at the same discursive text will be able to agree on the DQI and its components. This is an important result, as it greatly increases the confidence one can place in the DQI. The instrument satisfies the measurement criteria that we outlined earlier in the chapter. First, the instrument is rooted in political theory, capturing Habermas's discourse ethics more completely than previous measures (Gerhards 1997; Holzinger 2001). Second, this measure is rooted in observable behavior such as that reflected in parliamentary debates. Third, the measure is general, in that it can be used in a variety of contexts. Finally, the measure is reliable, as our empirical illustration has demonstrated. In conclusion, the DQI is the kind of measurement instrument that could help bridge the gap between political theory and empirical research.

This is not to say that the DQI is without limitations. One limitation arises within the Habermasian theoretical framework. Habermas has placed considerable emphasis on the truthfulness of claims, an aspect of discourse ethics that the DQI ignores completely because of its unobservable nature. However, we believe this omission does not detract from our claim that the DQI is a very good fit to discourse ethics. Another limitation of the DQI arises because it is located within the Habermasian framework. Not all theorists accept this framework as the proper definition of deliberation. For instance, Basu (1999) criticizes Habermas for leaving humor out of his conception of deliberation. Whereas Habermas appears to view humor as a vice, Basu views it as a virtue, since it may contribute to openness in a debate. Clearly,

---

reversed. Finally, there were two disagreements about the code for speeches for which the category was deemed applicable by both coders.

[19] There were six disagreements. In three cases, coder 1 deemed the category applicable, while coder 2 did not. In two cases, the reverse pattern occurred. Finally, there was one instance where both coders deemed the category applicable but disagreed on the code.

the DQI does not contain any coding categories for the humor in a speech. Others criticize Habermas for being excessively procedural in his focus. As a result, there is insufficient attention to the substance of the arguments that are made (Gutmann and Thompson 2002). The DQI does not incorporate these elements into its coding.

A third limitation of the DQI is that it is limited to discursive texts. Nonverbal communication is not coded as part of the DQI, nor is the tone of voice in which speeches are delivered. These omissions are of some potential importance, since psychological research shows that nonverbal cues influence the interpretation of messages (Walthier and D'Addario 2001). A final limitation concerns the application of the DQI to parliamentary debates. This application domain has some peculiar features, especially in terms of participation. Members of parliament face rather mild restrictions on participation, the worst of which is probably being cut short in a debate. Clearly, access to participation can be a considerably greater hurdle in other deliberative arenas, with some citizens being precluded from participating altogether. The present DQI does not capture such restrictions, but they should be included if the instrument is to be used in other contexts.

For the moment, we believe that these limitations are best addressed by making extensive notes for each speech. Coders should make such notes anyway in order to justify their DQI codes. With a little extra effort they could note their impression of the truthfulness of a speech or their impression of the role of humor. When appropriate, similar comments could be added concerning nonverbal cues and the substance of the arguments. While these notes are not codified into the DQI, they could help researchers to understand the context and character of the debate.

Further reliability tests of the DQI

With coding procedures there is always a problem if the developers of the coding categories are also the coders, because they are so familiar with the categories that a high reliability is not very surprising. The really hard test comes when the coding is done by persons who were not involved in the development of the coding categories. We submitted the DQI to two such tests with students at the University of Bern and the University of North Carolina at Chapel Hill. The difference between the two settings was that at Bern students got extensive training before using the index, whereas at Chapel Hill they got no prior training before working with the DQI. The purpose of the test at Bern should show us what level of reliability is attained if coders get extensive training in the application of the DQI. The Chapel Hill test, on the other hand, should show whether the instructions in the

DQI speak for themselves so that the index can be applied without prior training.

The students at the University of Bern were Felizitas Arnold and Barbara Koch. In their master's thesis they investigated the discourse quality in a 2001 debate on abortion in the lower house of the Swiss parliament, both in plenary session and in committee (Arnold and Koch 2002). Theoretically, they were interested in whether the discourse quality varied between the two parliamentary arenas. They made long and careful preparations for their coding task. First, they took a research seminar dealing with deliberative politics. Within this seminar, the DQI was explained at great length, and students had to do extensive coding exercises. Secondly, before beginning actual coding for their master's thesis, Arnold and Koch further practiced their coding skills with a previous 1975 abortion debate, also in the lower house of the Swiss parliament. Thanks to all these preparations, they reached a reliability in the high range attained by Steenbergen and Steiner. These encouraging results indicate that, with the necessary training, the DQI can also be used in a highly reliable manner by persons, including students, who were not involved in the development of the coding categories.

At Chapel Hill the reliability test took place in an undergraduate seminar in the fall semester of 2002.[20] The debate that was coded took place on December 19, 1997, in the British House of Commons on "Welfare to Work." The seminar had twenty-two participants, mostly sophomores. Students were directly assigned their coding tasks without any prior coding training. They coded the first eleven speeches of the debate, with two students randomly assigned to each speech, so that there were eleven coding teams. The coding was graded pass/fail to avoid any pressures that students might feel to arrive at identical codes. Since each coding team coded only one speech, we cannot compute the same reliability statistics that we computed before. However, we can compute the overall RCA for each pair and look at the mean RCA and its range. Each team made nine coding judgments. On what proportion of these was there agreement? The RCA ranged between 0.555 and 1.000, with a mean of 0.700 and a standard deviation of 0.141. While not nearly as impressive as the previous results, this type of inter-coder agreement is still reasonable. The important point to take away from these results is that the undergraduate students lacked familiarity with the DQI. They were also not very familiar with the political context of the debate in the House of Commons they were coding. In light of such limited training, it

---

[20] Participants in the seminar were Cuttino Alexander, Colby Day, Ginny Franks, Becca Frucht, Nikki Gallagher, Sarah Hench, Cassie Hoffman, In Joon Hwang, Tre Jones, Kristin Keranen, Elizabeth Makrides, Nicole Martin, Sunil Nagaraj, Patty Robbins, Lauren Shepard, Rob Squire, Susie Thompson, Laurel Wamsley, Geoffrey Wessel, Lily West, Crystal Zeager, and Brian Zimmerman.

should not come as a surprise that the DQI does not perform as well as when the coders are well versed in the instrument and the debate that is coded. As a general rule, we suggest that proper training of the coders is necessary. But if this is not possible, using untrained coders may still produce reasonable agreement between coders.

In chapters 5 and 6, the empirical core of the book, the coding was done by André Bächtiger and Markus Spörndli. As we will see in these chapters, their coding was also in the high range of Steenbergen and Steiner and Arnold and Koch. This is not surprising since in our research team Bächtiger and Spörndli had the main responsibility for the development of the DQI. For some of their analyses, Bächtiger and Spörndli subdivided some of the coding categories into finer subcategories.

4

Understanding the real world of deliberation: hypotheses about antecedents and consequences

Deliberation in a Habermasian sense is an ideal type. As we discussed in chapter 3, the real world of political discourse may well fall short of this ideal. Thus, we think of discourse quality as a continuum, ranging from low levels at one extreme to the Habermasian ideal on the other. Political actors, both individuals and institutions, are located somewhere along this continuum. Our DQI seeks to measure this location.[1] However, establishing the location of an actor on the deliberative continuum is only the first step. We would also want to know why the actor is located where s/he is and what the implications of this location are for political outcomes. This chapter is concerned with those questions. Our starting point is that the quality of discourse is not randomly determined. Rather, we believe that it is contingent on institutions, as well as the nature of the issue that is being deliberated on. These factors do not predetermine the level of discourse, but they explain meaningful variations in deliberation. This variation, in turn, has implications for political outcomes. That is to say that discourse quality influences outcomes over and beyond institutional rules.

A theoretical framework

To understand both the preconditions and consequences of deliberation, we first need to understand how it is situated in the field of social action.

---

[1] We should make clear that while individual actors may score very low or very high on discourse quality, we expect a smaller range for institutional actors such as legislatures. It is simply inconceivable that a successful institution can exist at a very low level of discourse. At the same time, deliberated consensus is probably the exception rather than the rule for most institutions, especially those characterized by partisan divisions.

By comparing deliberation to other modes of political action we can see how it is different. Risse (2000) has laid much of the groundwork for this type of analysis. He conceives of different logics of social action, which can be distinguished in terms of the goals of action. Drawing from March and Olson (1989, 1998), Risse starts by distinguishing between a "logic of consequentialism" and a "logic of appropriateness." The consequentialist logic is closely associated with rational choice models of political behavior and stipulates that actors are driven by the goal of finding the most effective means to accomplish an end. The end reflects a *fixed* a priori preference, which may or may not be purely self-interested. Thus, the overriding goal is for *individual* actors to find out "what works", i.e. what course of action is most likely to generate an outcome consistent with their preferences. This is quite far removed from the logic of appropriateness, which understands action on the basis of "what is right" from the perspective of an institution's norms and culture. The emphasis here is on the *collective*: individual behavior depends on and is, apart from random "error," predetermined by the institution. A process of socialization implies that, over time, actors acquire the norms of the institution and that their behavior becomes increasingly predictable just by considering these norms.[2] The norms and culture are usually considered *fixed* in these more sociological understandings of action.

While the distinction between the logic of consequentialism and the logic of appropriateness is a useful starting point, Risse makes a compelling case that there is a third and distinctive logic of social action – a logic of arguing or deliberation. Deliberation departs from both other logics in that it does not assume that the parameters of action, be they norms or preferences, are fixed. Rather the process of arguing can transform existing norms and preferences and produce new ones. We have discussed this premise of deliberative theory extensively in chapter 2. Risse's analysis does provide an interesting starting point with regard to our understanding of the determinants of the logic of deliberation or arguing.

On the one hand, the fact that institutional norms are to some extent variable suggests that institutions cannot fully determine the character of deliberation. After all, deliberation itself can produce shifts in those norms, although we expect this to be a slow and cumulative process most of the time. More immediately, deliberation can cause actors to choose from among a range of competing norms (March and Olson 1989, 1998), a common situation since there is rarely a one-to-one mapping of a decision task onto a specific norm.

---

[2] See Searing (1994) for a detailed analysis of the socialization process in the British House of Commons. He also provides a critical analysis of this understanding of institutions.

On the other hand, it is inconceivable that institutions have no impact on deliberation. Deliberative theorists have acknowledged that the design of institutions can influence the potential of deliberation. In this regard, it is useful to quote Dryzek (1992): "If we allow that there is such a thing as communicative rationality . . . then the political challenge becomes one of constructing institutions for its promotion" (p. 411).[3] What this leaves us is the need for a theoretical framework that allows deliberation to be institutionally determined but not overdetermined. We need an understanding that allows institutions to influence actors without assuming that the processes of arguing and deliberation are completely determined by institutional arrangements. We think such a framework can be found in Scharpf's (1997) *actor-centered institutionalism.*

A first thing to note is that Scharpf applies a broad definition of institutions. While there has been a vehement debate on this matter, in particular between rational choice and sociological institutional approaches, we believe that a broad and flexible definition yields the best opportunity for understanding the interplay between institutional structures and deliberative behavior by political actors. Thus we agree with sociological institutionalism that institutions provide norms of behavior (March and Olson 1989, 1998) as well as cognitive templates or scripts for behavior (DiMaggio and Powell 1991). We also agree with rational choice institutionalism that institutions can be conceived in terms of the "rules of the game," which structure the costs and benefits of action, creating constraints and opportunities for the behavior of actors (Hall and Taylor 1996; North 1992; Ostrom 1998; Thelen and Steinmo 1992).

Second, Scharpf believes that institutions reduce variance in behavior, although they do not eliminate it. Institutions, as defined above, provide actors with shared understandings and a sense of predictability of the range of behaviors that they can expect from each other. Correspondingly, they make it costly to violate institutional arrangements, if only because the future may be less predictable. But, as Scharpf aptly argues, the impact of institutions on actors can never be complete. Actors have diverse backgrounds and socialization histories that cannot be equalized through any set of institutional rules. Thus, any institutionalism should be *actor-centered*; actors operate within, but cannot be reduced to institutions.

If actors are to be taken seriously, how should they be conceived? Scharpf defines actors along two dimensions: *capability* and, more importantly in our context, *interaction orientations.* The latter define the way an actor perceives his or her relationship with other actors. This can be cast in terms of

---

[3] Some scholars have begun to think about the nature of institutions that can shape deliberation. This is truer at the mass level than at the elite level. For example, Fishkin (1997) has proposed issue forums as a stage for deliberation among citizens.

the weight that an actor gives to the interests of the other actors. These orientations, which may range from the complete disregard of the other to the exclusive focus on the other, influence how one interacts in an institution. This should have important implications for deliberation, in particular in terms of respect shown toward others, as we will discuss in the next section.

Interaction orientations exert an influence on the *modes of* interaction:[4] Scharpf distinguishes between four such modes: unilateral action, negotiated agreement, majority vote, and hierarchical direction. For our purposes, the distinction between negotiated agreement and majority vote is particularly interesting, as it relates to the distinction between "talk-centered" and "vote-centered" models of decision making discussed in chapter 2. Within the class of negotiated agreements there are further important distinctions, in particular between "distributive bargaining" and "problem solving." These distinctions too hold important implications for deliberation.

Interaction orientations and modes of interaction reflect to some extent the choices of individual actors. But Scharpf also notes the critical importance of institutions. Institutions influence the salience of different interaction orientations and they make certain modes of interaction more or less feasible. Of course, if actors hold interaction orientations strongly enough or the need for a particular mode of interaction is sufficiently compelling, then they may choose to adjust institutional arrangements that interfere with them. However, since institutional change is costly and usually difficult, it is more likely that institutions will limit the nature of the interaction orientations and modes of interaction, although they do not rule out variance in those dimensions.

Two other aspects of Scharpf's theory need to be highlighted. First, institutions are not the only influence on actors. The nature of the problem that is being discussed also has an important influence. Different problems make salient different orientations and different modes of interaction. For example, if the issue is allocating money for a project in the district of legislator Y, then X may be willing to entertain Y's interests along with his/her own interests, an orientation that Scharpf calls solidarity and that could produce logrolling (all interests being considered). But if Y proposes the legalization of marijuana and X disagrees fundamentally with this idea, then it is much more likely that X will respond individualistically, i.e. without regard for Y's interests. In terms of interaction modes, the logrolling example shows negotiated agreement, which would be much less likely for the marijuana issue, which might be settled simply by majority rule. Second, the ultimate

---

[4] Scharpf (1997) conceives of this influence as indirect, i.e. mediated by actor constellations. In a game-theoretic sense, the constellation captures the players, strategies, payoffs, and preferences. We shall ignore this aspect of political action, since it is not critical to our understanding of deliberation.

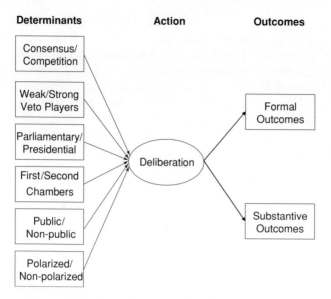

Figure 4.1 A schematic presentation of the determinants and outcomes of deliberation

focus of Scharpf is on policies and this is also the focus of much deliberative theory. Institutions, issues, interaction orientations, and modes of interaction combine to shape the nature of policies. It is thus important to look at the character of these policies and how it is related to deliberation as shaped by different institutional arrangements.

With a broad theoretical framework in place, we can now elaborate on it and develop hypotheses. We shall first consider the question of which institutional preconditions are likely to enhance the quality of discourse. Next, we consider the question of how the quality of discourse influences decision outcomes and policies. The hypotheses developed in this chapter will be evaluated in the empirical chapters that follow. The key elements considered in these hypotheses are illustrated in figure 4.1.

Institutional and issue antecedents of political discourse

If political discourse is conceived of as a continuum, then what determines whether an actor scores high or low on this continuum? Since our focus in this book is on democratic legislatures, we ask more specifically what circumstances cause a legislature to score high or low on the Discourse Quality Index (DQI). We believe that two sets of factors play an important role in determining the level of discourse, namely institutional factors and issue characteristics. We focus on five institutional factors (see figure 4.1): (1) consensus versus competitive democracy, (2) the influence of veto points and veto players, (3) presidential versus parliamentary systems, (4) second versus first chambers, and (5) public versus non-public arenas. We consider one issue characteristic: polarized versus non-polarized issues. While this list of factors is obviously not exhaustive, we believe that it goes a long way towards explaining cross-national, cross-institutional, and cross-issue variation in political discourse, as we shall elaborate below.

Consensus versus competitive democracy

The distinction between consensus and competitive democracies plays an important role in contemporary work in comparative politics. It was introduced by Lijphart (1984, 1999) as a device for understanding decision making, conflict resolution, and representation in modern democratic societies. Consensus democracy, which is best exemplified by Belgium and Switzerland, is based on executive power sharing in broad coalition cabinets, an executive–legislative balance of power, a multiparty system, proportional representation, interest group corporatism, federal and decentralized government, strong bicameralism, constitutional rigidity (requiring supermajorities to change the constitution), judicial review, and in some cases referenda. Competitive democracy, also known as the majoritarian or Westminster model, is best exemplified by New Zealand (until 1996) and the United Kingdom and serves as the antithesis of consensus democracy.

While the distinction between consensus and competitive systems has informed much empirical research in comparative politics (Lijphart 1984, 1999; Reynolds 1999, 2000, 2002), it has not yet been used to understand political discourse. Nonetheless, this distinction has a great deal of relevance for the analysis of speech acts in legislatures, especially in light of the older literature on consociationalism which may be viewed as its precursor. As discussed in chapter 1, the term consociationalism was developed in the 1960s to account for the politics of small European democracies such as Austria, Belgium, the Netherlands, and Switzerland, whose populations were deeply divided along mutually reinforcing lines but whose elites showed a great deal of cooperation. Lijphart (1968) defined consociationalism in terms of several characteristics: grand coalitions, the principle of proportionality, mutual veto power, segmental autonomy, and a "spirit of accommodation" among the elites. This spirit of accommodation is reminiscent of Johannes Althusius's (1563–1638) notion of the covenant or "consociatio." The covenant was an arrangement in which people would live together in mutual benevolence, striving for consensus by way of open communication. Consociationalism thus assumes communication, a mode of decision making in which participants strive to build a consensus through the provision of information and of arguments, showing mutual respect for each other's positions and a willingness to change positions. This, of course, is very similar to Habermas's ethics of discourse. Although the concept of consensus democracy places much greater emphasis on institutional rules, and much less emphasis on the behavior of actors, than consociationalism, it is easy to see that it is still highly consistent with high-quality discourse.

One institutional mechanism of consensus systems is particularly important in promoting deliberation: the existence of grand coalitions. The requirement that decisions are made in broad coalitions of social interests generates a logic of joint decision making which, in turn, provides incentives for deliberation. It is not a foregone conclusion that different coalition partners operating in this type of democracy agree a priori about the best policy. Indeed, there may be serious differences in situational definitions, cognitive problem representations, factual understanding, and standards of appropriateness, fairness, and justice. But the reality is that to ensure a successful government record actors will need to discuss their differences, present arguments and listen to counterarguments and, most of all, treat each other with respect. Thus it is necessary for actors in a consensus democracy to adopt a cooperative interaction orientation (Scharpf 1997), which makes possible a logic of arguing.

Two other mechanisms may further enhance the deliberative potential in consensus systems. First, not only is the very purpose of grand coalitions to make parties more cooperative, they also reduce the importance of electoral competition between coalition partners, since each of them has some influence on government policies and politics is not a zero-sum game for any of them.[5] Second, grand coalitions obscure policy making clarity, which reduces the possibility that actors can use political successes for partisan electoral advantages (Powell and Whitten 1993). Reduced competition makes it more likely that parties will engage in open discourse and will deliberate about policies.

But how much deliberation truly occurs in consensus democracies? Is it not just a process of bargaining based on self-interest that occurs within grand coalitions rather than anything resembling Habermas's ideal speech situation? We believe that there is room for real deliberation in consensus democracies. First, the distinction between bargaining and deliberation should not be drawn too sharply, as Holzinger's (2001) research nicely demonstrates. Thus, careful argumentation and respect, key elements of Habermas's ethics of discourse, may be essential conditions for successful bargaining (see also Ulbert et al. 2004). Second, mere bargaining may be

[5] We thank Klaus Armingeon for clarifying this point.

much more characteristic of distributive situations than of problem solving situations. If the goal is to explore solutions to problems by creating new policies, rather than distributing resources tied to an existing policy, then bargaining may not be sufficient to find agreement. In these problem solving situations, which usually entail a positive-sum game (Scharpf 1997), high levels of deliberation may be observed in consensus democracies, precisely because this is a key method for a grand coalition to agree on policy.

The situation in competitive systems is quite different. Here the party in government can usually safely ignore the opposition and usually stands to gain little by arguing its policies and treating the opposition with respect. Opposition parties that are "cooperative" must always fear that voters assign political successes to the government instead of them (Fiorina 1981; Lewis-Beck 1988). The attribution of success and failure looms large in the priorities of both the government and the opposition. After all, elections are a zero-sum game in which the stakes are a limited number of seats in parliament and ultimately control of the government. In Scharpf's words, "the cooperative search for mutually acceptable solutions will be blocked by the overriding interest of the opposition to demonstrate the impotence of the government and by the equally strong interest of the government to expose the irresponsibility and incompetence of the opposition" (Scharpf 1997: 192). Thus actors in a competitive system are motivated to dissociate, to sit on their positions, and to draw out their differences as clearly as possible. Such an environment is not conducive to an open discourse, not even in a problem solving situation (Scharpf 1997).

It is important to point out that these predictions refer to general trends that we expect to see; they are not deterministic. First, let us note that it would be misleading to think that grand coalitions simply prevent competitive interaction orientations. Not only must coalition partners face the electorate on their own account, parties might also have an interest in strengthening their position in elections, as this continues to make a difference in the allocation of ministerial posts. This creates incentives to uphold a political identity and defend the interests of their clientele and thus sets a basic constraint on parties' cooperative and deliberative capabilities, which, of course, is further reduced when parties face electoral insecurity or decline.

Likewise, it is inappropriate to conceptualize the interaction orientations of parties in a competitive system as merely competitive. There may be exceptional circumstances (e.g. war) where the government embarks on policies that are so far-reaching that it would like them to be backed by the opposition in order to claim a broad social support base. In this case, the normal competitive mode may be temporarily suspended, opening a window for deliberation with the opposition. More generally, self-interested actors in a competitive system may be interested in entering a discourse to correct false information, to enlarge their understanding about the outside world, and to learn the preferences of their interaction partners (Risse 2000). Furthermore, Chwe (1999) argues that a self-interested majority may sometimes allow the minority to "enforce" its favored decision, since this provides an incentive for the minority to participate and hence improves the information levels of the majority. However, these are exceptions to the rule; in general, neither the government nor the opposition has an incentive to share information.[6] Our first hypothesis is then as follows:

Hypothesis 1: Consensus democracies are characterized by a higher level of parliamentary deliberation than competitive systems.

The role of veto points/players

A second factor that is important for deliberation is the role of veto points and veto players. Veto points are defined as "structural incentives providing windows of influence" (Kaiser 1997: 437); one can think of them as places in the decision making process where the consent of one or more players is required if the process is to move forward (see also Immergut 1992). Veto players are actors whose consent is required to bring about policy change. There are institutional veto players, who are generated by the constitution, and partisan veto players, who are generated within the political game that takes place within the constitutional boundaries (Tsebelis 1995, 2002).[7]

As an explanatory construct, veto points/players are not independent of the distinction between consensus and competitive systems discussed previously. Indeed, one way to conceptualize consensus systems is in terms of the presence of numerous veto points or veto players. In this connection, Kaiser (1997) speaks of "consociational veto points," i.e. arrangements that lead to power sharing and consensual decision making in the executive. Likewise, Tsebelis (2002) conceives of consociational and consensus democracies in terms of veto players whose assent is required to formulate policy. By contrast, competitive systems are characterized by far fewer or perhaps no veto points/veto players.

---

[6] Austen-Smith and Feddersen (2002) refute such reasoning altogether and claim that there are more opportunities for deliberation under majority rule than under unanimity. But this formal result rests on several strong assumptions, in particular that actors value the common good in the same way, sharing essentially the same moral values. Under majoritarian decision making, this may create a serious motivational problem for deliberation, as politicians may simply not be willing to listen to minority demands or counterarguments. Hence, only if actors have veto power are other actors "forced" to listen and deliberate.

[7] There are important differences between the concepts of veto players and veto points (see Kaiser 1997), but for our purposes we discuss them jointly.

The correlation between veto points/players and consociationalism is not perfect, however. As such, it becomes useful to consider different combinations of these dimensions (Czada 2000) and think about their implications for deliberation. First, consider a competitive system without institutional veto points. This is the classical majoritarian situation as in the United Kingdom where a self-interested majority can overrule a dissident minority without taking its demands and arguments deliberatively into account. Thus, we should expect a low quality of discourse. Next, consider a competitive system with institutional veto points that give opposition parties veto power. This is a situation of divided government, which is likely to produce discursive cross-pressures, for example in Germany when the second chamber (Bundesrat) is of a different political orientation than the first chamber (Bundestag). On the one hand, party competition gives actors an incentive to attack the political opponent, which should reduce the level of discourse, specifically in terms of respect and constructive politics. On the other hand, the government needs the opposition to pass legislation and this may improve deliberation. Specifically, the governing parties have an incentive to provide a justification for their policies and to frame their arguments in a more inclusive and respectful way.

Now consider consensus democracies. Although it is true that these systems always contain a number of veto points/players, there is important variance on this dimension. In some consensus systems, institutional veto points may be available as an additional resource to actors (see Hug and Tsebelis 2002). A good example is the Swiss referendum: if a coalition party objects to a policy proposal and has public opinion on its side, then it can credibly threaten a referendum. In this case, the remaining parties will have to consider the objections of the actor, even if they control a majority. Consequently, we would expect deliberation to increase: the majority will have to justify its position, take the counterarguments of the dissenting party seriously, and try to develop some consensual solution, lest they accept a policy that is defeated in the referendum.

Just as there are circumstances under which a party in a grand coalition will find its veto power enhanced, there are also situations where this power is diminished. The ultimate weapon of any governing party is the threat to leave the government, which may deprive the grand coalition of its legislative majority. But not all such threats are credible (see Strom 2000: 280). Moreover, there may not be a viable exit option because no other coalition is conceivable in the near future (Scharpf 1997). Even if an exit option is available, it may be too costly for a governing party to use because it may condemn itself to an opposition role in which it cannot accomplish much. In these cases, a dissenting party in the government may have little de facto veto power, which means that the other parties may rule without engaging in a deliberation with the dissenter. However, it is unlikely that the majority will consistently treat the dissenting party with disrespect. After all, this could do irreparable harm to the coalition, possibly even causing the party to leave the government, and this might prove costly in the future when the participation of all members of the coalition is required to pass new legislation (e.g. if a supermajority is required). In sum, while we expect veto points/players to be a lubricant for deliberation, their presence or absence does not wipe out the effects of grand coalitions or majority-opposition settings. Put differently, veto points/players are an added component to consensus and competitive systems, enhancing the quality of deliberation within them. Our second hypothesis is as follows:

Hypothesis 2: There is a positive relationship between the level of parliamentary deliberation and the number of veto points/players.

Presidential versus parliamentary systems

One of the most important organizational differences between legislatures is the distinction between parliamentary and presidential regimes. Using Strom's minimal definition, a "parliamentary government is a system in which the prime minister and his or her cabinet are accountable to any majority of the members of the parliament and can be voted out of office by the latter, through an ordinary or constructive vote of no confidence" (Strom 2000: 265). In contrast, presidential systems lack the dependence of the executive on legislative confidence. This difference has major implications for the possibilities and the scope of deliberation in legislatures.

The confidence procedure of parliamentary systems places a premium on cohesive voting by the parties that make up the government. To ensure the stability of the government, the legislators of the governing parties have to vote with their government and generally cannot redraft its policy proposals. Dissent on the part of government MPs, especially when it occurs in public, is an embarrassment to the government and may severely undermine its stability. Indeed, it is not uncommon for governments to collapse after a single major defeat in parliament. As Diermeier and Feddersen (1998) demonstrate through a game-theoretic model, the confidence procedure creates an incentive for actors who profit from the current government to vote for the government's proposals. In addition to this incentive, party leaders generally also sway party members to adhere to party discipline (Searing 1994) and, if that does not work, an array of coercive means are available to keep MPs in line with the party. Such party discipline is not limited to the governing parties; the opposition too typically places a premium on cohesion if only to be more effective in attacking the government.

What does this imply for deliberation? The confidence procedure comes close to a situation of bounded mandates, which Elster (1998a) considers to be deleterious for deliberation. That is, legislators have a strong a priori incentive to defend or oppose the proposals of the government, depending on whether their party participates in the government or in the opposition, which means that argumentative lines have been fixed before the debate. This should not be the case in presidential systems, where party discipline is typically lower because it is less essential to governmental stability and survival. Although it is still true in a presidential system that the legislators' electoral fortunes are tied up with the success of the government (Cox and McCubbins 1993), thus creating a tendency to vote with one's party, there is much more room to deviate from one's own party than in a parliamentary system. As a result, MPs from the governing party are in a better position to engage in an open discourse with members of the opposition, which may lead to constructive political proposals in a way that should be less common in parliamentary systems.

Now that we have outlined the main effect of the presidential–parliamentary divide we can ask how it interacts with our earlier distinction between consensus and competitive systems. First, consider the combination of a competitive system and a parliamentary regime. Here we should see comparatively low levels of deliberation because the presence of a parliamentary system serves to strengthen competition between the government and the opposition. As Saalfeld puts it, ministers and legislators of the same party are "in the same boat" in a continuous election campaign against other parties (Saalfeld 2000: 357). Attacks on other parties are a normal part of this campaign so that parliamentary debates are characterized by low levels of respect. For instance, Ismayr (2001) describes how legislators in the German Bundestag are "advised" by their peers to "enrich" their speeches with attacks on political opponents. Constructive politics with the opposition is normally out of the question, even if legislators may privately agree with the arguments and proposals of other parties.

If a competitive system is combined with a presidential regime, then there should be more space for deliberation. Not only may legislators be more receptive to arguments across party lines, actors from the same party may also find themselves in opposing camps on certain policies. This blurs the divide between governmental and opposition parties and dulls the competitive game that exists between those parties. It does not eliminate party competition, however. At the end of the day, parties will have to compete with each other over the control of government. Legislators realize that their electoral fortunes are tied to those of the party (Cox and McCubbins 1993), so that they cannot be expected to stray from their party too often. Thus competitive presidential settings should produce better deliberation than competitive parliamentary settings, but we do not believe they will reach the quality of discourse found in consensus systems.

Does it matter if consensus systems are presidential or parliamentary? As an empirical matter, many consensus systems are parliamentary in nature, prime examples being Austria, Belgium, and the Netherlands. Nevertheless, we do not explicitly consider this combination here because we do not believe that there will be much in the way of deliberation specifically in the *legislature*, at least not in the Habermasian sense of managing disagreements. Rather, disagreements are settled in the *executive*, which serves as the legislative agenda setter (Tsebelis 2002). Coalition committees and intra-coalition summits are used to iron out the differences between the coalition parties. The resulting compromises will have to be voted on in the legislature, but we should not see much deliberative action, with coalition MPs primarily defending the government's proposals. With party discipline strong, leaders of the coalition parties can preempt deliberation among coalition MPs, which could undermine the compromises worked out by the government and hence could jeopardize the coalition. The opposition may wish to have real deliberation, but is generally too weak to force debate, especially if the coalition is oversized. Thus, any real deliberation is relegated to the government, not the legislature.[8]

Presidential consensus systems should have a relatively high level of discourse quality.[9] Here the legislature has an independent role to play and lower party cohesion should make it possible to have open deliberation about policy proposals from the coalition government. This deliberation should occur between coalition parties, for reasons that we have discussed before, but in a presidential system deliberation may also extend to the opposition since MPs do not have to vote with their party. Thus, we formulate the following hypothesis:

Hypothesis 3: There is more parliamentary deliberation in presidential systems than in parliamentary systems.

[8] A common complaint of opposition parties is that they feel shut off from the debate because coalition parties hide behind the agreements reached within the government. There may be exceptions to this rule (see Bächtiger 2004), but they seem sufficiently rare for us not to have to entertain them here.

[9] At first glance, presidentialism and consensus systems seem to be at odds with one another. As Lijphart (1999: 49) notes, the standard form of a presidential regime with a single president and presidential cabinet consisting merely of advisers might be difficult to reconcile with the grand coalition idea where all partners are equal decision makers. Yet the real world of presidential regimes involves more variety in this respect. In the Swiss cantons, for instance, we find directly elected collegial grand coalition executives which are not in a confidence relationship with the respective legislatures.

First versus second chambers

Bicameralism is a feature of many legislatures and the division between first and second chambers holds important implications for deliberation. Specifically, second chambers contain properties that allow higher levels of deliberation than we see in first chambers. From the time of the ancient Greeks onward, there have been staunch advocates, such as Aristotle, Cicero, Mill, and Madison, of a council of elders who could bring their experience and wisdom to the government. The political science literature frequently conceives of second chambers as places where policy proposals can be given more thorough thought before they are enacted into law (Tsebelis and Money 1997). This process of expressing "second thoughts" allows for more deliberation than we typically see in the first chamber. Several factors lubricate this deliberative process: members of the second chamber are typically older, usually have extensive prior political experience, are usually elected for longer terms, and work in a smaller chamber than their first-chamber peers. In addition, second chambers typically have strong "civility" norms which also favor deliberation. In the American context, the civility norms of the Senate have been contrasted with those of the House, causing scholars to argue that there is more opportunity for deliberation in the Senate (Loomis 1990). Thus our fourth hypothesis is:

Hypothesis 4: The quality of parliamentary deliberation is higher in second chambers than in first chambers.

Public versus non-public arenas

Observing parliamentary debates in the French National Assembly of the eighteenth century, the conservative philosopher and advocate of more tranquil politics, Edmund Burke, found it anything but deliberative. He considered it a sham: the French parliamentarians were playing

> the farce of deliberation with as little decency as liberty. They act like the comedians of a fair before a riotous audience; they act amidst the tumultuous cries of a mixed mob of ferocious men, and of women lost to shame, who, according to their insolent fancies, direct, control, applaud, explode them, and sometimes mix and take their seats amongst them, domineering over them with a strange mixture of servile petulance and proud, presumptuous authority (Burke 1987: 60).

In a study of the constituent assemblies in Philadelphia in 1787, Paris in 1789–91, and Frankfurt in 1848–9, Elster (1998b) found that speaking in public was indeed not conducive to calm and impartial deliberation. Behind closed doors, however, actors talked much more seriously (although there was also more bargaining).

This is not to say that public speaking only has negative implications for deliberation. In another paper, Elster (1998a) has pointed out that public discourses tend to have a "civilizing" effect on the participants, in the sense that explicitly selfish interests can rarely be defended and justified in the public sphere. Goodin (1996), too, believes that public speech acts require a greater focus on the common good, which has a moralizing effect on debate. There may be other beneficial effects of public deliberation as well. For example, legislators may feel a greater need to justify their positions because their audience does not only consist of fellow legislators but also, at a distance, the citizenry.[10]

Nonetheless, and although secretive and exclusive arenas are likely to horrify deliberative theorists, many argue that this very exclusiveness might actually benefit deliberation (Checkel 1999). Non-public legislative bodies such as parliamentary committees allow legislators to deliberate without external interference, lower the pressures to follow the wishes of constituents, and make it easier for politicians to reflect, to show respect for the claims of others, or even to change their opinions. Furthermore, committees are small face-to-face groups that operate over an extended period of time, which may create habits of working together and friendships, as well as knowledge about each other. These outcomes, in turn, may foster trust and, as such, lubricate the deliberative process.[11] Thus, our fifth hypothesis is as follows:

Hypothesis 5: Non-public arenas are characterized by a higher quality of parliamentary deliberation than public arenas.

Polarized versus non-polarized issues

So far, we have only considered institutional determinants of deliberation. But institutional scholars increasingly recognize that the interaction of institutional features and issues is the key (see Scharpf 1997; Tsebelis 2002). Of particular importance is the distance in the policy preferences of actors: what one could call the ideational (or, more narrowly, ideological) dimension

---

[10] The importance of justifications is highlighted in McGraw's (1991) research (see also Fenno 1978). Although this work is limited to blame avoidance and thus views justifications in the context of policy choices with negative outcomes, the general idea that citizens respond to policy rationales seems applicable across the entire range of issues and policies. Obviously, this only applies in public debates.

[11] Of course, they may also cause groupthink (Janis 1982), which could quite easily hamper open deliberation.

of policy issues, or what constructivists and postmodernists might call the "policy discourse" (Dryzek 2000).

To capture the divergence of issue preferences we distinguish between polarized and non-polarized issues, viewing these as endpoints on a continuum that captures the divergence of issue preferences.[12] Non-polarized issues are characterized by a consensus of the elites on key values and goals, while polarized issues are marked by sharp disagreements on these matters. Even if the elites agree that some goal is desirable, an issue may still be polarized because the elites fundamentally disagree about the best means to achieve this goal (von Beyme 1997). Moreover, "less polarized" issues are, in general, less salient for partisan electoral success. How does the polarization dimension affect deliberation? If an issue is not very polarized, then we should expect a more cooperative interaction among the political elites (Scharpf 1997). And even those actors whose self-interest is in conflict with the values of the discursive consensus might be rhetorically constrained, as it is difficult and costly to undermine a prior discursive consensus or a highly valued goal. This should promote more consensual decision making and, as such, should lead to higher levels of discourse.[13] This should be quite different when issues are more polarized. In this situation, there may not be a consensual outcome because there is a fundamental conflict in the basic values of legislators and parties. Our sixth hypothesis is as follows.[14]

Hypothesis 6: Non-polarized issues are characterized by a higher level of parliamentary discourse than polarized issues.

---

[12] We prefer this language to the distinction between positional and valence issues introduced by Stokes (1963), since we believe that all issues are valenced in the sense of being affectively charged. However, if the reader prefers the more traditional distinction, positional issues may be substituted for polarized issues and valence issues may be substituted for non-polarized issues without a loss of generality.

[13] If the issue is perfectly non-polarized, i.e. there is absolute agreement on the goals, policies, and implementation, then we may find little discourse because it is unnecessary to deliberate. Since very few issues fall into this category, we shall not consider it any further.

[14] With respect to issue specificity, other hypotheses might be formulated. For instance, one might argue that deliberation is more prevalent in the context of regulative issues than in the context of mere distributive issues (e.g. Elgström and Jönsson 2000: 701). We shall not consider this hypothesis since it is quite difficult to properly distinguish between regulative and distributive issues empirically, as most real-world issues are complex mixtures of both. Moreover, as Holzinger (2001) notes, basic questions of justice and fairness turn up in the context of distributive questions as well. Furthermore, uncertainty surrounding an issue might matter for deliberation too, in the sense that issues with high levels of uncertainty could be a strong incentive for actors to deliberate (Lascher 1996). However, the level of uncertainty surrounding an issue cannot be "objectively" determined but would require interviewing legislators about their respective perceptions, a task which goes beyond the confines of this study.

The hypotheses developed above lay out five institutional factors and one issue characteristic that we believe to affect the level of political discourse. In practice, these factors do not work in isolation but will combine to form constellations that facilitate or hinder parliamentary deliberation. From this perspective, we should observe the highest level of parliamentary deliberation in consensus presidential systems with strong veto players, when a non-public debate occurs in the second chamber concerning a non-polarized issue. The lowest level of parliamentary deliberation should occur in competitive parliamentary systems with weak veto players, when a public debate occurs in the first chamber concerning a polarized issue. Other constellations will be located between these two extremes, depending on how many facilitating factors and how many debilitating factors are present. It may also be possible that some of the factors interact, giving rise to configurations in Ragin's (2000) sense. While we do not have a strong a priori theory to suggest particular interactions, we shall revisit the possibility of configurations in the next chapter, which tests our hypotheses concerning the role of institutional factors and issue characteristics.

We should also note that not all aspects of discourse quality may be affected equally by institutional and issue characteristics. We expect to find particularly powerful effects in the areas of respect, level of justification, and constructive politics. To start with the latter dimension, how much constructive politics one observes in a debate depends critically on whether the political system is competitive or consensual, how many veto players there are, and whether or not an issue is polarized. The presence of oversized coalitions in consensus systems typically means that a sizable number of political parties need to be brought together on an issue, and this should enhance constructive political debate. The same holds true when veto players have to be brought into the fold. Moreover, the opportunity for constructive political debate may be much greater when the issue is not polarized than when it is.

Similar arguments can be given for the discourse dimensions of respect and level of justification. In consensus systems, it is important to convince numerous actors of the validity of a policy. This is done by providing strong arguments in support of the policy, but also by treating policy critics with respect. After all, disrespect could alienate some of the actors, which could decrease the likelihood of passing the policy or something like it. Clearly, majority actors in competitive systems do not need the minority and this should decrease the levels of justification and respect. If there are powerful veto players, then this too may enhance the levels of justification and respect, for the simple reason that the veto players have to be convinced that they should support a policy or at least not veto it. And non-polarized issues should make it easier to show respect than polarized issues, since the differences in initial issue positions are relatively small and there is likely to be widespread agreement about policy fundamentals, including the need to have a policy.

Outcomes of political discourse

What outcomes are associated with parliamentary deliberation? Does it matter if a policy was derived through extensive parliamentary deliberation, or is talk cheap and inconsequential as some rational choice theorists have argued (see Austen-Smith 1992)? This question is the focus of the next set of hypotheses, to be tested in chapter 6. To provide better leverage on this question, we distinguish between two outcome dimensions (see figure 4.1). First, we consider a *formal dimension*, which concerns the degree of unification in a decision: does a decision carry the support of all or most of the decision makers, or is it passed by a narrow majority? Second, we consider a *substantive dimension*, which focuses on the effects of a decision on social justice (to be defined later): does a decision generate or sustain a policy that enhances social justice, or does it detract from social justice? Both of these dimensions pertain to the final stage of Scharpf's (1997) actor-centered institutionalism and are influenced by the factors considered in the previous section, by way of parliamentary deliberation.

Formal consequences of deliberation

The formal dimension of political outcomes concerns the degree of unification in decision making. In deliberative political theory, the term unification is typically interpreted as consensus – a convergence of preferences that produces agreement that a particular policy is optimal under the prevailing circumstances. In practice, unification may also refer to compromises, i.e. agreements between actors that do not involve a fundamental change in preferences (Chambers 1995). Here, we consider both types of unification simultaneously. This partially reflects a pragmatic orientation: it is usually difficult to distinguish between real consensus and compromise because we do not know if preferences have changed. However, we also believe that consensus and compromise, as long as they are reasoned, are not incompatible: they can both be considered discursive (Dryzek 2000).

The connection between unified decision making and deliberation is well established in political philosophy. Advocates of deliberative politics typically argue that a deliberative process unencumbered by time constraints and other limitations should produce consensus because it continues until an agreement is reached (see chapter 2). Thus it seems obvious to hypothesize that deliberation promotes unification in parliamentary decisions. However, there is sufficient criticism of the deliberative position that we need to scrutinize this hypothesis before accepting it at face value. Much of the criticism concerns the practicality of unification in real-world political settings.[15] Even hardcore advocates of deliberation accept that real-world conditions rarely allow for unencumbered deliberation, but the critics go further. Some deny that deliberation can produce the kinds of preference transformations that deliberative theorists assume (Johnson 1998). Indeed, deliberation may only touch aspects of an actor's worldview, without affecting the fundamentals of this view (Chambers 1995). Thus, deliberation may only be able to affect preferences on specific policies (policy core) while being unable to influence ontological convictions such as core beliefs and values (the deep core, see Sabatier 1998: 104, 112). By implication a real consensus is typically out of reach, although a reasoned compromise on specific policies may still be possible.

But some deny even the possibility of unification through compromise. As Mason argues, "disagreement over which positions are reasonable is often just as intractable as disagreement over which position is correct" (Mason 1993: 145). In other words, actors may disagree not just on matters of principle, but also on matters of policy; the policy core may be just as contested as the deep core. In this vein, Shapiro has called attention to the potentially polarizing effect of deliberation: "People with opposed interests are not always aware of just how opposed those interests actually are. Deliberation can bring differences to the surface, widening the political divisions rather than narrowing them" (Shapiro 1999: 31). If we accept this position, the end result of deliberation may well be *less* unification instead of more. Shapiro's position finds support among many political psychologists; in this regard, we call attention to the psychological critique of deliberation by Lupia (2002).

So why is it that we should expect deliberation to have a positive effect on unified decision making? What specific mechanisms allow unification to take place? The most obvious of these mechanisms is constructive politics. As discussed in chapter 3, constructive politics implies that actors are willing to revise their original position in light of counterarguments and alternative demands. This produces mediating proposals, whose goal is to bridge the gap between the different sides on an issue, thus opening a window for the development of a reasoned compromise if not a genuine consensus.

Another mechanism through which deliberation may produce unified decision making is mutual respect. As Gutmann and Thompson have argued, "mutual respect . . . requires an effort to appreciate the moral force of the

---

[15] There are also criticisms of the normative value of unification, in particular consensus, which are addressed in the works of Dryzek (2000), Manin (1987), Sanders (1997), and Young (2001), as well as chapter 2 of this book.

position of people with whom we disagree" (Gutmann and Thompson 1990: 85). This not only has a civilizing effect on deliberation (see also Daele 2001), but it also makes it difficult to dismiss the opponent's position out of hand. This forces actors to listen to each other, which may open the window of opportunity for unified decision making. Consensus is by no means a necessary outcome of the process of listening, but it could lead to reasoned compromise. That is, actors may not be able to agree on fundamentals, but they may be able to find mutually acceptable solutions by respecting the fundamental principles of their opponents.

Finally, the level of justification contributes to unified decision making. On the one hand, justification has a signaling function, at least in non-public settings: if an actor goes through the trouble of formulating arguments for a particular position, this shows that s/he takes seriously the opportunity for deliberation.[16] On the other hand, justifications, when done well, may convince other actors of alternative viewpoints. Perhaps this will not produce a genuine consensus, but it may permit the development of compromise solutions. The level of justification is, in fact, the critical test of the hypothesis that higher levels of deliberation result in more unified decisions. The reason is that it is easy to reverse causality for constructive politics and respect. If an issue or policy is non-controversial or non-polarized, then actors may quickly realize that they agree and will then, as a result, show mutual respect and adopt a constructive stance; any other discourse might jeopardize the preexisting agreement. Thus, skeptics could argue that constructive politics and respect are merely an indication that a particular policy domain is non-polarized. But if this were true, it is unlikely that we would also see a high level of justification (at least in the non-public sphere), for there is no clear rationale why actors would spend much effort on arguments if everyone was in agreement. Therefore, high levels of justification suggest that decision makers seek unity in policy domains where it is currently missing. Thus we expect low levels of justification if actors do not see an opportunity for a unified decision but also if actors know that a unified decision is an almost certain outcome. Hence our seventh hypothesis is as follows:

Hypothesis 7: Unified decisions, in the form of a genuine consensus or a reasoned compromise, are more likely when there is a high level of parliamentary deliberation.

---

[16] This may not be true in public debates because, as we have seen, the primary audience in these debates may be constituents. Thus a high level of justification in a public debate may merely signal that the actor takes seriously his or her constituents, not his or her opponents. For this reason, our empirical analysis of the consequences of deliberation will focus on the non-public sphere.

Substantive consequences of deliberation

Deliberative theorists have had remarkably little to say about the substantive quality of decisions that have been derived through deliberation. Political legitimacy is not judged in terms of substantive outcomes, but rather in terms of the quality of the deliberative procedure. As we have discussed in chapter 2, this viewpoint has been criticized for being agnostic about the possibility that perfect deliberative practice may generate perfectly unjust outcomes (Cohen 1996; Gutmann and Thompson 1996). In the words of John Rawls, "legitimacy allows an undetermined range of injustice that justice might not permit" (Rawls 1996: 428).[17] It is thus clear that an analysis of the outcomes associated with deliberation will have to engage a substantive dimension.

At first, it may seem impossible to theorize about the substantive dimension. A true adherent of deliberation would have a difficult time specifying a universal criterion by which to judge political consequences. After all, any and all principles of justice are subject to discussion, which is the very reason why some critics believe that deliberative practice can easily produce negative substantive outcomes – there is no meta-deliberative moral principle guiding the discourse (Gutmann and Thompson 1996; Young 2001). On the other hand, deliberative theorists typically agree that the discourse should appeal to the common good. This suggests that not all standards for judging outcomes are equally valid; those appealing merely to selfish interests are deemed morally inappropriate. Several notions of the common good can be identified. As discussed in chapter 3, it may be construed in terms of Bentham's utilitarianism ("the greatest good for the greatest number") or in terms of Rawls's "difference principle." Here we focus on the latter for reasons that we shall discuss momentarily.

The difference principle implies that "social and economic inequalities are to be arranged so that they are . . . to the greatest benefit of the least advantaged" (Rawls 1971: 83). In practice, this implies an egalitarian doctrine of social justice (Rawls 1996). Specifically, the difference principle is associated with a weak form of egalitarianism, which treats equality as a means toward the end of improving the situation of the least advantaged (Shapiro 1997). That is, the redistribution of resources from the advantaged to the disadvantaged is deemed legitimate if it helps improve the situation of the latter. In contrast with the principle of strong equality, which stresses the leveling of social differences as the main goal (Niño 1996), weak inequality tolerates differences. However, such differences should not put

---

[17] The distinction between substance and procedure is similar to Scharpf's (1997) distinction between input and output legitimacy.

the weakest in an intolerable situation, nor should they be based on completely arbitrary criteria such as group distinctions (based on race, class, sex, nationality, religion, ideology, or whatever other ground – see Deutsch 1985).

It is now easy to see why there is a natural connection between deliberation and weak equality. Weak equality provides the opportunities that allow the least advantaged to become participants in the deliberative process. In addition, "it supports the basis for mutual respect" (Deutsch 1985: 146), precisely because arbitrary distinctions are eliminated. Since deliberative theorists care deeply about these aspects of the deliberative process, it makes eminent sense to judge the outcomes generated by this process in terms of their consequences for weak equality. There are other reasons for assessing deliberation in terms of the difference principle. First, Rawls (1971) arrives at this principle through the idea of the veil of ignorance, which may itself be viewed as a deliberation of sorts, not between individuals but within the individual. Second, utilitarian notions of the common good do not comport as well with the tenets of deliberation as the difference principle. Utilitarianism, after all, postulates that individual preferences can be aggregated through a fairly enumerative principle, a position that Habermas would find difficult to accept as legitimate.

But the question remains, what is it exactly about the deliberative process that ensures (weak) egalitarian consequences? In light of the widespread skepticism of critics such as Gutmann and Thompson (1996) and Young (2001), it is important to answer this question with precision. We expect that the content of justification plays a critical role in ensuring positive substantive outcomes. One would expect egalitarian outcomes only if actors discuss a policy in terms of the common good stated as the difference principle. This is not to say that an appeal to the difference principle guarantees a socially just outcome; only if a sufficient number of players accept this principle is it likely that egalitarian policies will be enacted. However, if appeals to the common good were absent, it would be fortuitous at best if a policy served equality. Indeed, that situation could well produce policies that would hurt the least advantaged.

The content of justification is likely to interact with the level of justification. That is, appeals to the difference principle may be more persuasive if they are carefully argued and justified. This makes it more likely that the consensus or compromise that decision makers reach reflects egalitarian considerations. The content of justification may also interact with respect toward groups. That is, appeals to the difference principle will generally carry little weight if they are accompanied by disrespect toward disadvantaged groups. On the other hand, respect for the disadvantaged may not lead to egalitarian policies unless an explicit argument is made that they should be helped.[18] However, levels of justification and respect by themselves should have little bearing on the level of equality of the decision outcomes. Thus our eighth hypothesis is as follows:

Hypothesis 8: (Weak) egalitarian decision outcomes are more likely when there is a high level of parliamentary deliberation, defined in particular in terms of the content of justification.

In this section, we have argued that parliamentary deliberation influences both the formal and the substantive dimensions of decision outcomes. On the one hand, deliberation promotes unified decision making. On the other, it enhances the likelihood that decisions promote equality. These dimensions do not act independently. Egalitarian decisions require that agreement can be reached about the appropriateness of the difference principle in a particular context. Making an appeal to the common good by invoking the difference principle may also help build a consensus better than a raw appeal to self-interest would. However, any correlation between the dimensions has to be imperfect, for there are examples of unified decisions that do not enhance equality and of majority decisions that do have this effect. Understanding how these dimensions play out in practice is an important empirical challenge that we take up in chapter 6.

In this chapter, we have developed a foundation for understanding the real world of deliberation: how does deliberation play out in practice? Focusing on parliamentary institutions, we have at once specified the conditions for deliberation and its outcomes. Thus deliberation has become the mediating variable between institutional factors and issue characteristics, on the one hand, and outcomes, on the other (see figure 4.1). By situating deliberation in this manner, we have moved beyond deliberative political theory, which typically has little to say about preconditions or consequences. Nonetheless, in deriving our hypotheses we have paid close attention to the formal requirements of deliberation that we discussed in chapter 2 and operationalized in chapter 3.

Our approach fits in the actor-centered institutional framework of Scharpf (1997). Treating institutions as an important determinant of behavior, we do not mean to imply that speech acts can be reduced to the factors outlined in hypotheses 1–6. Rather, those factors guide the behavior of parliamentarians, thus creating differential tendencies in deliberation. But variance in these tendencies does not eliminate variance in the speech acts

---

[18] Other factors seem less relevant for the substantive dimension. Participation matters in as far as proponents of the difference principle are not shut out from the debate. Constructive politics matters in as far as mediating proposals cater to the least advantaged.

of those operating within the same institutional context, since institutions only partially determine behavior. This is an important point to emphasize because it influences how we think about the outcomes associated with a logic of arguing. If deliberation could be reduced to institutional factors, then, by implication, formal and substantive decision outcomes could also be reduced to those factors. As hypotheses 7 and 8 suggest, however, we believe that deliberation has an independent effect on decision outcomes, which is precisely why the study of political deliberation is so important.

In the next two chapters we will take up the empirical investigation of deliberation. In chapter 5, we consider the antecedents of parliamentary deliberation, providing an evaluation of hypotheses 1–6. Chapter 6 then considers the consequences of parliamentary deliberation, focusing on hypotheses 7–8. Through these empirical analyses we are able to obtain a comprehensive picture of the role of deliberation as a mediator in the political process of parliaments.

5

Antecedents of deliberation: institutions and issues

The preceding chapters laid out the theoretical framework for our study. It is now time to engage in an empirical analysis of political discourse as it can be found in the real world.[1] We start by considering the institutional antecedents of discourse quality. Under what institutional arrangements does discourse in legislatures flourish? Which aspects of discourse are affected by those institutional arrangements? And how do issue attributes affect those aspects? These are the central questions of this chapter.

In this chapter, we test the first six hypotheses that were laid out in chapter 4 (the remaining hypotheses are tested in the next chapter). Thus discourse quality is correlated with five different institutional characteristic and one issue characteristic. The institutional characteristics, again, are: (1) consensus versus competitive democracy, (2) the influence of veto points and veto players, (3) presidential versus parliamentary systems, (4) second versus first chambers of the legislature, and (5) public versus non-public arenas. The issue characteristic is the extent to which prior positions on an issue are polarized. As we argued in the previous chapter, these institutional and issue characteristics provide a great deal of leverage on understanding the antecedents of discourse quality, and hence we expect them to give good insight into the conditions under which legislative discourse flourishes.

Our empirical analysis takes us to a variety of debates from four legislative settings: Germany, Switzerland, the United Kingdom, and the United States. These countries were selected because they provide variance on key institutional factors. Specific debates were selected in part to obtain leverage

---

[1] This chapter is based on the Ph.D. dissertation of André Bächtiger (2004).

over issue characteristics. Through a detailed quantitative and qualitative analysis of our countries and debates, we show that institutions matter for deliberation and that certain arrangements are more conducive to high-quality discourse than others. Before moving to these results, however, we should address in greater detail our research design.

Research design

The foundation of our research design is the idea of typological or theoretical sampling (Lamnek 1995; McKeown 1999). As the name suggests, a typological sample starts with a typology or set of theoretical categories. In contrast to random sampling, the case selection is purposive with respect to the typology. That is, cases are selected to fill out the categories, whereby the goals are to select cases that capture the extremes of the independent variables entailed by the categories and to select cases that are comparable in other regards. One can think of selecting extreme cases as finding ideal cases, i.e. ones that represent a category in its purest form. As Van Evera (1997) has argued, this helps in controlling for the effects of omitted variables.

Typological sampling was developed in the context of qualitative sociological research. We depart from this legacy by conducting statistical analyses on the debates that are selected through this type of sampling, in addition to performing more qualitative analyses. The goal of this statistical approach is not to produce generalizable inferences, since that would require case selection through random sampling. Rather, our goal is to use statistics to summarize information and to determine how much discourse quality varies across institutional settings as opposed to within those settings. In other words, we seek to detect if there is meaningful variation between groups relative to the variation within groups.

One may wonder why we do not use random sampling in this chapter (or in the next chapter). We see two main reasons for this. First, random sampling requires a well-defined population and sampling frame. While it is already difficult to construe what exactly a population of debates is, especially across countries and time, it is nearly impossible to find a proper sampling frame. There are no lists of debates that permit us to draw a random sample. To be sure, one can lay one's hands on listings of bills, but that sampling frame is insufficiently detailed because a bill can trigger multiple debates. Second, even if a sampling frame had existed, we would be wary of drawing a random sample because we want to select debates that matter. A random sample might have yielded a selection of debates on relatively minor issues. That might have been correct from a statistical viewpoint, but it would have been of little theoretical interest. When we ask which antecedents promote discourse, and which ones hinder it, we are especially interested in discourse over important issues – ones that matter for the polity. A purposive sampling technique is more likely to select such issues than random sampling.

While typological samples cannot be generalized in a strict statistical sense, we think that they can serve several useful functions. Similar to case studies, typological samples can be an indispensable first step toward tests with a large number of randomly selected cases (Achen and Snidal 1989). Moreover, as McKeown (1999) notes, the inability to make generalizations may not be important. The goal of typological sampling is to generate a set of "critical cases" (Eckstein 1975), i.e. cases for which we would expect the theory to hold true, if it is going to hold true at all. If we were to find that the theory does not hold true for those cases, this would cast serious doubt on the theory, regardless of the fact that the cases do not constitute a random sample.

Case selection

Typological sampling requires that one selects cases – legislatures and debates – that are "ideal" and "most comparable." That is, the cases should best satisfy the conditions specified by the theory and keep confounding factors to a minimum. This approach caused us to study the legislatures of Germany, Switzerland, the United Kingdom, and the United States, and debates on major issues such as social and economic policies, abortion, disability rights, animal welfare, crime prevention, and trade. The debates cover a period running from the late 1980s through the 1990s.

Legislatures

An assessment of hypotheses 1–6 requires that we select consensus presidential, competitive presidential, and competitive parliamentary systems, and that we consider legislative settings with both strong and weak veto power. In addition, we need to be able to study debates in two legislative chambers and in two different arenas: public and non-public. The selection of Germany, Switzerland, the United Kingdom, and the United States satisfies these criteria.

Switzerland represents the best empirical approximation for a consensus system. Since 1959, this country has had an institutionalized grand coalition.[2] It is the only consensus democracy that has presidential features

[2] In the seven-member Federal Council the three largest parties each have two seats, the fourth-largest party one seat. On December 10, 2003, there was a readjustment because the Swiss People's Party had moved from fourth to first place in parliamentary elections and correspondingly now got two seats. The Christian Democrats had fallen to fourth place and had to give up one of their two seats. Such readjustments are in the spirit of an institutionalized grand coalition.

(analysts frequently call it "semi-presidential" or "directorial"): although the parliament, in a joint session of its two chambers, elects the government (the Federal Council), the legislature cannot stage a vote of no confidence during the term of the government. If a government proposal is defeated by the Federal Assembly, then it is not necessary for the government to resign (Steiner 1974). Since the government's existence does not depend on legislative majorities, party discipline tends to be lower than in other European parliamentary systems (Kriesi 1998), and parliamentarians have a great deal of autonomy in drawing up legislation.

The Swiss system might leave the impression that all governmental parties have strong veto powers. However, this impression would be incorrect because parties of the grand coalition often form smaller coalitions in parliament, which makes it possible to bypass certain coalition partners. Indeed, this happens frequently (Kriesi 1998; Linder 1999), suggesting that veto players are not so much partisan in nature as they are institutional (Tsebelis 1995, 2002).

The main institutional veto device in Switzerland is the referendum. It poses an ever present danger to policy proposals by the government, as the historical evidence makes abundantly clear: the rejection rate for policy proposals in optional referenda was 43 percent between 1947 and 1995 (and the rate was 23 percent for mandatory referenda; see Linder 1999; Neidhart 1970; Trechsel and Sciarini 1998). However, not all decisions are subject to the referendum. Thus, we are able to consider deliberation under conditions of high (referendum threat) and low (no referendum threat) veto power.

We selected the United States as a representative of a competitive presidential system. This is a classical presidential democracy with a competitive two-party system and comparatively low party cohesion. The level of party cohesion is a topic of considerable debate. Traditionally, students of the US Congress have downplayed the role of political parties, focusing instead on the median votes on the floor of both Houses and on the committee structure. Accordingly, party cohesion was not considered a major factor in the legislative process. More recently, however, the responsible party government model has argued that, under the right conditions, political parties play a major role in the legislative process and that party cohesion, at times, has been very high in the US Congress (Aldrich and Rohde 2000; see also Cox and McCubbins 1993). Still, by comparative standards, party cohesion is not nearly as important as it is in countries such as Germany and the United Kingdom.

For most of the period that we are studying, the government was divided, with Republicans controlling the presidency and Democrats controlling the Congress under President George H. W. Bush, and Democrats controlling the presidency and Republicans controlling (part of) the Congress under

President William J. Clinton. The American system allows us to study deliberation under conditions of both strong and weak veto power. From an institutional perspective, the US constitution provides multiple veto points, with the president being able to veto legislation passed by the Congress, the Congress being able to override this veto given sufficient votes, and both chambers being able to control each other. In practice, veto threats are not always credible. We define strong veto power in terms of decision situations in which there were clear and credible veto threats, for example in the form of a presidential veto threat or a filibuster in the Senate that would empower the minority party. We define weak veto power in terms of situations in which it was clear to legislators that a bill would pass with a majority and that this majority could override a veto. This requires some judgment on our part, and we have tried to be conservative, making sure that most legislators would have been aware that veto threats were not credible.

We selected Germany as an exemplar of a competitive parliamentary system. The German legislature is characterized by strong party competition and party cohesion. The government depends on the support of the coalition parties, thus necessitating party discipline in ways not found in Switzerland and the United States. In this respect, Germany is much like the United Kingdom, where party discipline is also critical (Bowler, Katz, and Farrell 1999; Searing 1994).

Unlike Britain, however, veto players do exist in the German system. One of the legislative veto players is the Federal Council (Bundesrat), which has veto power over certain areas of legislation, namely statutes requiring assent (*Zustimmungsgesetze* – see chapter 6). Since the Federal Council has been controlled by the opposition with some regularity, the government parties in the Federal Diet (Bundestag) may face a credible veto threat (Schmidt 2003). This threat gives rise to two different scenarios. First, the opposition may enter into direct negotiations with the government even before the parliamentary stage of the legislative process. In this scenario, it is impossible to observe the management of disagreement in the legislature; the negotiations are conducted outside the parliamentary process and, if a deal is struck, party cohesion requires all parties to go along with it without much in the way of deliberation. The second scenario is that no agreement between the government and the opposition can be found prior to the parliamentary stage. In this case, it is likely that the bill will go to the Mediation Committee (Vermittlungsausschuss – Schmidt 2003). This scenario allows us to observe the management of disagreements in the legislature through deliberation. Consequently, these are the cases of central focus in this analysis (they are also the exclusive focus of chapter 6).

The last legislature that we consider is the British House of Commons. The House of Commons serves as another example of a competitive parliamentary system. It is perhaps the strongest counterpoint to the Swiss legislature (see Lijphart 1999). Instead of a grand coalition, a single party controls a majority of the seats in the House and hence the government. Instead of weak party discipline, the House of Commons is characterized by very strong party discipline and strong norms against voting with the opposition (Searing 1994). Thus our analysis will draw comparisons between the Swiss and British legislatures to elucidate the effect on deliberation of vast institutional differences along the competitive–consensus divide.

The British case is also interesting for purposes of comparison with the United States. Both of these countries are competitive in nature, but they differ in terms of the presidential–parliamentary dimension. While we can also draw comparisons in this regard between the United States and Germany, adding Britain to our case base will help amplify our findings concerning the impact of presidentialism–parliamentarism on deliberation.

Our motivation for the selection of the German, Swiss, British, and American legislatures has focused primarily on the dimensions that underlie the first three hypotheses, namely the consensus–competitive, strong–weak veto player, and presidential–parliamentary dimensions. What about the remaining two hypotheses, i.e. those concerning bicameralism and public versus non-public arenas? To shed light on the effect of second versus first chambers, we consider the German, Swiss, and US legislatures. Each of these legislatures is bicameral and in each case the second chamber can be considered a powerful actor. Thus we consider differences between the National Council and the Council of States in Switzerland, between the Federal Diet and the Federal Council in Germany, and between the House of Representatives and the Senate in the United States. We do not consider the House of Lords in Britain, since this chamber has relatively little power.

Our analysis of public versus non-public arenas of deliberation focuses on the German and Swiss cases. Here we contrast floor debates (public arena) with committee debates (non-public arena). Indeed, the German–Swiss comparison is appropriate due to strong similarities in the institutional workings of committees. In both cases, committee deliberations are non-public and committees have considerable power, for example in terms of rewriting government proposals (Döring 1995). We exclude the United States from the analysis because committee meetings are usually public and there are few other forums in which legislators deliberate behind closed doors. This problem comes into play also with the House of Commons. In addition, committees in the House do not have the prerogative of rewriting legislative proposals, which necessarily curbs the character of their deliberations.

Debates

Comparing debates across different national legislatures raises a fundamental problem. To demonstrate empirically that institutions matter for
deliberation we have to control somehow for the impact of different preference profiles that different institutional systems face (Hammond and Butler
2003). After all, differences in preference profiles may account for differences
in deliberation, which would make it difficult to tease out institutional factors from preference effects. Our attempt to control for different preference
profiles consists of choosing topics of debate for which actor constellations are similar (for example, social and economic issues with polarization
between leftist and rightist parties). This approach is not foolproof: it is
generally impossible to find debates on exactly the same set of issues in different legislatures. However, we try to draw comparisons only if the broad
parameters of debate are comparable, which means that at least the topic
should be comparable.

We select a total of fifty-two debates, mostly from the late 1980s and
1990s,[3] from the four countries described earlier. A key selection criterion
for the debates is that they should focus on critical decision cases, as opposed
to minor issues, and that they should cover topics found in at least two legislative settings. A key differentiating factor is the level of polarization of the
issue that is being debated. According to our sixth hypothesis, the level of
polarization of an issue should have important effects on the quality of discourse. To draw the distinction between low and high levels of polarization
we build on a useful classification developed by Kriesi (2001), which considers two issue dimensions: the degree of polarization and salience. Using
German data, Kriesi classifies social and economic policies according to the
level of polarization, a practice that we shall follow here since these issues
are tied closely to the left–right ideological divide that has structured the
political party systems of Germany, Switzerland, the United Kingdom, and
the United States since (at least) the early twentieth century (see Lipset and
Rokkan 1967).[4]

Identifying issues with low levels of polarization is more difficult, but we
have found several such issues. One of these concerns the rights of disabled
people: while actors differ on policy specifics, they all care for disabled
people. Animal welfare, especially policies preventing cruelty to animals, also

---

[3] The exceptions to this timeframe are the debates in the German Mediation Committee. Those
debates are drawn from the 1970s and are a subset of the debates that will be discussed in
chapter 6.
[4] Bächtiger (2004) finds supportive evidence by analyzing the party manifesto dataset (Budge
2001) for differences in party positions on the issues of free market capitalism and the
welfare state. On those important economic issues, party differences between the left and
right are sizable in all four countries, suggesting a high degree of polarization.

shows a low level of polarization, with all actors agreeing that animal welfare should be protected (see Garner 1998), although this agreement does not extend to issues such as hunting or sports involving animals. Kriesi (2001) argues that crime prevention also fits in the category of less polarization, since most parties agree that crime rates should be lowered even if they do not agree on the details of how this should be done. Compared to rights for the disabled and animal protection, crime is a high salience issue, according to Kriesi. Because of this aspect we shall analyze crime separately from the other less salient and non-polarized issues.[5]

The specific debates that we analyze are as follows.[6] For Germany, we analyze a crime bill as an example of a less polarized issue with strong veto power for the opposition, an animal welfare bill as an example of a less polarized issue with weak veto power for the opposition, nursing care insurance and abortion as examples of highly polarized issues with strong veto power for the opposition, and store closing times as an example of a highly polarized issue with weak veto power for the opposition. All of these debates occurred in the period 1990–6. We also coded debates from the Mediation Committee, all of which occurred in the 1970s. Those debates were selected to overlap with the debates that are analyzed in chapter 6. The less polarized committee debates cover several issues: indemnity for victims of violent crime, privacy protection of personal data, free public transport for severely handicapped people, and legal assistance and representation for low-income people. The highly polarized committee debates include tenants' rights and limits on rent increases, change in the rules of the pension system, promotion of home ownership in social housing, the social code, adjustment in pensions and improvement of the financial basis of the pension system, and income tax.

For Switzerland, we analyze the language bill as an example of a less polarized issue with strong veto power, animal welfare as an example of a less polarized issue with weak veto power, a revision of the labor law, the minimum wage, and abortion as examples of highly polarized issues with strong veto power, and labor law revision and a cantonal initiative concerning mass layoffs as examples of highly polarized issues with low veto power. Note that the same labor law revision is considered twice and is classified as an example of both strong and weak veto power. The reason for this dual classification is the referendum threat discussed before. Early on, debate over the labor law revision took place in the context of a credible referendum threat; accordingly, we describe the debate as one in the context

---

[5] We have also analyzed other issues that are non-polarized, but those issues are unique to particular countries.

[6] More detail can be found in Bächtiger (2004) and Spörndli (2004), as well as on our project website (http://www.ipw.unibe.ch/discourse/).

of strong veto power. Later on, the referendum threat had been carried out and, correspondingly, veto power was low. All of the Swiss debates occurred in the period 1991–2001.

For the United States, we analyze crime prevention as an example of a less polarized issue with strong veto power for the minority party, rights for the disabled as an example of a less polarized issue with weak veto powers for the minority party, the minimum wage and partial birth abortion as examples of highly polarized issues with strong veto powers for the minority party, and the minimum wage as an example of a highly polarized issue with weak veto powers for the minority party. We consider two different minimum wage bills. The first one, from 1989, was debated under Republican President George H. W. Bush. He threatened to veto the bill that was proposed by the Democratic majorities in the House and the Senate, and eventually did so, creating a situation of high veto power for the minority party in the legislature. A second minimum wage bill was debated in 1996. By then, Republicans had taken control of the Congress. While the Democratic minority and Democratic President Clinton opposed some of the provisions of the bill, it was obvious that a veto was unlikely and could be overridden. Thus, the debate took place in the context of a low veto threat. The US debates cover the period from the late 1980s until the mid-1990s.

We analyze three debates from the United Kingdom. The first of these debates concerns the minimum wage and it forms a nice counterpoint to the Swiss debate on this issue. This debate reflects the classical features of a highly competitive parliamentary system, i.e. strict party discipline and no veto points for the opposition. The remaining debates concern disability and trading hours. We include these debates because they have the unusual feature that party discipline was low. This allows us to judge discourse in a competitive parliamentary system that operates under conditions that may ease the normal partisan divides.

One element of the case selection deserves special emphasis. In an ideal world, we would have a full design in which we would consider the impact of bicameralism, issue type (polarized versus non-polarized), and arena (public versus non-public) for each of the four countries that we selected. Unfortunately that approach is not feasible for a variety of reasons. First, certain cells of the design are empty (for example, non-public arenas in the United States). Second, other cells are not empty but we were unable to detect debates with sufficient numbers of speech acts (at least ten). Comparability was also a concern, in that we were sometimes unable to find truly comparable debates (for example, comparing the debate on the rights of the disabled in the US House of Representatives to the debate in the Senate was meaningless because the latter did not entail major disagreements, whereas the former did). Our inability to fill out all of the cells reflects the case study character of our research; this is not an experiment but rather an analysis of debates as they occur in the real world. However, one implication is that we have to be very careful of how the analysis is conducted, as will become apparent below.

Measures

Predictors

The predictors in our analysis are the various institutional and issue characteristics contained in hypotheses 1–6. Each characteristic is measured as a dichotomy: either a debate possesses the characteristic or it does not. While one could think of more precise measures, using dichotomies has the advantage of casting the influence of the characteristics in the starkest possible manner.

Dependent variable: discourse quality

The dependent variables in our analysis are various indicators of discourse quality. As discussed in chapter 4, we are particularly interested in the levels of justification, respect, and constructive politics. These dimensions, as well as other components of our Discourse Quality Index (DQI), were coded for all fifty-two debates. This entailed coding over 5,500 speech acts. The coding was conducted by André Bächtiger.

The coding scheme is identical to that described in chapter 3, except for a couple of instances in which we chose to elaborate on the DQI codes because it provided useful additional detail. For example, we added additional codes for respect toward demands and respect toward counterarguments, so that the highest code is now acceptance of the demand or counterargument. Acceptance of a demand means wholehearted acceptance of a demand, i.e. acceptance of the demand when it is clear that such acceptance is not given reluctantly or under force. Acceptance of a counterargument means that an actor comes to accept a counterargument, even if this does not cause a transformation of his or her preferences vis-à-vis a demand. This is one step above valuing and including counterarguments, since the latter does not require agreement with the counterarguments.[7] Moreover, we recoded

---

[7] In the coding scheme presented in chapter 3, the category "counterarguments included and valued" could include situations in which an actor comes to agree fully with a counterargument. However, a speech act would also be placed in this category if an actor indicated that someone had made a valuable point that would have to be taken seriously without completely accepting the point. The present scheme differentiates situations of full acceptance from other situations in which counterarguments are valued. A similar phenomenon occurs with respect to demands. The highest code in the DQI is "explicit respect" toward

the respect toward counterargument indicator: the lowest score, 0, is given to actors who degrade counterarguments; ignoring counterarguments is counted as 1, being neutral toward counterarguments as 2, valuing them as 3, and accepting them as 4. The rationale behind this recoding is that, in practice, ignoring counterarguments is not only a feature of bargaining, but frequently also a feature of calm debates, an essential characteristic of Habermasian discourse ethics. Assigning it the lowest code might give a distorted view of deliberative quality. This is further validated by the fact that there are numerous instances where actors "weighed" the merits of demands without directly going into counterarguments. Hence, it seemed more appropriate to assign a higher code to ignoring counterarguments, although it remains a low-quality discourse category in the recoded version.

For the analysis, we use three respect indicators. We constructed a first respect index, combining respect toward demands, counterarguments and groups in an additive fashion. This indicator is called "overall respect." It ranges from 0 to 9, with higher scores indicating a greater level of respect and therefore a better level of discourse. While the "overall respect" indicator is particularly important in the context of the philosophical debate on deliber-ation, it might be somewhat misleading when it comes to testing the causal mechanisms we have proposed in the hypothesis chapter. For instance, it is not so obvious why actors in consensus systems should be more respectful toward groups since actors in competitive systems might also have strong incentives to be respectful because certain social groups might constitute potential or actual constituents. Therefore, we use a second respect indi-cator which only includes toward demands and toward counterarguments. We call this the "respect toward demands/counterarguments" indicator. It ranges from 0 to 7. Since the "overall respect" and the "respect toward demands/counterarguments" indicators are both very close to a continuum, we report means for them in the analysis.[8]

A final modification of the DQI is that we expanded the categories of the constructive politics indicator. Here we distinguish between four levels. Positional politics form the lowest level of the indicator. This is followed by alternative proposals, i.e. proposals that attempt to mediate but that do not fit the current agenda. In these two categories, the coding in this

---

the demand. Again, this category comprises two situations: (1) a demand is explicitly valued *and* accepted and (2) a demand is explicitly valued but not accepted. The current coding scheme separates these two possibilities, giving the highest code to cases where a demand is fully accepted.

[8] For simplicity and transparency reasons we have simply added the different indicators of respect without giving them different weights. However, as the different indicators have unequal numbers of categories, some indicators might distort overall scores and findings. We have rerun all analyses with weighted indices but found no differences.

Table 5.1 *Inter-coder reliability for the debates in the analysis*

Category	RCA	κ	r	α
Participation	1.000			
Level of justification	0.970	0.953** (0.046)	0.965**	0.982
Content of justification	1.000			
Respect toward counterarguments	0.919	0.881** (0.066)	0.941**	0.969
Constructive politics	0.970	0.954** (0.045)	0.983**	0.991

Notes: RCA = rate of coder agreement; κ = Cohen's kappa (with estimated standard errors in parentheses); r = Spearman's rank correlation; α = standardized reliability. $N = 185$. **$p < 0.01$.

chapter is identical to the coding presented in chapter 3. Where the present coding deviates is on the next category, which we label "consensus appeals." Consensus appeals are calls for compromise and consensus that are pertinent to the current agenda but that are unspecific. For example, a call to "bridge our differences" would be a consensus appeal if it did not contain a specific mediating proposal. The highest level of constructive politics is the same as was presented in chapter 3, namely mediating proposals that fit the current agenda. By breaking out consensus appeals from mediating proposals, we can get a better handle on different forms of "willingness to compromise," which can be quite concrete but also quite abstract.

The coding of these indicators requires some subjective judgments, so that there is a risk that the resulting measures are quite idiosyncratic and could not be replicated by another coder. To avoid that possibility, we checked the inter-coder reliability for a subset of the debates. André Bächtiger and Markus Spörndli coded two debates from the German Mediation Committee (namely the debates on changing the rules of the pension system and on tax relief and promotion of investment), as well as samples from the debates on the language bill in Switzerland, taken both from committee deliberations in the National Council and from the discussions on the floor of the Federal Council. The German debates are also used in chapter 6, so that our reliability check is also relevant for the results reported in that chapter. In total 185 coding decisions were made by the two coders, covering the following indicators: participation, level of justification, content of justification, respect toward counterarguments, and constructive politics. Statistics concerning the inter-coder reliability are reported in table 5.1.

As this table shows, the inter-coder reliability was quite high. Overall, the two coders agreed on 167 judgments, corresponding to an overall rate of coder agreement (RCA) of 90 percent. Breaking the inter-coder reliability down by category, we see perfect agreement on participation and on content of justification (RCA = 1.000). The rates of coder agreement on the remaining categories are also very high, with none of them dipping below 0.90 – the conventional cutoff for the RCA. Since the rate of coder agreement does not take into account that two coders may agree by chance, we also compute Cohen's kappa (κ) which does adjust for chance agreement.[9] All of the estimated kappa values are well above 0.8, which indicates near-perfect agreement (Landis and Koch 1977). For the ordinal indicators of the DQI (namely, level of justification, respect toward counterarguments, and constructive politics), it is also possible to define inter-coder reliability in terms of the Spearman rank correlation and the standardized coefficient alpha (α). These statistics are shown in the last two columns of table 5.1. Again, there is a very high degree of inter-coder reliability, with none of the correlations and standardized alphas falling below 0.9.

The bottom line is that there was a lot of agreement between the coders, despite the fact that judging discourse quality entails an interpretative element. The reliability reported in table 5.1 is in line with that reported in chapter 3. It instills us with confidence about measuring discourse quality and, more specifically, about the data that we shall use in this chapter and the next. With that said, let us now turn to an evaluation of our hypotheses.

The analysis takes up the hypotheses one at a time. Our primary analytic vehicle is to present the frequency distributions of the indicators of the DQI for different levels of the predictors (in the case of "overall respect" and "respect toward demands/counterarguments" we report the means). This is the least technical way of presenting our results. For readers who are interested in statistical significance testing, the text also makes reference to a series of analysis of variance (ANOVA) tests. These tests compare the variance in discourse across levels of the predictors with variance within each of those levels. For instance, in the comparison of consensus and competitive systems, which we shall discuss next, we can ask if the DQI indicators vary across those systems. We can also ask how much variance there is within consensus systems and within competitive systems; such variance would be due to peculiarities of the countries, debates, and speakers that are grouped inside a particular type of system. The ANOVA compares the variance across systems with the variance inside each system. Roughly speaking, ANOVA

---

[9] Kappa can be computed only if the rate of coder agreement is not perfect. Hence it is not reported for the categories of participation and content of justification.

determines if the variance across systems is sufficiently large compared to the variance inside systems to allow the conclusion that it did not occur by chance. In this case, we say that system type has a statistically significant effect.[10]

Consensus versus competition

Our first hypothesis concerns the level of discourse in consensus versus competitive systems. As discussed in chapter 4, we expect discourse to be higher in consensus systems than in competitive systems. Does our data support this expectation? To answer that question we begin by drawing a comparison between Switzerland and the United Kingdom. As discussed before, Switzerland represents the archetypical case of a consensus system. By contrast, the United Kingdom is one of the classic examples of a competitive system. Thus, by drawing the comparison between these two cases we are in a position to assess political discourse when institutional differences are maximal.

The debates on which we base our Swiss–British comparison concern adjustments to the minimum wage. This issue played a prominent role on the political agenda of both the British and Swiss legislatures, roughly during the same period. In the United Kingdom, the debate possessed all the classic features of a competitive parliamentary democracy. The minimum wage bill was an important bill for government and opposition alike, and party discipline was therefore high. Moreover, the government knew that it had a clear majority for the bill, leaving the opposition without veto power. Under these circumstances, one would expect discourse quality to be low on all three of the key dimensions – level of justification, respect, and constructive politics. This is exactly what we observe in table 5.2, which shows descriptive statistics for the dimensions of the DQI. The tendency is toward low scores on all of these dimensions. There are no consensus appeals or mediating proposals; overall respect levels hover around a mediocre mean score of 2.27 (out of a maximum of nine); respect toward demands/counterarguments is at 1.24 (out of 7). There are no instances of speakers accepting the demands or counterarguments of their opponents, while instances of explicit respect

---

[10] The ANOVA takes into consideration that our data are unbalanced, i.e. we do not have the same numbers of speech acts for each of the levels of the predictors. Details about the adjustments that we made to the ANOVAs can be found in Bächtiger (2004). The ANOVA makes a strong assumption that the discourse quality indicators are at least interval scales, which is questionable at best. Thus, we complemented the ANOVAs with ordered logistic regression analysis (for details see Bächtiger 2004). In most cases, the ANOVAs proved to be the more conservative of the two tests, so this is what we report here.

Table 5.2 *Discourse quality in consensus and competitive settings: a Swiss–UK comparison*

Discourse quality dimension	Consensus (Switzerland)	Competitive (UK)
Level of justification:[a]		
No justification	10.80	12.90
Inferior justification	8.10	29.00
Qualified justification	13.50	12.90
Sophisticated justification	67.60	45.20
Overall respect (mean):[b]	3.54	2.27
Respect demands/counterarg. (mean):[b]	2.41	1.24
Constructive politics:[a]		
Positional politics	86.50	93.50
Alternative proposal	2.70	6.50
Consensus appeal	8.10	0.00
Mediating proposal	2.70	0.00

Notes: Table entries are percentages (which add up to 100 percent in each column). The analysis is based on the Swiss and UK minimum wage debates.
[a] Interjections excluded ($N = 68$ speech acts).
[b] Interjections included ($N = 82$ speech acts).

are rare (2.2 percent) and instances of disrespect frequent (73.3 percent).[11] In terms of levels of justification, sophisticated justifications, while not rare, constitute only a small number of the speech acts. In sum, the British debate is characterized by a rather low level of discourse that is indicative of a decision making process in which deliberation plays a minor role at best.

When we contrast this with the Swiss minimum wage debate, the poor level of discourse in Britain becomes even more evident. The Swiss debate occurred in a context in which consensus was important, in which party discipline was comparatively low, and in which there were credible veto points. These are conditions under which deliberation should flourish, and this is reflected in the much better discourse quality that we observe in table 5.2. In the Swiss debate, respect levels are much higher: overall respect is at 3.54 and respect toward demands/counterarguments is at 2.41. Not only do we find that instances of disrespect are much lower (29.7 percent), we also find

---

[11] This is based on a categorical "respect toward demands/counterarguments" indicator, which collapses respect toward demand and counterargument in one dimension, involving four categories: disrespect toward demands and/or counterarguments, a neutral category, explicit respect toward demands and/or counterarguments, and acceptance of demands and/or counterarguments.

instances of explicit respect (18.9 percent) or even agreement with demands and counterarguments (5.4 percent). Sophisticated justifications were the norm in the Swiss debate, constituting a majority of the speech acts. Even on the constructive politics dimension, the Swiss debate compares favorably: while positional politics dominated the debates in both Switzerland and the United Kingdom, the Swiss debate at least saw some instances of consensus appeals and mediating proposals. The differences between the Swiss and British debates are so strong that they are highly significant in an ANOVA (at the 0.01 level), with the exception of constructive politics.[12]

Our comparison of two extremes of the consensus–competitive dimension suggests that institutional differences matter a great deal for political discourse. Before we accept that conclusion, however, we should address a contrasting explanation. The difference in discourse between the British and Swiss legislatures may simply be cultural in nature. More specifically, different logics of appropriateness (March and Olson 1989, 1998) in each legislature may dictate different norms of parliamentary conduct and, therefore, a different deliberative space.[13] Perhaps the norms in the British House of Commons mitigate high-quality discourse, while the norms of the Swiss National Council favor it, quite independently of any institutional differences between those legislatures.

If this argument is correct, then we should see the level of discourse in the British House of Commons remain low even if we change some of the institutional factors in a direction that favors deliberation. That is not the case, as is evident from the debates on disability and on Sunday trading time. First, consider the disability debate. While conducted in an otherwise competitive system, the circumstances of this debate were quite unusual for Britain. The bill prompting the debate was not introduced by the government, but by a coalition of advocates of the disabled that spanned all parties represented in the House. The government was opposed to the bill, claiming that it was too costly, but it found itself unable to block legislation and eventually, though grudgingly, accepted it. The existence of a multiparty coalition not only reflected low party cohesion, but also introduced somewhat of a consensus element to the debate. Correspondingly, our institutional explanation would predict higher levels of political discourse, and this is precisely what we observe. In the disability debate, a majority (63.6 percent) of the speech acts contained sophisticated justifications. Respect scores were much higher than in the minimum wage debate, with 3.27 for overall respect and 2.18 for respect toward demands/counterarguments. While positional politics

---

[12] The significant differences for both respect indicators are robust when interjections are excluded.

[13] On the role of norms in the House of Commons, see Searing (1994).

was the norm in the disability debate, just as it had been in the minimum wage debate, consensus appeals occurred more often (6.8 percent). Thus, the disability debate attained relatively high levels of discourse quality for Britain, where institutional factors often align to generate a sharp divide between the government and opposition that debilitates deliberation. Indeed, speakers in the debate seemed to be quite aware of the unusually high level of discourse; as Nicholas Scott, the Conservative Minister for Social Security and Disabled People, stated: "It may be useful if I intervene to clarify the Government's position on the motion and the Bill to which it relates; I congratulate all the hon. Members who have spoken in a universally high-quality debate; the issue of disability affects every single constituency in the country and therefore every hon. Member, irrespective of party or region" (*House of Commons*, February 26, 1993, col. 1175).

We observe a similar pattern in the debate on Sunday trading time. Here an open vote was held, so that party discipline was low. In addition, numerous proposals were circulating, none with a clear a priori majority, which necessitated some negotiation. Again, these circumstances are quite favorable for deliberation, and we again predicted that discourse in this debate would be of a higher quality. This is what we found, at least in terms of the respect dimension. In this debate too, respect levels were considerably higher than those we observed in the minimum wage debate: overall respect was at 3.11 and respect toward demands/counterarguments was at 2.00. On the other dimensions of discourse quality, the competitive character of the British system once again manifests itself. All of the speech acts in this debate could be characterized as positional politics. In terms of the level of justification, sophisticated justifications never occurred, although the debate fared better than the minimum wage debate in the much smaller incidence of absent or inferior justifications (5.3 and 10.5 percent of speech acts, respectively).

Our analysis of the British debates clearly shows that institutions matter for political discourse. While we do not deny the relevance of culture, it is not the entire story. Changes in the institutional parameters can have a profound effect. In this case, moving a competitive system in the direction of a consensus system with weak party discipline and veto players resulted in marked improvements in political discourse. Such shifts in discourse cannot be accounted for by shifts in cultural norms and have to be attributed to changing institutional factors.

A comparison of Switzerland and the United Kingdom can teach us a great deal about the way in which consensus and competitive systems shape discourse, but it is important to consider other cases as well. An obvious choice is to compare the Swiss and German legislatures. Germany too is a competitive system, and like Britain, party discipline is usually high. Unlike the United Kingdom (under normal circumstances), however, veto players

Table 5.3 *Discourse quality in consensus and competitive settings: a Swiss–German comparison*

Discourse quality dimension	Consensus (Switzerland)	Competitive (Germany)
Level of justification:[a]		
No justification	10.10	20.90
Inferior justification	13.60	17.80
Qualified justification	27.30	21.50
Sophisticated justification	49.00	39.80
Overall respect (mean):[b]	3.62	3.12
Respect demands/counterarg. (mean):[b]	2.48	2.11
Constructive politics:[a]		
Positional politics	81.00	86.20
Alternative proposal	8.20	6.60
Consensus appeal	6.20	5.00
Mediating proposal	4.60	2.20

Notes: Table entries are percentages (which add up to 100 percent in each column). For a description of the cases entering this analysis see http://www.ipw.unibe.ch/discourse/.
[a] Interjections excluded ($N = 1,383$ speech acts).
[b] Interjections included ($N = 1,896$ speech acts).

do play a role in Germany: as discussed earlier, if the opposition controls the Federal Council, then it becomes a pivotal player in the legislative process. In this regard, Germany is similar to Switzerland and it would be interesting to see how the consensus–competitive divide in discourse holds up when veto players are present.

The results from this analysis are shown in table 5.3. This table reveals important differences between Switzerland and Germany. First, consider the level of justification. Qualified and sophisticated debates were far more common in the Swiss debates (76.3 percent) than in the German debates (61.3 percent). The mean levels of both respect indicators are also higher in Switzerland; the mean difference is 0.50 for overall respect and 0.37 for respect toward demands/counterarguments.[14] Finally, consider constructive politics. This is the only indicator for which the differences between Switzerland and Germany are small, although there is a slight tendency toward greater consensus appeals and mediating proposals in the Swiss system

[14] The significant differences for both respect indicators are robust when interjections are excluded.

(10.8 percent versus 7.2 percent in Germany). ANOVAs reveal that the differences on levels of justification and respect are statistically significant (at the 0.01 level). Only the difference on constructive politics fails to achieve statistical significance.

The Swiss–German comparison corroborates our earlier finding that discourse quality is greater in consensus systems than in competitive systems. At least, this is true for two of our three indicators. But the comparison suffers from several limitations. First, it is confounded in two different ways. The Swiss and German legislatures do not only differ in their level of competitiveness, but also in their level of party cohesion and in the fact that one legislature operates in a presidential system while the other operates in a parliamentary system. Second, our analysis of respect is based on all speech acts, including interjections. Since interjections may be less respectful, it would be useful to see how their exclusion affects the respect scale.

To overcome the limitations of the Swiss–German comparison we now present an analysis in which interjections are excluded. Moreover, this analysis draws a contrast between Switzerland, as a consensus system, and Germany and the United States, as competitive systems. By including the United States we alleviate the confounding factors discussed before, since the United States, like Switzerland but unlike Germany, is a presidential system with comparatively low party cohesion. The results of this analysis are reported in table 5.4.

This table again shows important differences in the level of respect between consensus and competitive systems. While these differences are not as large as they were in the Swiss–German comparison, they are still unmistakable. Respect levels in our consensus system remain higher: the mean levels of overall respect are at 3.67 for Switzerland and 3.37 for the United States and Germany; the mean levels of respect toward demands/counterarguments are at 2.53 for Switzerland and 2.27 for the United States and Germany. An ANOVA shows that these differences on the two respect indicators are highly significant (at the 0.01 level).

In terms of constructive politics, table 5.4 does not reveal major differences between consensus and competitive systems. In contrast with table 5.3, there are also no major differences in the level of justification. For both of these indicators, an ANOVA failed to show a significant effect for the consensus–competitive system comparison. Thus, adding the American debates to the competitive side of the ledger has wiped out the differences in justification that we observed earlier.

These results suggest important differences between consensus and competitive systems, in particular with regard to respect. Respect levels are considerably higher in the Swiss consensus system than in competitive systems, a result that takes on additional meaning if one realizes that Swiss

Table 5.4 *Discourse quality in consensus and competitive settings: a Swiss–German/US comparison*

Discourse quality Dimension	Consensus (Switzerland)	Competitive (USA and Germany)
Level of justification:		
No justification	10.60	8.10
Inferior justification	13.70	15.50
Qualified justification	26.30	30.00
Sophisticated justification	49.40	46.40
Overall respect (mean):	3.67	3.37
Respect demands/counterarg. (mean):	2.53	2.27
Constructive politics:		
Positional politics	81.50	81.30
Alternative proposal	7.70	7.00
Consensus appeal	5.80	8.40
Mediating proposal	5.00	3.30

Notes: Table entries are percentages (which add up to 100 percent in each column). For a description of the cases entering this analysis see http://www.ipw.unibe.ch/discourse/. $N = 2,409$ speech acts.

coalition parties are not much concerned about coalitional stability and that the coalition parties became increasingly polarized during the 1990s, the timeframe of our debates (see Hug and Sciarini 1995). An example may illustrate the willingness of Swiss actors to respect or accept proposals and counterarguments from political opponents. In the heated public debate on labor law revision, in which the Social Democrats found themselves in opposition to the proposed legislation, Christiane Brunner (SPS – Social Democrats) nonetheless declared: "concerning the proposition of the Christian-Democratic group, it is an interesting one because it has at least the advantage of protecting the neediest employees" (Nationalrat, March 22, 1995, p. 849).[15] This example illustrates that there is a space for respectful political dialogue in consensus democracies.

In competitive settings, this space is much smaller. Indeed, there is an incentive to undermine and ridicule the demands and arguments of political opponents. Consider, for example, the German debate on animal welfare. While this was a less polarized issue – all parties agreed that something should be done to protect animal welfare – it still generated a considerable amount

---

[15] "quant à la proposition du groupe démocrate-chrétien, elle est intéressante parce qu'elle a l' avantage de protéger au moins les plus fragiles parmi les salariés."

of vitriolic speech. Commenting on the proposal of the Kohl government (a coalition of CDU/CSU and FDP), Charlotte Garbe (Greens) exclaimed:

> What the government and coalition fractions present here as the core of their animal protection conception is a shameful caricature of the demands animal lovers in Germany have been pushing for years ... My dear colleagues, one cannot see an earnest will of yours to codify changes in our society's treatment of animals that would be more than a cosmetic change of the civil law (Bundestag, June 20, 1990, pp. 17080–1).[16]

In polarized debates, respect levels can drop even lower. In the German abortion debate, for example, Claus Jäger (CDU/CSU – Christian Democrats) interjected that "You deserve a slap in the face for that!" (Bundestag, September 26, 1991, p. 3688).[17]

While there are important differences in the levels of respect found in consensus and competitive systems, our evidence shows few differences in constructive politics.[18] This suggests that respect does not necessarily translate into a more constructive political approach. Or, put differently, positional politics is the norm in both the consensus and the competitive systems that we have studied. While this may be disappointing to advocates of deliberation, we should note that the hurdle for constructive politics is quite high in multiparty settings. The existence of partisan divides suggests that legislators are divided on numerous substantive issues, and this makes it a priori unlikely that policy compromises can be worked out for all but a small subset of issues even in consensus democracies.

The weak findings on constructive politics should not be taken to mean that respect is meaningless in parliamentary debate. Over time, respect could become an important resource that binds legislators together and that may make future cooperation easier. Moreover, from a deliberative perspective, respect is important in its own right. It signals a willingness to take seriously one's opponents and to entertain their ideas and arguments. Even if, at the end of the day, one does not put forward a compromise proposal, a

[16] "Was die Bundesregierung und mit ihr die Koalitionsfraktionen uns hier als angebliches Herzstück ihres Tierschutzkonzepts zur Beschlussfassung vorgelegt haben, ist eine beschämende Karikatur dessen, was die Tierfreunde in der Bundesrepublik Deutschland seit Jahren gefordert haben ... Verehrte Kolleginnen und Kollegen, bei Ihnen ist der ernsthafte Wille nicht erkennbar und nicht vorhanden, Änderungen im Umgang unserer Gesellschaft mit Tieren festzuschreiben, die mehr wären als eine kosmetische Anpassung des BGB."
[17] "Also, für das Argument gehört Ihnen eine runtergehauen!" On average, discourse quality in this debate is not even the worst. That is, German debates on other polarized issues often sank lower in terms of discourse. One reason may be that party discipline was somewhat relaxed in the debate; we shall return to this possibility later in the chapter.
[18] With respect to levels of justification, we would say that the evidence is mixed. Some of our analyses show higher levels of justification in consensus systems, while others show no difference between consensus and competitive systems.

Table 5.5 *Discourse quality in the contexts of strong and weak veto power*

Discourse quality dimension	Strong veto power	Weak veto power
Level of justification:[a]		
No justification	12.90	12.80
Inferior justification	14.60	15.70
Qualified justification	22.40	28.60
Sophisticated justification	50.10	42.80
Overall respect (mean):[b]	3.38	3.20
Respect demands/counterarg. (mean):[b]	2.28	2.10
Constructive politics:[a]		
Positional politics	84.70	88.30
Alternative proposal	8.50	5.90
Consensus appeal	4.30	3.90
Mediating proposal	2.60	1.90

Notes: Table entries are percentages (which add up to 100 percent in each column). For a description of the cases entering this analysis see http://www.ipw.unibe.ch/discourse/.
[a] Interjections excluded ($N = 1,352$ speech acts).
[b] Interjections included ($N = 1,860$ speech acts).

serious consideration of opposing views at least validates the fact that other viewpoints are reasonable. It may also mean that one's final opinions are better informed, since one has made the effort to entertain all sides of an issue (see Fishkin 1997).

The role of veto players

Our second hypothesis suggests that the ability of some actors to veto decisions forces other actors to deliberate. If this expectation is correct, we would expect the levels of justification and respect, as well as constructive politics, to be higher in the presence of strong veto players. Is this true? Table 5.5 lends only weak support to the hypothesis.

Our results indicate only a small effect on the level of justification. If veto power is strong, then the incidence of qualified or sophisticated justifications is 72.5 percent. This drops slightly (to 71.4 percent) when veto power is weak, but this difference is not statistically significant in an ANOVA. We also fail to obtain statistically significant differences on constructive politics, although there is a slight tendency for positional politics to increase when veto power decreases.

The most important differences, again, are found for respect. On average, both overall respect and respect toward demands/counterarguments are lower when veto power is weak. ANOVAs reveal that these differences are statistically significant (at the 0.05 level).[19]

Two cases can illustrate the effect that veto power has on political discourse. First, consider the US minimum wage debates conducted in the House of Representatives in 1989. The first debate, on April 11, occurred under a direct presidential veto threat, but there was hope of finding a compromise that would either avoid a veto or have such widespread support that a veto could be overridden. By the time of the second debate, on July 14, hopes for a compromise had faded; Democrats and Republicans had been unable to forge a compromise that was mutually acceptable. As the Democratic House majority pushed its bill, it faced a strong veto threat from President George H. W. Bush. Now it was clear that the required two-thirds majority to overrule this veto could not be achieved. Thus, whereas the first debate had been focused on coalition building, the second debate pitted the Democratic majority against the Republican minority, turning the debate into a competitive one.

The impact of this shift was quite visible, especially in terms of the respect dimension of discourse quality. The number of disrespectful speeches increased from 40 percent to almost 60 percent from the first to the second debate. At the same time, explicitly respectful speeches or speeches that accepted demands/counterarguments decreased from 10 percent to nothing. Thus, while disrespect was high even in the initial debate – something we should expect in a competitive system – it became much more prevalent once it was clear that the majority and minority could not come to an agreement.

A second example is the Swiss debate on labor law reform in 1996. The issue here was to overhaul certain labor regulations in an attempt to improve the competitiveness of the Swiss economy. The government proposal sought to improve gender equality by abolishing regulations that made it impossible for women to work at night. There was some opposition to this proposal, since some feared that it would lead to a massive expansion of night shift work, which according to leftist groups was detrimental to workers' health. To address these concerns, the government proposal provided for bonus payments during night and Sunday shifts. However, this compromise solution was dismantled when a group of right-wing deputies challenged the legitimacy and need for bonus payments. As they withdrew support for the bill, the Swiss Federation of Trade Unions began collecting signatures for a referendum. This severely polarized the debate. Since parties from the right

---

[19] The significant differences for both respect indicators are robust when interjections are excluded.

knew that they would probably lose in a referendum, their ability to veto the government proposal decreased significantly. It was clear that the decision making process had been transformed from consensual to majoritarian. In the words of Georg Stucky (Free Democrat), "Now we can do whatever we want, as we are facing a referendum vote anyway" (Nationalrat, March 6, 1996, p. 152).[20]

The change in atmosphere was palpable. Prior to the referendum threat, respectful speeches had outnumbered disrespectful speeches in the first chamber debate. About 38 percent of the speech acts had been explicitly respectful or accepting of the demands/counterarguments of others, while only 23 percent of the speech acts had been disrespectful. After the threat, explicitly respectful or accepting speech acts vanished, while disrespectful speech acts increased to 80 percent. The usually consensual Swiss legislature had transformed itself in the course of discussing the labor reform bill, and the metamorphosis was so stark that an unwitting observer might have wondered if she was experiencing a debate in a competitive setting.

The importance of veto players for political discourse can also be illustrated through the German debate on nursing care insurance. Here the Kohl government faced an opposition of Social Democrats and Greens that controlled the second chamber, the Federal Council. This put the opposition in a position of strong veto power. While the overall debate achieved low respect scores, there were still a few coalition MPs that tried to build "deliberative bridges" to the opposition. For example, Gebhard Glück (Christian Democrat) used his speech to point out the similarities between the government and opposition positions: "Yet coalition and opposition do agree on fundamental questions; I do not see the danger that people in true need of care could be barred from services; of course, we will have to talk about this in the Mediation Committee, at the latest, if the SPD wishes to do so" (Bundestag, October 22, 1993, pp. 15852–3).[21] But in the same speech Glück also stated that the criticisms of the SPD (Social Democrats) were overdrawn. This perfectly illustrates the discursive cross-pressures in a competitive setting, where actors like Glück, on the one hand, try to encompass the demands and counterarguments of a powerful political opponent, yet still have strong incentives to degrade them.

Our results, then, suggest that respectful discourse is more likely when opposition forces hold veto power. We do not observe corresponding

---

[20] "Wir können jetzt machen was wir wollen, wir stehen ohnehin vor einem Referendum."
[21] "Koalition und Opposition stimmen doch in grundsätzliche Fragen weitgehend überein; ich sehe auch nicht die Gefahr, dass wirklich Pflegebedürftigen zu Unrecht Leistungen versagt werden könnten; selbstverständlich werden wir aber spätestens im Vermittlungsverfahren über dieses Thema sprechen müssen, wenn die SPD dies wünscht." The SPD (Social Democrats) had objected to the government proposal that it would hurt the truly needy.

differences in the level of justification or in constructive politics. However, the fact that the majority begins to pay respect to minorities, and vice versa, even in competitive settings, suggests that veto players matter for discourse.

An important question is whether this finding can be interpreted as deliberation in a strict sense. The question is whether the increase in respect is authentic or merely strategic, in the sense of greasing the wheels of a negotiation process that the majority would have liked to avoid by imposing its will on the minority but could not avoid because of the minority's veto power. As always, arbitrating the authenticity of speech is a difficult task, but our guess is that much of the change in respect is strategically motivated. This might disappoint deliberative theorists, but we cannot underestimate the practical importance of changes in speech, even if they lack authenticity. Politicians adapt to changing circumstances and incentive structures, and in this sense they are purely strategic creatures. But without such adaptations it would be impossible to pass legislation, to address problems, or to ever change the status quo. Negotiation is an essential fact of political life, and our findings here suggest that political actors realize that they need to adjust their speech acts in order to facilitate negotiation, or they risk never passing any legislation. In this regard, our findings corroborate Holzinger's (2001) argument that deliberation is an essential part of negotiation. If the need to negotiate arises, respectful talk becomes an important instrument for forging winning coalitions, although we will have to wait until the next chapter to see how successful this instrument is.

Presidential versus parliamentary systems

Our third hypothesis argues that, within the subset of competitive democracies, discourse quality should be higher in presidential systems than in parliamentary systems. As discussed in chapter 4, the impetus for this hypothesis is that party cohesion is generally higher in parliamentary systems. This makes it less important for members of one party to develop relationships with members of another party, hence removing an important incentive for respectful and constructive dialogues across party lines. In presidential systems, lower party cohesion should cause legislators to forge cross-party links, which should be associated with higher level of discourse.

To test this hypothesis we pit discourse in the United States, a presidential system, against discourse in Germany and the United Kingdom, two examples of parliamentary systems. The results are displayed in table 5.6. On the whole, these results produce some support for our hypothesis, but they also contradict it in important ways. The contradictions are found on the level of the justification and constructive politics dimensions. Sophisticated

Table 5.6 *Discourse quality in the contexts of presidential and parliamentary competitive systems*

Discourse quality dimension	Presidential (USA)	Parliamentary (Germany and UK)
Level of justification:[a]		
No justification	11.40	11.20
Inferior justification	18.60	13.40
Qualified justification	29.30	8.40
Sophisticated justification	40.70	67.00
Overall respect (mean):[b]	3.24	2.62
Respect demands/counterarg. (mean):[b]	2.11	1.61
Constructive politics:[a]		
Positional politics	89.90	83.00
Alternative proposal	6.10	8.70
Consensus appeal	3.70	6.90
Mediating proposal	0.30	1.40

Notes: Table entries are percentages (which add up to 100 percent in each column). For a description of the cases entering this analysis see http://www.ipw.unibe.ch/discourse/.
[a] Interjections excluded ($N = 497$ speech acts).
[b] Interjections included ($N = 1,031$ speech acts).

justifications are more common in parliamentary systems (67 percent) than in presidential systems (40.7 percent), a finding that runs counter to our expectations. In addition, pure positional politics was less common in parliamentary systems (83 percent) than in presidential systems (89.9 percent) and this, too, contradicts our third hypothesis. In an ANOVA, these results are statistically significant (at the 0.05 level or better).

There is support for our third hypothesis when we consider the respect dimension. The respective mean differences are 0.62 (overall respect) and 0.50 (respect toward demands/counterarguments). ANOVA and regression tests show these effects to be statistically significant (at the 0.01 level).[22]

Overall, then, support for the third hypothesis is a mixed bag. We can think of two, somewhat ad hoc, explanations for this outcome. First, we relied on the assumption that party cohesion was comparatively low in our example of a presidential system, i.e. the United States. That assumption may

[22] The significant differences for both respect indicators are robust when interjections are excluded.

be incorrect, since studies of voting behavior in the House of Representatives demonstrate the existence of clear partisan voting patterns, especially after the Republican takeover in 1995 (Aldrich and Rohde 2000). Second, all of the debates in our analysis are public in nature, which may blur differences between parliamentary and presidential systems, in that party cohesion may be less of a concern when there is an audience of citizens that can be reached for the purpose of securing votes in the next election.

However, a qualitative analysis of the debates clearly reveals some in-stances in which the results are more clear-cut. First, the effect of party discipline is clearly demonstrated in the German abortion debate. When we compare this debate to debates about similarly highly polarized issues (nurs-ing care insurance and trading times), we find much higher levels of respect. Much of this had to do with lower party cohesion in the abortion debate. As Konrad Elmer (SPD – Social Democrats) notes in the abortion debate: "When the fronts are once not exactly along fraction lines, a much more productive debate is possible . . . Many bills might ultimately be more qual-ified if this happened more frequently." (*Ausschuss für Frauen und Jugend*, June 3, 1993, p. 30/64).[23]

As a second example, it is instructive to compare discourse in the German Federal Diet and Federal Council to discourse in the Mediation Committee. As a rule, discourse in the latter is much higher than in the two chambers of the German legislature. Members of the Mediation Committee operate under relaxed party cohesion. Indeed, as discussed in greater detail in the next chapter, they are given a mandate to work out compromise solutions (at least within reasonable limits). As a result, mutual respect and constructive politics often flourish in the Mediation Committee, whereas their develop-ment is much more circumscribed in the Federal Council and Federal Diet (unless party cohesion is lifted there as well).

Further evidence for the parliamentary–presidential divide may come from less polarized issues. The debate on disability rights in the US House of Representatives produced a gentle discourse, at least in comparison with the debate on the polarized minimum wage issue conducted in that same institution, in which speakers showed respect for each other's positions and arguments. By contrast, the German debates on animal welfare and the pro-tection of privacy, similarly less polarized issues, showed relatively low dis-course quality. While these comparisons are not conclusive because the issues are somewhat different, they suggest that the parliamentary–presidential

---

[23] "Gerade wenn die Fronten einmal nicht genau den Grenzen der Fraktionen entlang gingen, sei hier eine viel sinnvollere Diskussion möglich . . . Viele Gesetze wären vielleicht am Ende viel qualifizierter, wenn dies öfter der Fall wäre" (speech delivered in the Committee on Women and Youth).

divide accounts for some of the differences in political discourse that we observe.[24]

In conclusion, the comparison between parliamentary and presidential competitive systems suggests relatively robust differences in respect. These differences are in the expected direction and suggest better opportunities for respectful discourse in presidential settings. We also observe some counterintuitive effects on discourse, whereby parliamentary systems produce higher levels of justification and constructive politics. These results are a puzzle for the moment. While we have hinted at possible explanations, these are ad hoc. Clearly more theoretical development is required to account for the results, although this should not distract from the finding that respect behaves as we had predicted.

First versus second chambers

According to our fourth hypothesis, second chambers are better equipped for deliberation than first chambers. This is due to institutional provisions, as well as norms of civility. Consequently, we should expect to see higher levels of discourse, in particular in terms of respect and constructive politics. To see if this is true, we consider a series of debates that are constant across chambers in terms of the underlying issues (and perforce issue polarization) and other aspects. Thus, differences in discourse can be safely attributed to chambers, since alternative explanations are being controlled for.

The results of our cross-chamber analysis are shown in table 5.7. As this table shows, discourse is indeed of a higher quality in second chambers than in first chambers. Consider first our indicators of respect. In second chambers, the mean difference in the overall respect indicator is 0.37 and in the respect toward demands/counterarguments indicator it is 0.35. These effects of chamber on respect are statistically significant in the ANOVA and the regression tests (at the 0.01 level).[25] In addition to these powerful effects, we see a slight tendency in first chambers toward greater positional politics compared to second chambers. An ANOVA reveals this effect to be significant as well (at the 0.05 level). The only difference that is not statistically significant is that on levels of justification; those are comparable in first and in second chambers.

But what drives discourse in second chambers? Here we can learn a great deal from senators' reflections on their own institution, in particular concerning norms of civility. Consider, for example, Clairborne Pell's

---

[24] We omitted these debates from the analysis reported in table 5.6 because of the small number of speech acts.

[25] The significant differences for both respect indicators are robust when interjections are excluded.

Table 5.7 *Discourse quality in first and second chambers of the legislature*

Discourse quality dimension	Second chambers	First chambers
Level of justification:[a]		
No justification	15.00	12.70
Inferior justification	14.70	15.50
Qualified justification	22.00	26.40
Sophisticated justification	48.30	45.70
Overall respect (mean):[b]	3.77	3.40
Respect demands/counterarg. (mean):[b]	2.64	2.29
Constructive politics:[a]		
Positional politics	82.60	85.20
Alternative proposal	7.70	8.60
Consensus appeal	6.10	3.60
Mediating proposal	3.60	2.60

Notes: Table entries are percentages (which add up to 100 percent in each column). For a description of the cases entering this analysis see http://www.ipw.unibe.ch/discourse/.
[a] Interjections excluded ($N = 3{,}694$ speech acts).
[b] Interjections included ($N = 4{,}096$ speech acts).

(Democrat, Rhode Island) reflections during the debate over partial birth abortion, a highly polarized issue that could have easily produced a disrespectful discourse between proponents and opponents of this procedure: "The Senate has a long and established tradition of careful deliberation precisely because of its rules and procedures for legislating such difficult issues with thorough and adequate review" (November 8, 1995, S16790). In the same debate, Carol Moseley-Braun reflected that "the Senate's job is to be as rational as possible in our discussion of volatile issues like this one and to consider what is really at stake" (September 26, 1996, S11358).

US senators are not alone in their assessment of their institution. In the Swiss language debate, Carlo Schmid (Christian Democrat), a member of the Council of States, made the following observation: "In this club atmosphere we think that we ought to be good, that we have to live up to a higher form of decency, that we have to defend ideals. Each of you will subscribe to this" (June 15, 1994, p. 706).[26] And in the German debate on nursing insurance, Federal Councilor Norbert Blüm (Christian Democrat) noted

[26] "Wir haben in dieser Klubatmosphäre irgendwie die Auffassung, dass wir gut sein müssen, dass wir eine höhere Form der Anständigkeit pflegen müssen, dass wir Ideale zu vertreten haben. Das wird jeder von Ihnen unterzeichnen."

"the special ability of this High House to find factual policy solutions, to achieve consensus" (October 15, 1992, p. 446).[27]

These observations are in line with the prediction of sociological institutionalism that deliberative norms can become inscribed in an institution, with actors following these norms as a normal part of the institutional routine. However, we should not overlook the fact that second chambers also contain "rational" mechanisms – procedures as opposed to norms – that promote deliberation. For instance, the filibuster in the American Senate is an anti-majoritarian mechanism that frequently "forces" senators to adopt more cooperative attitudes in order to pass desired legislation. This mechanism clearly played a role in the background of the crime debate. The bill sponsored by the Democratic majority contained provisions on habeas corpus and gun control that were objectionable to Republicans. When Republicans threatened to filibuster, Democratic Senators were forced to engage in a more open-ended debate that would produce a compromise solution. In the House of Representatives, the debate never became compromise-oriented; here the Democratic majority could proceed as it desired, since the minority Republicans had no effective means of blocking the bill.

Another facilitating element for deliberation is that party cohesion is typically lower in the Senate compared to the House, although this does not generalize to all second chambers. Weaker party cohesion means that it is easier to form cross-party coalitions. As a result, senators from different parties become more respectful, as they work together on legislation and need to keep open the possibility of future collaboration. Thus, even when senators strongly disagree with the demands and arguments of their opponents, it is unlikely that they will become very disrespectful, since this not only violates norms of senatorial conduct but also jeopardizes good working relationships. A fairly typical example in this regard is Senator Orrin Hatch (Republican, Utah), a staunch opponent of the 1989 minimum wage bill that was sponsored, among others, by Senator Edward Kennedy (Democrat, Massachusetts). Despite his opposition, Hatch praised Kennedy for his integrity and personal achievements: "The minimum wage goes up, as Senator Kennedy would like it to do and I know he is sincere in what he is doing, and I admire him for the facts he wages, albeit how wrong they are" (April 6, 1989, S3421). Later Hatch would co-sponsor legislation with Kennedy, a possibility that might well have been blocked had he been less respectful toward him.

In federalist systems, another aspect of second chambers may come into play, namely that senators are not just representatives of parties but also of

---

[27] "die besonder Befähigung dieses Hohen Hauses, zu sachgerechten Lösungen, zum Konsensus zu kommen."

their states. This can produce mixed motives: on the one hand, senators are expected to play a partisan role and oppose legislators from other parties but, on the other hand, collaboration with those legislators may be beneficial if it brings benefits to their state. These cross-pressures may favor more open and respectful debate than one would find in first chambers.

Finally, it is important to consider the size of second chambers. These chambers are much smaller than first chambers (by about a factor of 8.8 in Germany and about a factor of 4.3 in Switzerland and the United States). This puts fewer constraints on speaking time, which helps deliberation. In addition, close working relationships across parties are more likely to form in second chambers due to their smaller size. There may be other explanations for better discourse in second chambers, which account for specific examples. For instance, in the Swiss Council of States parties are ideologically more proximate than in the National Council. Incumbents in the Council of States also have a greater probability of being reelected (Wiesli and Linder 2000), which may take off some competitive pressure and enhance a more collaborative ethic.

Regardless of the precise explanation, the evidence strongly suggests that second chambers are beneficial for deliberation. Debate in these chambers tends to be more respectful and also slightly more constructive. This is true regardless of whether they operate in a consensus system or in a competitive system. From a deliberative perspective, then, the presence of these institutions should be welcomed.

Public versus non-public arenas

In our fifth hypothesis, we followed Elster (1998b) and argued that closed or non-public arenas are more conducive to high-quality discourse than open or public debates. Does this hypothesis comport with our data? Here we consider the usual three dimensions of discourse – level of justification, respect, and constructive politics – as well as a fourth dimension: content of justification. The reason for considering this dimension is that appeals to the common good may be far more common in public debates than in non-public debates, since the former are cast in terms of a broader audience that may be sensitive to such appeals, including the media and citizens.

Table 5.8 shows the results of our analysis. As this table reveals, there are marked differences in the discourse found in public and non-public arenas, i.e. committees. First, consider the aspect of justifications. The level of justifications is significantly lower in non-public than in public arenas. Only about 60 percent of the speech acts in closed arenas contained qualified and sophisticated justifications, while the percentage of such speech acts approached 90 percent in open arenas, a statistically significant difference. This

Table 5.8 *Discourse quality in public and non-public arenas*

Discourse quality dimension	Non-public	Public
Level of justification:[a]		
No justification	21.10	5.80
Inferior justification	19.20	6.00
Qualified justification	30.10	12.10
Sophisticated justification	29.60	76.10
Content of justification:[a]		
Group interest	5.00	8.80
Neutral	86.30	60.70
Common good (utilitarian)	6.10	17.00
Common good (difference principle)	2.60	13.50
Overall respect (mean):[b]	3.67	3.36
Respect demands/counterarg. (mean):[b]	2.61	2.21
Constructive politics:[a]		
Positional politics	83.20	83.40
Alternative proposal	7.20	8.10
Consensus appeal	5.10	6.30
Mediating proposal	4.50	2.20

Notes: Table entries are percentages (which add up to 100 percent in each column). For a description of the cases entering this analysis see http://www.ipw.unibe.ch/discourse/.
[a] Interjections excluded ($N = 3,086$ speech acts, except for content of justification where $N = 2,166$ speech acts).
[b] Interjections included ($N = 4,221$ speech acts).

clearly supports Elster's argument that publicity strengthens "civility" in that actors want to appear reasonable in public and therefore express more extended arguments. In non-public arenas, to the contrary, the need to always justify one's positions is clearly reduced. Moreover, non-publicity enhances bargaining which does not require justifications, at least not lengthy ones.

Public debates also contained significantly larger numbers of appeals to the common good than non-public debates: 30.5 percent versus 8.7 percent. Apparently, in public, actors seem to have a stronger pressure to make appeals to the common good in order to respond to the moral claims of their constituents.

Where non-public arenas fare much better than public debates is on the xrespect dimension. As table 5.8 shows, overall respect hovers at 3.67 in the non-public sphere and 3.36 in the public sphere. For respect for demands/counterarguments, differences are even more marked, with 2.61

in the non-public sphere and 2.21 in the public sphere. These effects on respect are statistically significant in an ANOVA (at the 0.01 level).[28]

It is interesting to note that open and closed settings do not show much difference in terms of explicit respect or the acceptance of demands/counterarguments. Where they are different, however, is in terms of disrespect. Disrespectful speech acts are much less common in closed debates (15.1 percent) than in open debates (41.9 percent).

An interesting question is whether the difference in respect between public and non-public arenas is limited only to competitive democracies. In those democracies, competition may be particularly vehement in the public arena because of the legislators' visibility to citizens. To the extent that disrespect is a tool that partisan actors use to score points over their opponents, one would expect high levels of disrespect that could well dissipate once the debate occurred behind closed doors, hidden from the audience. In consensus systems, where competition is less relevant, respect should be high, regardless of whether the debate is open or closed.

We probed this possibility by interacting the nature of the arena (public versus non-public) with the system type (consensus or competitive). In an analysis of variance, this interaction was highly significant.[29] It is in the expected direction. In consensus systems, the difference in respect between public and non-public debates tends to fade. In competitive settings, however, this difference is large. In non-public arenas, the respect levels approach those of a consensus system. On the other hand, public arenas in competitive systems are characterized by rather low levels of respect. When playing for an audience of citizens, legislators in a competitive system know that there is much to gain by discrediting one's opponents and little to gain from praising them.

The only area in which the difference between public and non-public debates is non-significant is constructive politics. Positional politics is the norm, regardless of whether one deliberates in public or behind closed doors. With this exception, however, it seems that discourse in public settings is a different animal than discourse in non-public settings. In public settings, discourse seems to be crafted to score points with an audience of citizens. Hence, appeals to the common good are cast in the form of well-crafted arguments, which are presented without much regard for the arguments presented by others. In non-public settings, discourse seems to be crafted more with an eye on one's colleagues. It is unnecessary to make elaborate

---

[28] The significant differences for both respect indicators are robust when interjections are excluded.

[29] $F = 59.43$, $p < 0.01$ for overall respect; $F = 39.32$, $p < 0.01$ for respect toward demands and/or counterarguments.

arguments for that audience, which consists of policy experts who can pick up on arguments and evidence quickly. There is also little need to appeal to the common good, although we suspect that such appeals, when they occur, carry much greater weight since they cannot be as easily discredited as "cheap talk." There is a strong need, however, for mutual respect, or at least the avoidance of disrespect and this is what we observe.

One may wonder why legislators behind closed doors would like to avoid disrespect. An important reason is that committees are small face-to-face groups, which exist for extended periods of time. The members of those committees work together day in and day out and it is unavoidable that they will get to know each other very well. This can create positive trust and even friendships. In the words of Herbert Werner, "I do not want to insinuate this to you because in the course of this discussion I have come to appreciate all of you far too much" (Bundestag, May 21, 1992, p. 15/99).[30]

In the light of the philosophical discussion on deliberation, where publicity is often viewed as a crucial aspect of deliberation, these findings might be troubling and reassuring at the same time. Reassuring should be the fact that public discourse is better in terms of the level and content of justification, although one may wonder about the authenticity of appeals to the public good. Troublesome should be the fact that public discourse can be quite disrespectful, at least in competitive settings. Respect, of course, plays an important role in forging policy coalitions in the present and in the future and, in this regard, Elster (1998b) appears to have been correct when he argued that deliberation benefits when it is insulated from the public.

The role of polarization

Our analysis so far has focused on institutional explanations of discourse quality. However, issue attributes may also have a role to play. According to our sixth hypothesis, we expect discourse quality to be the highest when issue polarization is low. When legislators agree on policy fundamentals, it should be easier to engage in an open-minded deliberation than when there is sharp disagreement on an issue.

Our data lend strong support to this hypothesis. Table 5.9 shows considerable differences in discourse quality between less polarized and highly polarized issues. First, sophisticated justifications are more common when issue polarization is low (46.7 percent) than when it is high (37.1 percent). Respect levels are also considerably higher in less polarized

---

[30] "Das will ich Ihnen nicht unterstellen, weil ich Sie alle im Laufe dieser Diskussion viel zu sehr schätzen gelernt habe." This statement was made in a debate of the special abortion committee of the Federal Diet.

Table 5.9 *Discourse quality and the level of issue polarization*

Discourse quality dimension	Low polarization	High polarization
Level of justification:[a]		
No justification	10.40	16.10
Inferior justification	15.80	20.10
Qualified justification	27.10	26.70
Sophisticated justification	46.70	37.10
Overall respect (mean):[b]	3.83	3.43
Respect demands/counterarg. (mean):[b]	2.72	2.33
Constructive politics:[a]		
Positional politics	81.60	82.00
Alternative proposal	8.30	8.70
Consensus appeal	6.20	7.00
Mediating proposal	3.90	2.30

Notes: Table entries are percentages (which add up to 100 percent in each column). For a description of the cases entering this analysis see http://www.ipw.unibe.ch/discourse/.
[a] Interjections excluded ($N = 2,995$ speech acts).
[b] Interjections included ($N = 3,516$ speech acts).

issues – the mean differences are 0.40 (overall respect) and 0.39 (respect toward demands/counterarguments).[31] In an ANOVA these effects were statistically significant (at the 0.01 level). The only area in which we fail to find a statistically significant issue polarization effect is constructive politics. There is virtually no difference in the incidence of positional politics when we compare less polarized and highly polarized issues. At the other end of the spectrum, differences in the incidence of mediating proposals and consensus appeals are also negligible.

When we focus on the comparison between less polarized and abortion debates, we obtain a similar pattern of results. A comparison of the abortion debates with less polarized issues reveals a greater likelihood of sophisticated justifications in the latter setting (55 percent versus 41.6 percent). In an ANOVA, this difference in sophistication levels is statistically significant (at the 0.01 level). We also observe much lower levels of respect in the abortion debates, with a mean level for overall respect at 4.07 for less polarized debates and 3.42 for abortion debates; for respect toward

[31] The significant differences for both respect indicators are robust when interjections are excluded.

Table 5.10 *Discourse quality and the level of issue polarization*

Discourse quality dimension	Low polarization	High polarization
Level of justification:[a]		
No justification	10.00	11.20
Inferior justification	13.10	17.60
Qualified justification	21.90	29.60
Sophisticated justification	55.00	41.60
Overall respect (mean):[b]	4.07	3.42
Respect demands/counterarg. (mean):[b]	2.91	2.30
Constructive politics:[a]		
Positional politics	83.20	86.00
Alternative proposal	7.80	7.20
Consensus appeal	5.40	3.10
Mediating proposal	3.60	3.70

Notes: Table entries are percentages (which add up to 100 percent in each column). For a description of the cases entering this analysis see http://www.ipw.unibe.ch/discourse/.
[a] Interjections excluded ($N = 2,196$ speech acts).
[b] Interjections included ($N = 2,219$ speech acts).

demands/counterarguments the scores are 2.91 for less polarized debates and 2.30 for abortion debates. These differences in respect are statistically significant in an ANOVA (at the 0.01 level).[32] The effect of issue polarization on constructive politics is again not statistically significant in an ANOVA.

These results suggest that issue polarization matters for deliberation. Higher levels of discourse can be achieved when issue polarization is low than when it is high. This is perhaps unsurprising, but it leads to a sobering conclusion. Most political issues are polarized, and particularly those issues where it may be difficult to achieve a high level of discourse in legislative settings. Of course, precisely on those polarized issues it would be desirable to get high-quality discourse.

We should hasten to add, however, that we have observed quite a bit of variance in the debates on polarized issues. Polarization does not preordain poor deliberation. Much depends on the mix of institutional factors that surround a polarized issue. In this regard, it is useful to contrast the American

---

[32] The significant differences for both respect indicators are robust when interjections are excluded.

and German/Swiss abortion debates. The American debate produced the
lowest value on our respect dimensions. This is not altogether surprising.
The partial birth abortion bill that spurred the debate was clearly a partisan effort on the part of Republicans, who acted as a unified party at the
time of the debate. The Republicans knew that the passage of the bill would
trigger a veto from President Clinton, which would allow them to make
the partial birth abortion ban – one of the most controversial forms of
abortion – into a campaign issue for the next elections. The Democratic
minority was keenly aware of this strategy and it wanted to broaden the
debate to discuss abortion more generally, which would allow it to por-
tray the bill as a first step in Republican efforts to do away with abortion
completely. Republicans, however, severely restricted the debate, contributing to a great deal of frustration among Democrats. There was no desire
for compromise, or to take seriously opponents' arguments and positions.
Rather, the abortion debate was played out as a partisan game, with the
objective of scoring points in public opinion. In this atmosphere and with
these institutional parameters, it is hardly surprising that the debate on
the laden partial birth abortion issue scored very low in terms of discourse
quality.

The institutional parameters in Germany and Switzerland were much
more favorable toward high-quality discourse. Although abortion was a
similarly controversial and polarizing issue in these countries, the institutional setting of the debates allowed legislators to explore common ground.
In Switzerland, the consensus character of the political system helped deliberation. In Germany, less party cohesion worked in favor of high-quality
discourse. The outcome, however, was similar in both countries. What could
easily have been a partisan debate on one of the most divisive moral questions of our time was transformed into a debate in which legislators at least
attempted to reconcile conflicting views, albeit not always successfully. The
relaxed party discipline in Germany, for example, allowed the debate to
become more personalized, although not devoid of partisan elements. In
the words of Horst Eylmann (Christian Democrat), "this is . . . a debate
of personal testimonies, moral appeals, strict positions, and sometimes of
big words too, but it also is a debate of critical and skeptical reflexivity"
(Bundestag, June 25, 1992, p. 8259).[33] And the words of Uta Würfel (Free
Democrat) in the same debate suggest the effort that was made to consider
opposing viewpoints: "We as the members of the special committee [on
abortion] have really tried to weigh the arguments of the other side without

---

[33] "Dies ist . . . eine Debatte der persönlichen Bekenntnisse, der moralischen Appelle, der
entschiedenen Haltungen, zuweilen auch der grossen Worte, aber auch eine Debatte der
kritischen and zweifelnden Nachdenklichkeit."

prejudice, and we have fought for the best way to protect the unborn life" (Bundestag, June 25, 1992, p. 8231).[34]

The bottom line, then, is that issues polarization makes it more difficult to achieve high-quality discourse. However, it is possible to arrange the institutional parameters of the debate in such a manner that some of this difficulty can be overcome. While such institutional arrangements may not end positional politics, they can at least contribute to a more respectful discourse with better arguments. And that may be very important. After all, on deeply divisive issues, especially when they are of a moral nature, it may be extremely painful to see one's viewpoints and arguments trivialized, or worse ridiculed. Such disrespect may entrench positions even further, making future solutions more difficult.

Conclusions

In this chapter, we have considered the antecedents of deliberation, both in terms of institutional characteristics and in terms of issue attributes. What have we learnt? The most important conclusion is that institutional design matters for the quality of political discourse. We have identified certain institutional features that promote deliberation, and others that hinder it. Our data suggest that favorable institutional antecedents include consensus institutions, the presence of veto players, debate in second chambers, and debate in non-public arenas. Debilitating factors include competitive settings, the absence of veto players, debate in first chambers, and debate in public arenas. We also saw a hint that presidentialism may further discourse, although this result is more mixed. These institutional factors work in tandem with issue attributes, and they can offset some of the negative effects on deliberation that we observed from issue polarization.

These findings have great relevance for those who are interested in designing institutions that promote deliberation. (Issue characteristics may be more difficult to manipulate, so we shall spend less time on them.) Institutional design may be particularly relevant in situations where political actors are polarized on key issues and where proper institutions may provide a window of opportunity for deliberation in an environment that would otherwise not be discourse-friendly. This may include countries that come out of civil war situations, or countries with strong ethnic and religious divisions, or newly developing democracies.

---

[34] "Wir Mitglieder im Sonderausschuss . . . haben wirklich vorurteilsfrei die Argumente des jeweils anders Denkenden abgewogen, und wir haben miteinander um den besten Weg zum Schutz des ungeborenen Lebens gerungen."

136 DELIBERATIVE POLITICS IN ACTION

Some might object that cultural factors are far more potent than institutions in shaping deliberation. Where countries have experienced long histories of conflict, a culture of mutual distrust may have developed that cannot be overcome no matter what set of institutions is designed. Our study was not designed to contrast institutional and cultural explanations. We do not study deeply divided societies or newly emerged democracies. But our results contain a hint that culture is not the entire story. As the British example shows, when institutional parameters are changed, it may be possible to improve deliberation even in contexts where discourse is usually of a low quality. We should keep in mind also that culture may be endogenous to institutions, being a product of institutional design as much as it is an impetus to such design (see Hall and Taylor 1996).

We should not exaggerate the impact of institutions on discourse. Some aspects of discourse quality showed little variation across institutional factors, while for other factors the changes lacked consistency. The constructive politics dimension showed remarkable resilience to institutional change. Only in the comparison between first and second chambers did we find an institutional effect in the expected direction. In the case of the parliamentary–presidential comparison, we observed an effect but in an unexpected direction. Otherwise, levels of constructive politics looked very similar across institutional settings, with positional politics being the norm. At least in legislative settings, it appears that it is very difficult to move actors away from positional politics in their speech acts and in the direction of consensus solutions. We suspect this may not hold true in other settings such as civic forums, where partisan divides are often less relevant and initial positions may not be crystallized, but this suspicion requires a different study than we have conducted here.

In terms of the level of justification, our findings are more mixed. Levels of justification do show some changes across institutional settings, but not always in the expected direction and not always robustly. The analysis of levels of justification also reveals that the dimensions of discourse quality do not always travel in the same direction when institutional parameters are changed. As the comparison between public and non-public debates shows, bringing a debate into the public arena greatly improves the level of justification of demands by speakers, but it hinders respectful discourse.

Our results suggest that respect is the most sensitive to institutional and issue attributes. In all of our analyses, we found that respect changed in the hypothesized direction as we compared different institutional settings and different kinds of issues. This suggests that institutional design may have the greatest payoff in terms of forging a respectful discourse. While such a discourse does not necessarily move actors away from their original positions, it is not unimportant. Especially in an atmosphere of mutual distrust, respectful interactions may be the first essential step in a process toward cooperation.

How much of an impact do institutional factors (and issue characteristics) have on political discourse? It is important that we do not exaggerate these effects. Not only are they inconsistent across different dimensions of discourse quality, the effects are often subtle. The legislatures that we analyzed in this chapter are, generally speaking, not worlds apart. We have not uncovered some settings in which discourse is absent and others in which it is perfect, although individual speech acts sometimes approach these extremes. We should not have expected this either. We selected four established western democracies, in which societal conflicts were comparatively mild in the period of our study. For this reason alone, we should expect to see some convergence in the levels of discourse across those institutions.

The differences that we observe between institutional settings are thus not categorical, but rather subtle shifts along a continuum. Earlier we argued that deliberation can be fruitfully conceptualized in continuous terms, although this conceptualization has not been the norm in political theory. Here we find that such a conceptualization is useful in order to register subtle movements in discourse that reflect institutional differences that would never be noticed in a categorical conceptualization.

But what is the use of subtle shifts, one might ask? Does it really matter if one setting is slightly more respectful than another, or slightly less positional, or slightly better in the justification of demands? We think it does. Such changes may be barely noticeable to casual observers, but to political actors operating in a particular setting, such changes send clear signals. That is, departures from the normal discourse, even when they are subtle, can indicate a great deal about other actors' willingness to work out a mutually agreeable solution. Seasoned politicians pick up on those signals; they represent windows of opportunity that should not be wasted.

There is another, perhaps more compelling reason why subtle shifts in discourse matter: they have the potential to change political outcomes. This brings us to the next chapter, in which we will take a closer look at the relationship between discourse and outcomes. Through a detailed study of the German Mediation Committee, we will see that discourse influences both formal and substantive decision outcomes. And the kinds of discourse that matter are exactly the nuanced and subtle shifts that we have observed here.

6

Discourse and its consequences

In the previous chapter, we considered the antecedents of political discourse. That chapter established a variety of institutional conditions that facilitate (or, conversely, hinder) high-quality discourse. But does the quality of discourse matter for political outcomes? While high-quality discourse may be beneficial in its own right, at least from the vantage point of political philosophy, institutional scholars will want to know if better deliberation also produces better outcomes. This chapter takes up this important question.[1]

It is useful to note at the outset an important design difference from the previous chapter. Whereas institutional features were the key variables in chapter 5, we hold them constant in the present chapter. Here we want to demonstrate that discourse matters for political outcomes independently of institutional characteristics. To that effect we study the implications of discourse in one institutional setting: the German Mediation Committee (Vermittlungsausschuss).

We focus on two aspects of political outcomes. First, we consider a formal dimension of outcomes, namely the degree of unification in a decision outcome. In chapter 4 we developed the following hypothesis for this dimension: unified decisions, in the form of a genuine consensus or a reasoned compromise, are more likely when there is a high level of parliamentary deliberation (hypothesis 7). The second aspect of political outcomes is the substantive dimension of social justice. Chapter 4 presented the following hypothesis for this dimension: (weak) egalitarian decision outcomes are more likely when there is a high level of parliamentary deliberation, defined in particular in terms of the content of justification (hypothesis 8). We address these two

---

[1] This chapter is based on the Ph.D. dissertation of Markus Spörndli (2004).

dimensions and their corresponding hypotheses later in this chapter. First, we say more about the research design and measurement.

Research design

How should one study the effect of discourse on political outcomes? One approach would be to select a set of debates, code their level of discourse quality, assess their outcomes, and then establish a correlation between discourse and outcomes. However, if these debates are drawn from diverse institutional contexts, we have an immediate problem. The previous chapter has demonstrated that discourse quality varies with institutional designs. We also expect political outcomes to vary with institutional designs. Thus there is a risk that the correlation between discourse and political outcomes is spurious.

To overcome this risk we have opted to keep institutional features constant so that we can establish an effect of discourse that is not confounded with institutional designs. In terms of research design, this means that we rely on a comparable cases strategy (Lijphart 1975) or a "most similar systems design" (Przeworski and Teune 1970). That is, we select our cases – parliamentary debates – in such a manner that they are comparable on institutional variables, while showing variance in the level of discourse quality. In our investigation, this means that the cases come from the same political institution, the German Mediation Committee. Thus our design enhances internal validity by maximizing the probability of uncovering a relationship between decision outcomes and discourse that is not spurious.

We should note an obvious drawback of our design. First, by focusing on a single institution, we limit the universe of cases that can be analyzed. This means that our statistical analyses can attain only a limited level of complexity because we have few degrees of freedom to work with. While we report several statistical analyses, we avoid putting all of the weight on quantitative methods. Qualitative analyses also play a critical role in this chapter, in particular in highlighting situations that are consistent with or deviate from the statistical findings. Thus, we can engage in a limited "process tracing" analysis (George and McKeown 1985), which allows us to put some flesh around the statistical barebones.

Another drawback of studying a single institutional context is that it reduces external validity. We do not claim that the findings with respect to the German Mediation Committee generalize to other contexts; this is an empirical question that requires further research. However, we would like to note that our selection of the German Conference Committee is not biased toward a particular end of one of the key institutional dimensions discussed in chapter 5. That is, the Mediation Committee does not represent a classical

competitive context, nor does it represent a pure form of consensus decision making. By being situated in the middle of the competitive–consensus
dimension, we think that the Mediation Committee may tell us something
about situations that are neither very favorable nor very unfavorable toward
deliberation. In practice, we believe that many institutions may fall in this
location.

Context: the German Mediation Committee

The institutional context that we choose for our analysis should be marked by
a potentially high degree of variance in discourse quality. For this purpose,
we have selected the German Mediation Committee or Vermittlungsausschuss (VA).[2] The VA is a constitutionally mandated institution that is concerned with mediating conflicts between the Federal Diet (Bundestag) and
the Federal Council (Bundesrat).[3] Prior to German unification in 1990, the
VA consisted of eleven members from the Federal Diet and eleven members
from the Federal Council (one for each state). Since unification, the number
of members has grown to sixteen members from each chamber of the legislature. Members of the government may also participate in the VA, or may
be required to do so at the behest of the VA, but they do not have any voting
power. The VA chairmanship fluctuates quarterly between a representative
of the Federal Diet and a representative of the Federal Council.

A mediation procedure in the VA can be initiated in two ways. For statutes
requiring assent (*Zustimmungsgesetz*), which concern issues that affect the
interests of the states, the mediation process can be initiated by the Federal
Council, which has veto power on such statutes, as well as the Federal Diet
and the government. For statutes not requiring assent (*einfachesgesetz*),
which form the most common type of legislation, the Federal Council can
demand mediation. In both cases, a simple majority in the Federal Council
is required for a request for mediation. In the case of statutes not requiring
assent, the Federal Diet can deny the mediation request, which requires
an absolute majority. Mediation requests can never be denied when they
concern statutes requiring assent, since the Federal Council has veto power
in such cases.[4]

---

[2] For discussions of the VA see Posser (1992), Schindler (1999), Schmidt (2003), and von
Beyme (1998).
[3] The Federal Diet currently consists of 603 members who are elected for a period of four
years. The Federal Council consists of sixty-nine members representing the governments of
the states (*Länder*).
[4] In an analysis of 150 key decisions, von Beyme (1998) notes that appeals to the VA have
been particularly common in the areas of education and economic policy. They have been
infrequent in the area of foreign policy, where the Federal Council has a much harder time
claiming jurisdiction (*Einspruch*).

The objective of the VA is to bridge the differences between the two chambers of the legislature and to reconcile conflicting interests. This is particularly important if the two chambers of the legislature are dominated by different parties, as during the SPD-FDP coalition (1969–82), the second half of the Kohl era (1990–8) and, most recently, during the red-green coalition. The VA engages in rewriting legislation so that both the Federal Diet and the Federal Council can agree on it. To facilitate this process, the VA meets behind closed doors in an atmosphere of secrecy that intends to minimize partisan or state pressures on the members. The VA can solicit expert testimony, hear representatives from the government, and discuss for extended periods of time.

Decision making by the VA is by simple majority. However, VA members know that their mediation proposals are referred back to the Federal Diet and the Federal Council for a formal vote. Proposals that garner a bare majority in the VA are likely to fail in these chambers. Hence, there is considerable pressure on the VA to make decisions via oversized majorities or by consensus. Correspondingly, Schmidt (2003: 84) refers to the mediation committee as "the institutional core of Germany's grand coalition state."

Mediation proposals by the VA are referred back to the Federal Diet, which discusses and votes on them (the so-called "fourth reading"). After the Federal Diet reaches a decision, the Federal Council evaluates the proposal and, depending on the legislation, can request an appeal, vote the legislation down, or accept the legislation. While the Federal Diet and the Federal Council are not bound by the mediation proposal of the VA, over 90 percent of such proposals are accepted (Schmidt 2003). Thus, the VA is rarely used as an instrument for obstructing the decision making process.

Our sketch of the VA reveals several attributes that enhance the deliberative potential of this institution. First, the German constitution gives considerable powers to the VA to bridge different positions through rational debate (Dästner 1995). Compared to other institutions in the legislative process (see chapter 5), the VA is much less prone to normal party pressures which may cause a deadlock, especially if the Federal Diet and Federal Council are in the hands of different party coalitions. Rather, as Lhotta (2000) points out, the VA limits veto power and legislative deadlock by emphasizing deliberation as a means to facilitate the coordination of diverse interests. In this connection, it is worthwhile noting that the institutional and political weight of the VA is much greater than that of comparable institutions in other parts of the world such as Switzerland and the United States (Tsebelis and Money 1997).

Second, the size and composition of the VA facilitate deliberation. The limited membership of twenty-two up to reunification and thirty-two afterwards makes it more likely that a symmetric exchange of information takes place than would be the case in a large legislative body. (As shown in the next section, all our cases are from the time before reunification.) Symmetry in the exchange of positions, ideas, and arguments is arguably an essential condition for deliberation. Deliberation is also helped by the fact that members of the VA are usually veteran politicians and policy generalists who have received a mandate from their parties to explore the possibility of compromise. There is also little turnover in the membership, which should have further helped deliberation.

Finally, the VA can do its work behind closed doors. Meetings of the VA are not open to the public or the media, and verbal protocols of those meetings are under embargo for a period of at least five years. All of these provisions are put in place to minimize pressures on the VA from special interests, from the states, and from party elites. As Elster (1998a) has argued, the quality of deliberation should be enhanced by these practices, even if a lack of openness may seem to be a far cry from the deliberative ideal.

Not all aspects of the VA are so advantageous for deliberation, however. Members of the VA are still also members of parties. This has at least two implications. First, VA members may not want to lose face in their own party by straying too far from the party line. There is a potential political cost for being too accommodating, and while VA members may be more protected from those costs than others would be, due to their veteran status and role, they cannot go too far. Second, VA members are aware that their decision is not the last word. Thus, they have to keep an eye on the political, i.e. party, realities of politics in the Federal Diet and the Federal Council, assessing what is feasible and what is not. To the extent that they do, a completely free deliberation may not take place. That is, strategic considerations may circumscribe deliberation, with strategic speech taking the place of authentic speech. Even more perversely, some VA members might consider the mediation process as a good opportunity to further partisan interests. As von Beyme (1998: 101) notes, "no party can claim not to have used the Federal Council and the conference committees to gain advantages for party political purposes."

In sum, the German Mediation Committee (VA) provides a good context for considering the effect of discourse on political outcomes. Not only are institutional features kept constant, but the VA also changed very little in its membership in the timeframe that we study. There is, however, also potential for variance on the key predictor of discourse quality. That is, while many attributes of the VA suggest that discourse quality should be high, other attributes may serve to suppress this under certain circumstances. Thus, the VA provides a good foundation for a most similar cases analysis.

Case selection

As in chapter 5, the cases for the analysis are debates. The selection of debates occurred in two stages. First, we selected the relevant time period. Next, we decided on individual debates. In terms of time period, we had access to VA debate protocols between 1949 and 1994 (between the first and twelfth election period). Within this timeframe, we decided to focus on 1969–82, since the Federal Diet and Federal Council were controlled by different partisan majorities in this period. Specifically, during this period a coalition of SPD and FDP, first led by Willy Brandt and then by Helmut Schmidt, controlled a majority of the seats in the Federal Diet (ranging between 51.0 percent from 1976 to 1980 and 54.6 percent from 1972 to 1976 and 1980 to 1982). However, for most of this period, the Federal Council was controlled by the CDU-CSU.

There are two reasons to focus on the period 1969–82. First, the VA plays its most significant role during periods of "divided government" because partisan conflicts are most likely to produce deadlock between the two legislative chambers under those circumstances. Second, during periods of partisan conflict, the federal dimension of mediation is the most likely to take a back seat, while conflicts over distributive, redistributive, and regulatory policy come to the fore. This kind of situation presents an important methodological advantage. In keeping with the most similar cases design, we would like to keep our analysis focused on similar kinds of issues. However, the kinds of issues that the VA considers are not always comparable, as they are positioned along two cross-cutting dimensions, one dealing with federalism and the other dealing with partisan politics. It is during periods of "divided government" that the issues are most clearly products of partisan battles and, in that sense, comparable. More precisely, under "divided government" federal questions are most likely to coincide with normal partisan conflicts, so that we do not end up comparing non-partisan federal issues with partisan non-federal issues (and vice versa).

In the period 1969–82, the mediation process was used 124 times (Schindler 1999). Many of the debates surrounding these mediation processes were very short, in fact too short to form a reliable foundation for the Discourse Quality Index (DQI). Shortness is often a reflection of the fact that only policy details are being discussed in the VA because there is already a consensus on policy principles. Therefore, by omitting short debates we tend to overselect instances of debate on fundamental policy matters. However, we would argue that such a bias is appropriate since the role of discourse is of particular interest when there are fundamental differences of opinion about policy. Thus, one of our selection criteria was protocol length, with ten pages being the minimum length for inclusion in the sample. A second selection criterion was that the mediation process should address questions of legal, labor, or social policy, since these questions define key partisan conflicts that might benefit the most from deliberation. Finally, we selected only debates on those issues that from the beginning were considered by the VA. This avoids analyzing debates on issues that had already been considered in subcommittees. These subcommittees are typically dominated by expert testimony, which could pre-commit VA members to a particular position, in this way circumscribing the deliberative space in the VA debates (Hasselsweiler 1981).

There is one more constraint on the case selection. Until 1971, verbatim protocols of debates in the VA were not available. Instead, summaries of the debates were provided, but these tend to be so cryptic that they may not reflect the true deliberative process. Thus, effectively our analysis concerns debates in the period 1971–82. When the other selection criteria are applied, we are left with twenty debates, encompassing 302 speeches. When evaluating our results, the reader needs to be aware that our selection criteria have led to a selection bias which may have an impact on the results. Therefore, generalizations beyond the twenty cases must always be made with great caution.

These debates pertain to the following issues: improvement of tenants' rights and limits on rent increases, change in the rules of the pension system, reform of matrimonial and family law, promotion of home ownership in social housing, the social code, indemnity for victims of violent crime, change in the law pertaining to conscription and alternative service, privacy protection of personal data, modernization of housing, adjustment in pensions and improvement of the financial basis of the pension system, tax relief and promotion of investment, income tax, free public transportation for severely handicapped people, legal aid, and legal assistance and representation for low-income people. This is a wide range of issues that covers important aspects of the political debate in the period 1971–82. The case selection includes debate on economic issues as well as social issues. The only area that is underrepresented is foreign policy, but the VA has played only a small role in this domain historically (von Beyme 1998). Note that some issues were debated on several occasions; each debate constitutes a separate case in the analysis.

Measures of the formal dimension of outcomes

The VA protocols contain information about the proportions of votes for and against a proposal. Instead of using these proportions directly, we have transformed them into an ordinal scale. The reason for this transformation is that it is difficult to infer the meaning of the vote outcome from the proportions. First, we need to consider the role of abstentions in judging the vote proportions, since abstentions may imply much more than indifference toward a proposal and could well reflect opposition. Second, the partisan distribution needs to be taken into consideration in judging vote outcomes, especially in ascertaining the meaning of a unanimous or near-unanimous vote. These two points suggest that an element of interpretation is inevitable in dealing with formal decision outcomes. In this light, using a metric scale would be misleading, as it would suggest more precision than there really is. Moreover, the practical value of a precise measure is questionable. We are concerned with qualitative differences in the vote outcomes such as (near) unanimity versus narrow majorities. Hence, it is not very important to put precise values on the outcomes.

Our measure of vote outcomes, then, contains the following four categories: (0) a narrow majoritarian decision, (1) a near-narrow majoritarian decision, (2) a near-unanimous decision, and (3) a unanimous decision.[5] Pure unanimity exists if all participants accept or reject the proposal under consideration. However, we use the unanimity category also if there are at most two abstentions in the vote. A near-unanimous decision is one in which there are at most two opposing votes and in which the number of abstentions is, at worst, small. On the other extreme, we define a narrow majoritarian decision as one in which the vote distribution reflects partisan lines, so that a partisan majority (e.g. parties of the government) win the VA vote but without the support of other parties. In the absence of abstentions, given a membership of twenty-two, this means that the majority carries twelve votes, with ten opposing votes (an 11:11 split would mean a balance of power; in this case, the original bill is adopted). We consider a decision near-majoritarian if there are at most two deviating votes, i.e. members from the other side who cast their votes with the partisan majority, and if the number of abstentions is limited. In our analyses, we usually combine the two unanimity codes and the two majority codes, to establish a simple distinction between (near-)majoritarian and (near-)unanimous decisions.

Measures of the substantive dimension of outcomes

Measuring the substantive dimension of outcomes is considerably more complicated than measuring the formal dimension. The substantive dimension focuses on the question of whether a decision reveals a (weak) egalitarian principle or whether it instead corresponds to a non-egalitarian principle such as equity. Put simply, to what extent does the decision reveal a commitment to (weak) egalitarianism in the sense of Rawls?

---

[5] In principle, we could add a fifth category, namely non-decision. However, this category did not apply to any of our debates and is therefore omitted.

One question arises immediately: can we ascertain the substance of a decision just by looking at it? Here we rely on Dunn's (1981) distinction between policies that regulate and those that allocate, as well as his argument that all policies can be placed into these two categories and that each category has distributive and redistributive implications. Dunn's argument implies that when a legislative body such as the VA makes a policy decision, it effectively also makes a decision about the distribution and redistribution of resources. Since questions of distribution and redistribution lie at the heart of conceptions of justice, it follows that we can say something about the fairness of a decision.

The verdict that measuring the fairness of a decision is possible in principle, of course, does little to alleviate the practical problem of rendering such a verdict in specific instances. We make a judgment merely about the *relative* fairness of a VA decision because the VA's jurisdiction is limited to weighting the proposals of the Federal Diet and the Federal Council, so that it can give more weight to the fairness claims of one chamber relative to the other but it has limited room to make proposals that bring in completely novel conceptions of fairness.

Our measure of substantive outcomes then focuses on the decisions reached by the VA and codes their fairness relative to the goals in the original legislative proposals. A careful reading of those proposals thus precedes the coding of the VA decisions. When coding those decisions we focus on the fundamental direction that they take, rather than trying to obtain an absolute measure of their fairness implications. This enhances the likelihood that other coders will draw similar conclusions, although we are aware that the coding of such an abstract concept as fairness will probably always entail some controversy. The specific fairness codes are as follows: (0) the decision works against the principle of weak egalitarianism, (1) the decision contains egalitarian principles but on the whole works against the principle of weak egalitarianism, (2) the decision is a distributional compromise and acts neutrally with respect to the principle of weak egalitarianism, (3) the decision is consistent with the principle of weak egalitarianism but contains inegalitarian elements, and (4) the decision is consistent with the principle of weak egalitarianism.

We should make clear that we do not measure the substantive effects of a policy *after* it is enacted, but merely the decision as made in the meeting itself. The reasons are, first, that the VA does not make the final policy decision, so that enacted policies may well differ from those decided on by the VA. Second, even if the VA had the last word, policies have unintended consequences and those would taint our measures of fairness once a policy is enacted.

Measures of the discourse quality

Our key explanatory variable is the Discourse Quality Index (DQI). While this measurement instrument was discussed in detail in chapter 3, it is important to discuss a few details in this chapter. In chapter 5, we elaborated on a few of the dimensions of the DQI where this was helpful for obtaining analytical leverage. These dimensions are respect, the content of justification and constructive politics, which all play an important role in our hypotheses.

The measure of respect that we use in this chapter is a combination of respect toward counterarguments and respect toward mediating proposals. Respect toward mediating proposals is similar to respect toward demands, as we discussed in chapter 3; since the most important demands in the context of the VA come in the form of mediating proposals, we decided to focus on them. We do not consider respect toward groups, in part because it showed relatively little variance in the VA debates and in part because we do not deem it very important for political outcomes. Our respect indicator has three categories: (0) counterarguments and mediating proposals are ignored or degraded; (1) either counterarguments or mediating proposals are treated with respect; (2) both counterarguments and mediating proposals are treated with respect. Thus, the respect indicator measures a speaker's willingness to entertain ideas that run counter to his or her original position.

Our indicator for the content of justifications focuses on conceptions of the common good. Our primary interest here is in the extent to which a speaker appeals to weak egalitarian principles, where those principles are understood in Rawlsian, i.e. instrumental terms: equality is a means to an end and not a goal in itself (Shapiro 1997). At the same time, our indicator is concerned with the breadth of the moral justification that a speaker offers. Thus our indicator of the content has three categories: (0) inegalitarian appeals; (1) appeals that are either egalitarian or neutral; and (2) appeals that are egalitarian and pluralistic, in the sense of engaging multiple conceptions of justice.

It is useful to analyze these categories in terms of the predominant principles of justice as they can be found in social choice theory and social psychology. Inegalitarian appeals are those that are rooted in utility and in notions of equity, desert, merit, or proportionality (see Scott et al. 2001). Appeals to utility typically stress efficiency (Schmidt 2000), which is usually understood as being incommensurate with weak egalitarianism, since the redistribution that the latter entails may disturb the market equilibrium. Likewise, notions of equity, desert, merit, or proportionality are fundamentally inegalitarian because their premise is that goods should be distributed in proportion to individual inputs and not individual needs (Deutsch 1985). Appeals to weak equality are rooted in the idea that everyone should have a fair chance to get ahead. Arrow's (1973) maximin principle also fits the egalitarian category, as do humanitarian conceptions that everyone's basic needs should be satisfied (Feldman and Steenbergen 2001; Katz and Hass 1988).

In addition to elaborating on the content of justifications, we added detail to the coding of the constructive politics indicator. This indicator consists of three categories: (0) positional politics; (1) neutral; and (2) mediating politics. Positional politics means that speakers sit on their position and do not make an effort to approach other speakers. We also count in this category alternative proposals (see chapter 3), as well as any proposal that aims to shift or delay the debate. The latter class of proposals may be subdivided into two categories. First, a proposal may suggest that certain issues should be debated and decided in the context of a different debate, typically on a related matter. Second, a proposal may suggest that these issues should be taken up at a later point in time, albeit in the context of the current debate. By placing alternative and shifting/delaying proposals in the category of positional politics, we opt for a cautious interpretation of those proposals. A more optimistic reading would see those proposals as a genuine effort to break open the debate, especially if there is an impasse that might be overcome by seeking common ground in another area. However, there is a real risk that such proposals constitute "cheap talk" because it is unlikely that they will be taken up when they do not fit the debate. An even more pessimistic reading would be that such proposals are entirely strategic, in that they seek to manipulate the agenda in order to influence final vote outcomes (on this point see Kameda et al. 2002). Given that we cannot rule out these alternative interpretations, we have decided to err on the side of pessimism.

At the other extreme, we find mediating proposals. Such proposals can be either formal or informal, and they can seek a compromise or a consensus. In a compromise, both sides back down from their original demands in order to meet somewhere in the center. In a consent solution, learning plays a central role: upon hearing certain arguments, and after evaluating possible counterarguments, the decision makers reach an agreement that a particular solution is reasonable. In between positional and mediating politics we find neutral speech acts, which cannot be classified as strictly positional or strictly mediating.

In addition to respect, content of justification, and constructive politics, we also coded the level of justification in the VA debates. Our indicator here is identical to the one described in chapter 3. We also coded participation, but we shall ignore it here because there was insufficient variation. Note that while our coding for three of the four indicators deviates from the description in chapter 3, it is always possible to recode those indicators so that they correspond strictly to the DQI indicators.

Coding of the DQI as well as the two dependent variables was performed by Markus Spörndli (see Spörndli 2004 for further details). For some of the debates, André Bächtiger served as a second coder. As reported in chapter 5, inter-coder reliability on the DQI was high, even for the dimensions that were coded in greater detail such as the content of justifications.

Before we turn to the analysis, let us take a look at the DQI indicators. A key concern here is that the indicators show variance, since it is variation in the DQI that we believe explains variation in political outcomes. With the exception of participation, there is considerable variation on the indicators. Consider, for example, the level of justification. This ranges from an average of 1.4 in the debate on conscription and alternative service, a level that is closest to an inferior justification, to an average of 2.6 in the debate on tax relief and the promotion of investments, a level that is closest to a sophisticated justification. Similarly, there is considerable variance on the content of justification. Using the three-point ordinal indicator, the average content ranges from 0 in the debate on tax relief and the promotion of investments to 1.4 in the debate on income taxes. Thus, on one hand, we have debates for which egalitarian appeals are nonexistent, while, on the other hand, we also have debates that make egalitarian (if not pluralistic) appeals. Respect also shows considerable variation, with a minimum of 0.4 (in the debate on conscription and alternative service) and a maximum of 1.3 (in the debate on income taxes). This shows that some debates were characterized by little respect, while other debates showed respect for either counterarguments or mediating proposals. Finally, there is considerable variation in the level of constructive politics: the minimum is 0 (in the debate on reforming matrimonial and family law), while the maximum is 1.5 (in the debate on free public transport for severely handicapped people). Thus some debates were characterized by positional politics, while others showed a real tendency toward mediating politics.[6]

The variation in discourse quality is also evident when we combine the indicators of the DQI. To do so, we first placed all of the indicators on a common 0–6 scale. When we combine all of the indicators the resulting index (DQI-4) ranges from an average score of 8.4 to an average score of 15 (out of a possible range between 0 and 24). If we omit the content

[6] Given the ordinal character of the DQI indicators, reporting means is somewhat perilous. Spörndli (2004) reports the frequencies with which different codes occur in the 302 speech acts that make up the twenty debates. These frequencies also reveal considerable variance on the DQI indicators, suggesting that our characterization of the dispersion across debates is not a statistical artifact.

Table 6.1 *A cross-tabulation of discourse quality and decision margins*

| | Discourse quality | | |
Decision margin	*Low*	*High*	Total
Majoritarian	8	1	9
Unanimous	2	9	11
Total	10	10	20

Notes: "Discourse quality" is a median split of the three-indicator DQI (DQI-3) described in the text. "Decision margin" groups majoritarian and nearly majoritarian decisions into one group and unanimous decisions and nearly unanimous decisions into another group. Fisher's exact test $= 9.404$ ($p = 0.005$); Goodman and Kruskal's tau $= 0.495$ ($p = 0.005$).

of justification (DQI-3), which is less relevant for understanding formal outcomes, then the range is between 5.8 and 13 (out of a possible range between 0 and 18). In the remainder of this chapter, we shall focus on these indices, although we shall revisit individual indicators where this is useful.

Results for the formal dimension of outcomes

Does the level of deliberation matter for the margins with which proposals are passed or defeated? Does deliberation produce greater unity in decision making, as deliberative theorists hope? We are in a unique position to answer this question because our data contain information about margins of defeat or victory for mediating proposals in the VA, as well as data about the deliberation that precedes the vote on those proposals.

Table 6.1 provides an initial answer to our question. This table describes the relationship between a dichotomized version of the DQI-3 and a dichotomized version of vote outcomes. The DQI-3 is an index that combines the respect, level of justification, and constructive politics indicators. Here we have used a median split to dichotomize this measure. The vote outcome measure contrasts (near-)majoritarian with (near-)unanimity decisions. As the table shows, of the ten (near-)majoritarian decisions fully eight had DQI-3 values that were below the median. On the other hand, of the ten (near-)unanimous decisions only one had a DQI-3 value below the median. Thus, there appears to be a strong relationship between the outcomes and discourse quality. This is borne out statistically: when we perform Fisher's exact test we obtain a test statistic of 9.404 with a probability value of 0.005, which means that we can soundly reject the null hypothesis that discourse quality and vote outcome are unassociated. Another way to look at the data is to use the DQI-3 to predict vote outcome. This yields a statistically significant (by an exact test) and substantively important value of 0.495 on Goodman and Kruskal's tau, which means that taking into consideration discourse quality helps us improve our predictions of the vote outcome by close to 50 percent.[7] Thus the results of the cross-tabulation suggest that there is a substantial relationship between vote outcomes and discourse quality, a relationship that is clearly statistically significant despite the small number of debates in the analysis. We take this as initial evidence of the importance of political discourse for the formal dimension of political outcomes.

Before we can take this evidence at face value, however, we need to rule out alternative explanations. As we noted at the beginning of this chapter, we have tried to make the debates as comparable as possible on dimensions other than discourse quality. But this does not mean that the cases are identical on those dimensions, and this leaves open the possibility that other aspects of the debates account for vote outcomes.

We can think of a number of those aspects. First, the majority distribution in the VA fluctuates across the debates and could influence both the level of discourse and the vote outcomes. When there is a balance in the VA seats controlled by the government and the opposition, then we expect discourse levels to increase because the government needs the opposition, which should increase the respect, level of justification, and constructive politics indicators. At the same time, the likelihood of unanimous vote outcomes increases because neither the government nor the opposition can pass a proposal on its own.

Another factor that needs to be considered is the initial level of polarization between government and opposition. If the government and opposition enter the mediation process with only minor differences of opinion, then one would expect discourse to be of a high quality, since the different parties are not in fundamental disagreement. At the same time, there is a good chance that the differences can be ironed out easily, so that a mediating proposal will have widespread support in the VA.

Finally, we consider the role of age. There is variation in the average age of the VA members across the different debates. Such variation may be consequential for discourse as well as outcomes. The key to this prediction

---

[7] Since we do not expect content of justification to influence vote outcomes much we have left it out of this analysis. However, we obtain similar results when we include this indicator in the DQI. Now the DQI is below the median for seven of the nine cases in which the decision was (nearly) majoritarian, while it was below the median in only two of the eleven cases in which the decision was (nearly) unanimous. Fisher's exact test is 6.748 with a probability value of 0.022, while tau is 0.355 with an exact probability value of 0.022. Thus, we can continue to rule out the hypothesis that vote outcomes and discourse quality are unrelated.

is that the VA is designed to include politicians who are able to withstand pressures from their parties and who have the wherewithal to work out compromises and agreements. Older politicians are typically in a better position to withstand pressures from the party leadership, and their years of experience have given them a keen sense of the political process, including the mediation process in the VA. Thus more experienced VA members should be better equipped for the mediation process. On the one hand, this means that we should expect them to be more successful at forging solutions that can be accepted by everyone or nearly everyone. On the other hand, it also means that we should expect more senior VA members to fare better in creating a discourse that facilitates compromise and consensus.[8]

The reason that we worry about these alternative explanations is that they may render spurious the relationship between discourse quality and formal political outcomes. The preferences of the actors precede discourse and outcomes, and they may be responsible for the high level of correspondence between these two variables in table 6.1. That is, if the modal preference of the VA membership is to be accommodating, then we should not be surprised that a compromise or consensus is found. Neither should we be surprised that the level of discourse is high, since an accommodating membership will avoid disrespectful speech acts or speech acts that jeopardize a constructive solution or that cast the debate in terms of narrow interests. On the other hand, if the modal preference is not accommodating, but is rather to push through one's own views, then decisions should be majoritarian and discourse should be of a low quality, since there would be no need for the majority to show respect for the minority and to be constructive in their speech acts. Of course, any temptation to attribute political outcomes to the level of discourse should be suppressed in this situation because prior preferences are the true causal agent.

Unfortunately, we have no access to the prior preferences of the VA members as they entered the debates. But some information can be gleaned from considering the distribution of power in the VA, as well as the level of polarization of the initial positions. We can almost think of these two variables as proxy measures of the initial preferences of the VA members. When the government has a clear majority in the VA, we would expect it to prefer passing a proposal that reflects the bill that was passed in the Federal Diet, as opposed to diluting the bill in order to accommodate the opposition. When the government and opposition differ about policy fundamentals, as in the case of polarized issues, we should expect there to be less initial willingness

[8] These three control variables do not exhaust the possible differences between debates. Spörndli (2004) tests a number of other variables, including the length of debates and speeches, the gender composition of the VA, the role of the VA chair, and the ratio of questions to answers within a debate. Most of these factors fail to achieve statistical significance at conventional levels. Even if they do, they do not nullify the effect of the DQI-3.

Table 6.2 *Logistic regression of decision margins*

Predictor	M1	M2	M3	M4
Discourse quality	1.105	1.601	1.776	1.602
	(0.028)	(0.034)	(0.031)	(0.075)
Majority distribution		4.678		
		(0.044)		
Polarization			2.692	
			(0.174)	
Average age				−1.495
				(0.038)
Constant	−9.411	−16.498	−17.151	61.338
	(0.031)	(0.032)	(0.038)	(0.053)
LR	18.433	10.076	16.071	9.773
p	0.003	0.000	0.003	0.000
Incorrect predictions	4	4	3	1

Notes: Table entries are maximum likelihood logistic regression estimates with two-tailed p values listed in parentheses.

to compromise, with a corresponding decline in discourse and the reduced likelihood of a unanimous outcome. To the extent that the relationship between discourse quality and vote outcome is preserved after controlling for these proxies for initial preferences, we would conclude that discourse has a real effect on political outcomes.

To test the influence of discourse quality on vote outcomes in the presence of the control variables, we ran several logistic regression analyses, in which the dependent variable is the same dichotomous vote outcome variable as found in table 6.1. In this logistic regression analysis, we predict the probability of a (nearly) unanimous decision as a function of the DQI-3, now in its original form, and the control variables. Logistic regression analysis is a commonly used technique for modeling dichotomous outcome variables, which makes it appealing to use in the present context. On the downside, this method uses maximum likelihood estimation to derive estimates of the effects of predictors, and while it is possible to demonstrate that maximum likelihood estimators have desirable statistical properties in large samples, it is not clear that they also do so in small samples like those we have. To minimize some of the statistical concerns, we entered the control variables one at a time (see Achen 2001). We also repeated the analysis using a linear probability model, but the results are comparable to what we report here (see Spörndli 2004). The results of the logistic regression analyses are shown in table 6.2.

The logistic regression results demonstrate that the effect of discourse quality on vote outcomes is robust: regardless of the specific control that is entered, the DQI-3 always exerts a statistically significant and positive effect on the probability of attaining a (nearly) unanimous decision in the VA. Indeed, its effect is actually enhanced slightly by including the control variables. First, consider the majority distribution in the VA, which is measured here in terms of whether government and opposition have parity. As expected, parity increases the likelihood of unity in the vote outcome, but it does not remove the effect of discourse quality. In other words, the relationship between discourse and vote outcomes cannot be reduced to a common underlying factor that measures the balance of power in the VA.

Next, consider polarization. This control variable also behaves as we had anticipated, although it is not quite significant. Thus, polarization shows a weak tendency to reduce the likelihood of unified decisions. However, discourse quality remains influential, suggesting that its effect on vote outcomes cannot be reduced to preexisting differences in the political preferences of government and opposition. Another way of putting this is that discourse quality can help overcome initial polarization as an obstacle to forging compromise and consensus.

Finally, consider age. This variable runs counter to our expectations. If the VA is composed of older politicians, then the likelihood of (nearly) unanimous decisions is actually reduced. It is surely possible to give a post-hoc rationalization for this finding. It is consistent with psychological research suggesting that old people may be more dogmatic in their beliefs than middle-aged people (Baltes, Staudinger, and Lindenberger 1999; Post 1980). Alternatively, we may be dealing with a cohort effect, with the oldest members of the VA coming of political age during the Nazi era and World War II, although it is less clear why this should have made them less willing to compromise.[9] Regardless of the explanation, the important point is that age does not wipe out the effect of discourse quality. While this effect is now only marginally significant in a two-tailed test, it remains powerful and substantively important.

A good feeling for the substantive importance of discourse quality can be obtained when we convert its effect into an odds ratio.[10] In the models

[9] We also tried more direct measures of political experience such as the average number of years that VA members had spent in national or state politics and the average number of years that they had spent in the VA. These measures also exert a surprisingly negative effect on unanimity, although they do not attain statistical significance.

[10] In a logistical regression analysis the impact of predictors is not linear, so that interpretation is complicated. However, by exponentiating a coefficient we can get a sense of a predictor's impact on the odds of obtaining a (nearly) unanimous decision versus a (nearly) majoritarian decision.

reported in table 6.2, the impact of a unit increase in discourse quality on the odds ranges between 3 and nearly 6. In the worst case, this means that an increase of one unit in discourse quality is expected to improve the odds of reaching a unified decision by a factor of three. Put differently, there is an over 200 percent increase in the odds of a unified decision. By any reasonable standard, this is a substantively important result.

Another way to ascertain the importance of discourse quality is to investigate how well it accounts for actual outcomes in debates. We can construct a predicted probability of a (nearly) unanimous decision by using the predictor values for each debate and the estimates reported in table 6.2. If the predicted probability exceeds 0.5, we could make a decision to classify that particular debate as one that should have ended in a (nearly) unanimous decision. If the predicted probability is less than or equal to 0.5, we could derive the alternative prediction that the debate should have ended in a (nearly) majoritarian decision. We can then compare these predictions to the actual outcomes and keep a tally of incorrect classifications of debates. This tally is reported at the bottom of table 6.2.

We see that predictions based on discourse quality alone do fare quite well. We would have misclassified four of the twenty debates, amounting to 20 percent. By considering control variables we can reduce these mistakes, with the best performance coming from a model that includes discourse quality as well as the average age of the VA membership: this model misclassifies only one of the debates. Notice that if we had ignored any information about the predictors, we would have fared much more poorly, running the risk of misclassifying nine of the debates. Thus, we can say that considering discourse quality greatly improves our ability to predict the outcomes of debates, with further gains being made when control variables are considered.

While a consideration of the DQI-3 improves our ability to predict decision outcomes, our predictive ability is not perfect. What can we say about the cases that are not classified correctly in terms of the formal outcomes of debates? Here we turn to a qualitative analysis of our data. The debates that are misclassified when analyzed in terms of discourse quality include those on pension reform, home ownership, aspects of the social code, and aspects of indemnity for victims of violent crime. What was it about these debates that caused them to be misclassified in our quantitative analysis?

For the debates on the social code and indemnity for victims of violent crime, our model underestimates the outcome. These are the only two debates of our universe of twenty debates that ended with an unambiguous consensus and not merely a compromise. But in these two particular debates, the overall discourse quality was quite low with a DQI-3 score of 7, which falls in the bottom quartile. This runs counter to our expectations, which suggest that consensus is more likely if the quality of discourse is high. That these particular debates behave anomalously has much to do with the fact that building a consensus was not difficult and appeared to depend almost exclusively on filling in information gaps, as opposed to rational persuasion in the sense of Habermas. It appears that differences between the two sides on those issues were the result of ignorance or false perceptions, both of which were overcome quickly with the exchange of information in the VA. Each side was able to offer credible information that the other side had previously not possessed or which it had interpreted incorrectly. For example, in the debate on the social code the government quickly realized that its proposal contained unintended consequences. In the words of Jahn (Marburg), a member of the majority coalition in the Federal Diet, the government's legislative proposal would have the unintended effect of creating "a deterioration vis-à-vis the previous legal status."(VA, November 16, 1978, Protocol 18, p. 3).[11] In the debate on indemnity for victims of violent crime, a majority of the Federal Council had opposed the bill that was proposed by the government. However, soon after the debate in the VA had started, this group realized that the original bill would fulfill their objectives and they wound up supporting it. The exchange of information to clarify legislative proposals and to fill in knowledge gaps is, of course, a critical element of parliamentary debate and of deliberation (Austen-Smith and Feddersen 2002). But this does not nearly require the deliberative effort that we find in cases where there are disagreements on policy fundamentals, which explains the comparatively low DQI scores in these two debates.

The debate on home ownership ended with a majority decision. The model that includes only discourse quality predicts a near-unanimous decision. Looking closely at the data, one sees that of all majority decisions this case is closest to the cutoff point towards near-unanimous decisions.

Finally, our model overpredicts the outcome for the debate on pension reform. In terms of discourse quality this debate scored in the top quartile, which would suggest a strong probability that the final vote would pass (nearly) unanimously. In reality, this debate resulted in a majoritarian decision. A model that takes into consideration the relative power positions of the government and opposition helps us understand this outcome. In this debate, the government had a clear majority in the VA. As such it was able to stick to the original bill that had passed in the Federal Diet. It is not so much the outcome, then, that is surprising as the rather high level of discourse in the debate. While the government knew that it did not need the opposition, and while the opposition realized its weak position, there was still an effort to persuade the other, in an atmosphere of respect that,

[11] "eine Schlechterstellung gegenüber der bisherigen Rechtslage mit sich bringt."

Table 6.3 *A cross-tabulation of discourse quality and substantive decision outcomes*

| | Discourse quality | | |
Decision outcome	Low	High	Total
Inegalitarian	2	4	6
Neutral	1	1	2
Egalitarian	6	6	12
Total	9	11	20

Notes: "Discourse quality" is a median split of the four-indicator DQI (DQI-4) described in the text. Fisher's exact test $= 0.746$ ($p = 0.811$); Goodman and Kruskal's tau $= 0.016$ ($p = 0.811$).

at times, was even characterized by constructive political debate. However, despite a positive debate, no agreement could be reached on policy fundamentals. While the government reasoned about pension reform in strictly egalitarian terms, the CDU-CSU majority in the Federal Council argued in terms of personal responsibility. This lack of agreement about policy fundamentals was the key reason why a (nearly) unanimous decision could not be reached.

Results for the substantive dimension of outcomes

The previous section demonstrated that discourse quality and formal political outcomes are linked in a robust manner. The question is whether discourse quality is also linked to substantive outcomes. As we discussed in chapter 2, critics of deliberative theory frequently argue that perfect deliberation may be perfectly unjust in the political outcomes that it generates (see, for example, the cautionary remarks of Gutmann and Thompson 2002). Do we find evidence of this in the VA debates? Or do we find evidence that high-quality discourse enhances justice, as advocates of deliberative politics hope and claim?

If we look at the simple relationship between discourse quality and the substance of decisions we are inclined to say that both the advocates and the critics of deliberation have it wrong. The reason is that there simply is no relationship between discourse and substantive outcomes, as table 6.3 makes abundantly clear. In this table, we have pitted our three-point substantive outcome measure against a dichotomous version of the

DQI-4. We use the DQI-4 here because, according to our hypotheses, content of justification plays a critical role in shaping substantive outcomes. The dichotomization is based on a median split of the DQI-4 index. As table 6.3 shows, egalitarian and neutral decisions occur equally frequently in low-quality and high-quality discourses. Proportionally speaking, inegalitarial outcomes are actually more common under a high-quality discourse than under a low-quality discourse. All in all, however, there is no evidence of a statistically significant relationship between discourse quality and the substance of outcomes: Fisher's exact test is 0.746 and not significant, while Goodman and Kruskal's tau is only 0.016, which is also not significant.

Upon further reflection, it appears that the substance of political outcomes has a great deal to do with the character of majority preferences. We can classify the majority distribution into three categories. First, there may be a majority in the VA with a clear preference for inegalitarian outcomes. Second, there may be a majority in the VA with a clear preference for egalitarian outcomes. Finally, there may be a relatively even balance between supporters of equality and their opponents. As one might expect, the presence of a clear majority on either side of the issue of equality has a strong effect on the final outcome. Indeed, this effect is nearly deterministic. For example, both debates in which the majority preferred an inegalitarian outcome also produced that outcome. And of the eight debates in which the majority – in this case the social-liberal government – favored equality only one failed to produce this outcome. Given the strong influence of initial majority preferences, it is clear that discourse quality cannot play much of a role in shaping substantive outcomes. This is a sobering thought for deliberative theory. If our insights from the VA can be generalized at all, then it seems that *power politics* – the politics of majority preferences – seems to dominate substantive outcomes. Discourse seems to be impotent at changing this, except under rare circumstances.

Only half of our debates showed clear majority preferences either way on the issue of equality. Perhaps discourse plays a more limited role, influencing the outcomes only for those cases in which a clear majority preference does not exist. At first glance this does not seem to be true either: within this subset of cases there is still no significant relationship between discourse quality and substantive outcomes (Fisher's exact test is 0.585, which is not statistically significant; tau is 0.005, which is also not significant). The bottom line of our analysis thus seems to be that discourse does not change the substance of political outcomes.

Before we accept this conclusion, however, we should think about the meaning of discourse quality in the context of substantive outcomes. As we argued in chapter 4, respect and constructive politics may not be all that important for substantive outcomes. Rather, the content of justification,

Table 6.4 *Logistic regression of substantive decisions*

Predictor	M1	M2
Content of justifications	2.598	
	(0.075)	
Content + level		1.448
		(0.057)
Initial majority position	4.268	3.206
	(0.057)	(0.054)
Constant	−4.331	−8.288
	(0.087)	(0.062)
LR	13.495	14.039
p	0.001	0.006
Incorrect predictions	3	3

Notes: Table entries are maximum likelihood logistic regression estimates with two-tailed p values listed in parentheses.

followed by the level of justification, seems to be much more important. Perhaps focusing on these indicators helps to get a clearer picture of the impact of discourse on substantive outcomes. Of course, such an analysis should also consider the majority position, as we have found this to be an important influence on outcomes. Analytically, we shift our strategy to logistic regression analysis, where we have dichotomized the outcome variable with 1 indicating egalitarian outcomes and 0 indicating neutral or inegalitarian outcomes.

Table 6.4 shows the results of this analysis. Let us first consider the model that contains only the content of justifications, coded as the portion of egalitarian arguments in a debate (codes 1 and 2 on our content of justification indicator). We see that this variable exerts a marginally significant and positive effect on our outcome variable. Substantively, this is an important effect: for a unit increase in egalitarian arguments we expect the odds of an egalitarian outcome to increase by a factor of 13. This effect is particularly impressive considering that the majority position also exerts a powerful influence.

It is important to note that the relationship between egalitarian arguments and egalitarian outcomes is not tautological. Our indicator of the content of justifications measures only how often VA members reason in terms of weakly egalitarian arguments. It does not measure in what direction these arguments are used. Arguments about equality can be used to support egalitarian policies, but also to oppose such policies. Indeed, for three debates we find that the opponents of egalitarian policies invoke egalitarian arguments,

and in a further two debates the use of egalitarian arguments is balanced
between proponents and opponents of egalitarian policies. Thus there is a
tendency for egalitarian arguments to be used by supporters of egalitarian
policies, but this tendency is far from perfect. Moreover, if we only count
egalitarian arguments for the proponents of egalitarian policies, then the
resulting measure, while exerting a positive effect on outcomes, is no longer
statistically significant. Even more telling, if we only count such arguments
for the opponents of egalitarian policies, we still find a positive effect on
outcomes, although this is again not statistically significant.

When we add the level of justification of egalitarian arguments to the
content indicator, then we retain a positive effect of discourse quality on outcomes that is marginally significant, as is demonstrated in the last columns
of table 6.4 (VA, November 16, 1978, Protocol 18, p. 3).[12] A unit increase
on this index is expected to raise the odds of an egalitarian outcome by a
factor of 4. Again, this is a substantively important effect, which shows that
the content and level of justification components of the DQI are influential
in determining substantive outcomes.

The logistic regression analysis with majority position, content of justification, and level of justification does a good job at predicting the outcomes
of the debates. There are only three debates that are misclassified in terms
of their actual outcomes. Had we ignored information about the predictors
and simply predicted debate outcomes on the basis of the model, then we
would have been wrong in eight instances.

What can we say about the three debates that are classified incorrectly? Let
us start with the debate on changing the income tax code. Here our model
predicts an egalitarian outcome, when in fact the outcome was neutral. This
outcome reflected a genuine compromise, in that the opposing factions of
the VA gave up their original positions in order to reach an agreement in
the middle. This compromise became a central focus early on in the debate.
For example, one of the first speeches makes the point that "The Committee
should really be able to concentrate on the questions for which there is a
possibility of arriving at a compromise. He [the chair] can only express
this as a request; according to his opinion there is a mutual obligation to
take account of the time pressures of each committee member."[13] As this
quote suggests, time pressures were one reason to seek a compromise. We
should also keep in mind, however, that this was also the second time that
the VA dealt with this issue and that the first effort was concluded without a

---

[12] We can also interact these two indicators, which yields comparable results, although they
are plagued by some degree of multicollinearity.

[13] "Der Ausschuß sollte sich wirklich auf die Fragen konzentrieren können, bei denen die
Möglichkeit besteht, zu Vermittlungsergebnissen zu kommen. Er [der Vorsitzende] könne
das nur als Bitte aussprechen; s.E. sei man es sich aber gegenseitig schuldig, auf die Zeit-
probleme jedes einzelnen Rücksicht zu nehmen."

unified proposal. Thus the different factions refrained from lengthy efforts to persuade one another and instead moved quickly in a compromise direction. Telling in this regard is also that the different factions seemed to rely on the arguments of the other side. Thus proponents of an inegalitarian outcome based most of their arguments (54 percent) on egalitarian conceptions of the common good. On the other hand, egalitarian arguments were relatively rare among the proponents of an egalitarian outcome. It was almost as if each side adopted the other side's logic in order to find common ground more quickly.

Another debate that was misclassified and that is similar in nature to the previous example is the debate on legal aid. Our model predicts this debate to produce an outcome in the middle range, when, in fact, the outcome was egalitarian. For the interpretation of this case one has to consider that from the beginning there was pressure to arrive at a compromise, as illustrated by the following quote:

> He [Jahn] considers it as not impossible that this [the first item of the demand] could be an issue on which a compromise is feasible. Therefore he asks for an agreement to postpone the final decision and to go first through all the demands in order to get a definitive picture whether an overall compromise is feasible. (VA, April 16, 1980, Protocol 36, p. 44)[14]

Given such pressure for a compromise, there was give and take for the final outcome, although according to our classification the outcome ended up as egalitarian albeit close to the cutoff point of the middle range. The important point to note is that the committee operated with a focus on compromise, which caused them to focus less on the substantive dimension and more on the need to forge a commonly acceptable solution. Thus it is no surprise that a model to predict the substantive outcome is not quite adequate. The main motivational forces in the committee were less geared to the substance of the outcome than to reaching a mutually acceptable agreement.

Finally, consider the debate on tax relief and promotion of investments, which is the most interesting instance where our model mis-predicts. This is the only debate in which the majority position was not reflected in the final outcome. That is, while a majority of the VA supported an egalitarian outcome, and while our model predicts this as well, the actual outcome was inegalitarian. One of the striking things about this debate is that the level of discourse is quite high: the DQI-4 score was 13, which falls in the top quartile of scores for these debates. When assessed in terms of the DQI-3,

---

[14] "Er [Jahn] halte es nicht für ausgeschlossen, dass dies [Nr. 1 des Anrufungsbegehrens] ein Punkt sein könnte, auf den man sich verständigt. Deshalb bitte er darum, damit einverstanden zu sein, die endgültige Entscheidung zurückzustellen, erst einmal die gesamten Anrufungsbegehren durchzugehen . . . um dann ein endgültiges Bild davon zu erhalten, ob es insgesamt einen Einigungsvorschlag geben kann oder nicht."

this debate has the highest discourse quality of all of the debates. One interpretation of this result is that discourse was able to overcome the initial majority position. More generally, one could argue that there is a biasing effect on the outcome when a debate starts with a clear majority favoring a particular position, and that discourse is unlikely to nullify or change this bias unless it is of truly exceptional quality. Whether this interpretation is valid in the present case and more generally should be assessed through other studies.

Conclusions

In this chapter, we have studied the political outcomes that are associated with deliberation. We have studied two outcome dimensions, namely a formal dimension that taps the degree of unity of a decision, and a substantive dimension that measures the extent to which a decision is consistent with Rawls's principle of weak egalitarianism. We have studied these dimensions by focusing on the German Mediation Committee or VA during a time period in which a social-liberal coalition (SPD and FDP) controlled the Federal Diet, while Christian-Democrats (CDU-CSU) controlled the Federal Council. We analyzed a total of twenty debates on a wide range of issues that are representative of the topics that the VA discusses. What have we learnt?

On the formal dimension of political outcomes, advocates of deliberative democracy have frequently expressed the hope, if not the belief, that deliberation produces more consensual outcomes. If political actors are allowed to engage in a high-quality rational debate on the merits of different policy choices, so the argument goes, then they will be moved by the non-coercive force of the better argument (see Habermas 1996a). In the ideal world, all will come to agree on what the better policy is and this will be the policy that is adopted unanimously.

Deliberative skeptics deem this view over-optimistic. Not only does it require a major cognitive effort to persuade people (Lupia 2002) which, given realistic time constraints, may mean that not everyone is persuaded and that decisions are not unanimous, it may even be the case that deliberation produces polarization, especially when the deliberative body is divided into factions such as parties. The argument is that a high-level discourse may cause actors to realize how fundamentally divided they really are on an issue (Shapiro 1999; Sunstein 1997). If deliberation polarizes, then unanimous decisions are less, rather than more, likely. Indeed, political actors might be better off not to deliberate at all, and to strike deals with a minimum of political discourse.

Our results on the VA suggest that deliberative skeptics may be too pessimistic. In the VA, unanimous or nearly unanimous decisions were typically associated with a high level of discourse in the preceding debates. Even when we controlled for rival explanations of the formal outcomes of debates, discourse quality continued to be an important factor. Rather than polarizing them, discourse thus helped different sides to find a commonly acceptable solution to an issue.

This is not to say that high-quality discourse is a necessary condition for unanimity. As we have seen, sometimes the differences between opposing factions are fairly small and a simple exchange of information is sufficient to forge an agreement. Under those conditions, discourse does not have to be of a particularly high quality in order to reach a compromise or a consensus. Thus we see deliberation as a facilitating force in the process of reaching commonly agreeable solutions, a force that is not always required but that can become quite important, especially if there are preexisting disagreements about policy fundamentals.

On the substantive dimension, too, we have seen that some are hopeful while others are skeptical about the virtues of deliberation. The advocates of deliberative politics argue that deliberation is by definition an egalitarian enterprise, since no one should be excluded from the debate. This makes it more likely that representatives of the least advantaged groups in society are heard in the debate. Moreover, a real deliberation focuses on the common good and this could easily be understood in Rawlsian terms, i.e. in terms of assisting the least advantaged in a society. Thus deliberation is expected to enhance social justice by forcing political actors to consider the plight of the least advantaged in society. In fact, deliberation may even cultivate an ability to empathize with disadvantaged groups (Shapiro 1997).

Skeptics of deliberation are pessimistic that just outcomes will prevail. Their argument is that deliberation is about the process and not so much about the substance of decision making. Any linkage between those aspects is speculative at best. At worst, such a linkage is plainly wrong because it is not at all difficult to imagine scenarios in which a perfectly fine deliberation leads to an outcome that is perfectly inegalitarian or otherwise unjust (see Gutmann and Thompson 2002).

What do we observe in the VA debates? First, we should note that the VA is of course not a forum in which everyone participates. Only representatives of the political parties represented in the Federal Diet and Federal Council get to participate. However, in the time period that we are studying, disadvantaged groups found strong advocates in the form of the SPD-led governments of Brandt and Schmidt. Moreover, appeals to the common good framed in egalitarian terms were not uncommon in the VA debates. We found that such appeals enhanced the likelihood of (weak) egalitarian outcomes, although this effect was only marginally significant.

What we did not find is an effect of deliberation framed more broadly. That is, apart from the content and the level of justifications, other elements of discourse quality do not seem to matter. When considering our most comprehensive measure of discourse quality, the DQI-4, we found no statistically significant effect on substantive outcomes. This suggests that other aspects of discourse quality such as respect and constructive politics do not improve the likelihood of egalitarian outcomes, and in fact may reduce it.

We should also keep in mind that the limited effect of discourse occurs in a context in which power politics very much shapes the final outcomes. When a clear majority favors an egalitarian outcome, or when a clear majority opposes such an outcome, it almost always gets its way. As Shapiro (1999) has argued, politics is about interests and power, and there is surely support for that claim in our data.

The distribution of support for egalitarian outcomes thus acts as a powerful control variable. That we manage to find some limited effects of deliberation is encouraging, when viewed in that light. Of considerable interest is also that we have one debate in which a strong preexisting majority did not get its way and that this debate was characterized by a high level of discourse. This suggests the intriguing possibility that deliberation may be able to offset the numeric force of prior preferences. However, lest we capitalize on chance, we should hold off from drawing any firm conclusions here until we have more evidence.

Thus our results suggest that high-quality political discourse enhanced the likelihood of unanimous vote outcomes in the VA and – less robustly – that certain aspects of a high-quality discourse also enhanced the likelihood of egalitarian outcomes. The question that remains is whether these results can be generalized. On the one hand, the VA has a peculiar set of features that are not found in all institutions. It operates in the greatest secrecy and its membership has a mandate to create mediating proposals. As Elster (1998b) has argued, closed institutions like the VA make for better deliberation than open institutions. We suspect that the mandate of VA members helps in this regard as well. On the other hand, the VA shares with most institutions the fact that it works under time pressure, so that deliberation cannot be unlimited. Moreover, partisan pressures may be diminished in the VA, but they are surely not absent and this, too, makes it not so atypical.

One way to think about the VA is that it sits somewhere in between the competitive and consociational ends of the political spectrum. We believe that this lends some generalizability to our results. However, only further research will tell whether other institutions follow the same patterns that we have uncovered here. We hope this chapter has shown that such research is both feasible and worthwhile.

Conclusion and research outlook

To our knowledge, ours is the first attempt to submit a measure of the level of deliberation to reliability tests. Since these tests proved to be successful, we were able to establish systematic variation in the discourse quality. Successful reliability tests, of course, do not automatically mean that the measure is valid. Does our Discourse Quality Index (DQI) really tap into the philosophical concept of deliberation? The answer would have been negative if we had been unable to explain the variation in the discourse quality in its preconditions and consequences in a theoretically meaningful way. As chapters 5 and 6 demonstrate, however, variables linked to the deliberative literature helped us to explain it to a large extent. The validity of a measure is always most difficult to prove in a final way, and we do not claim that we are absolutely sure that our DQI measures what philosophers understand by deliberation, but we are at least encouraged that we are on the right path.

Our results show that discourse quality is not a uni-dimensional phenomenon but a complex cluster of elements. If actors justify their arguments in the sense of the deliberative model in a sophisticated way, this does not always mean, for example, that they show respect for the arguments of other actors, another aspect of the deliberative model. This meant for our empirical analyses that quite often we had to break down the DQI into its individual elements. When comparing, for example, the discourse quality in full parliamentary sessions and committee meetings, we found that the level of justification was higher in the former, the level of respect in the latter. This means that often it is useful not to talk about the level of deliberation in general but about the individual elements of the deliberative model. This has to be kept in mind when using our data for the philosophical discussion on deliberation which is often too undifferentiated, lumping all

165

aspects of deliberation into a single category. We also took great pains not to limit ourselves to statistical analyses of quantitative data, but also to look at qualitative aspects of the various parliamentary debates. Such qualitative analyses often helped us to make sense of deviant cases from our general findings.

What is the agenda for further empirical research on the deliberative model? One direction is to refine the Discourse Quality Index (DQI). Although the index proved useful for the current project, the coding categories need to be further differentiated. As a starting point for our research, we wished to work with only a few clearly delimited categories, so that we could attain high inter-coder reliability. This goal has now been reached so that we can refine the coding categories. With regard to the respect shown toward the demands of others, for example, we lumped all speeches that contained exclusively negative comments in the same category. For future research, we will try to differentiate this category by distinguishing different levels of negative statements. Still unresolved is the question of how to get an empirical handle on the truthfulness of the statements made in a political discourse. One way to go would be to investigate the *perception* of truthfulness. If one could establish through interviews whether the statement of a particular actor is *perceived* as truthful or not by other actors, this would already be a good step forward in coming to terms in an empirical way with the concept of truthfulness. If an actor says, for example, that he or she truly respects the views of others and this statement is taken at face value by the other actors, we register an important phenomenon, whether or not the actor in his or her inner self really senses such respect. Perhaps the actor may not know what his or her innermost feelings are in a particular situation. Could in-depth interviews help further? We leave this question unanswered for the time being, but we may come back to it in our future research.

With regard to the application of the DQI, we need to move beyond the parliamentary arena, to other political arenas such as debates in cabinets, courts, advisory commissions, and bureaucracies. We also need to look at the discourse quality in the media. Most important, however, is that we expand the application of the DQI to the wider public sphere, which is so central to the deliberative model. Deliberative theorists postulate that opinions on political matters should be formed in informal debates among friends, neighbors, families, in the workplace and in voluntary associations (della Porta 2004; Kriesi 2004; Neblo 2004). Such opinions should then be transmitted in an effective way to the formal political arenas. Since informal debates in the public sphere by their very nature are not recorded, we will have to look for research methods other than the study of debate transcripts. Obvious choices are interviews and participant observation. Thanks to modern technology, a new form of discourse in the public sphere has developed with the internet, and for research purposes this new form has the advantage that debate transcripts are available for analysis (Kies and Jansen 2004).

From the perspective of political relevance, it will be urgent to study the aspect of discourse quality in deeply divided and unstable societies such as Bosnia-Herzegovina, Kosovo, Macedonia, Northern Ireland, Cyprus, Afghanistan, Iraq, Sri Lanka, Rwanda, and Colombia. Such a research orientation will bring us back to the starting point of the current project: consociational theory. We have to expect that discourse quality in such societies will be extremely low. Quite often, the representatives of the various groups will not even talk with each other. But we could study what they say about each other in speeches and interviews. We will certainly register much hatred and many threats in these speeches and interviews. Occasionally there may be hints of a willingness to bargain and even to deliberate with the other side. It will be particularly interesting to investigate the instances where the representatives of the various groups actually begin to talk with each other. In most cases we will not have minutes of such talks, but perhaps after the end of the talks the participants will convey in interviews and speeches some impression of what went on during the talks and perhaps even of how much deliberation took place. The data situation will certainly not be as good as in the current project where we could rely on verbatim minutes of the parliamentary debates. But as an empirical basis we would still have some texts to work with. Theoretically the question would basically be the same as in the current project, namely to explain the preconditions and the consequences of variation in the level of deliberation. A key variable would be the amount of violence among the various groups. How are deliberation and violence intertwined? Is a strong decrease or even a halt to violence a necessary condition for the initiation of some elements of deliberation? Or, on the contrary, does an increase in violence bring everyone to their senses so that some deliberation will begin to take place? Furthermore, does the signaling of a willingness to deliberate reduce the level of violence? Asked in the most fundamental way, is talk "cheap" in such crisis situations or has it any impact (Steenbergen et al. 2004)?

Making recommendations on the basis of such research, we would become policy advisers, a development that we would welcome. Ultimately, our research should have concrete political relevance, especially in crisis situations where human dignity and human life are at risk. We hope that we would be able to give such advice with the necessary modesty and humility. Consociational scholars such as Arend Lijphart are good examples for us in this respect. They have given useful institutional advice in many troublespots of the world. We intend to follow their lead and to give in our future research some supplementary advice on the behavioral aspect of deliberation, showing why deliberation is an important aspect of attaining political stability.

Just as important as expanding our research to deeply divided and unstable societies will be an expansion to the international level. In a time of globalization, it is becoming of crucial importance how conflicts at the international level are handled. Scholars such as Risse (see chapter 3) have convincingly argued that deliberation has a place in international politics too (Ehrensperger 2004; Ulbert et al. 2004). It will be interesting to investigate the discourse quality in international governmental organizations such as the World Trade Organization (WTO) and in non-governmental organizations (NGOs) active on the international scene, such as Amnesty International and Greenpeace. It will be particularly interesting to see what happens with regard to discourse quality when these two types of international organization interact with each other, for example at the World Economic Forum in Davos, Switzerland. In this international research area, Patrizia Nanz and Jens Steffek of the University of Bremen have already moved ahead with a large empirical project on deliberation (Nanz and Steffek 2004), and we plan to work closely together with them in our future research.

For the specifics of the research design in all future projects, the question of the units of analysis will be important. In the current project, the main units of analysis were debates on specific issues, although we also did some analyses on the discourse quality displayed by individual actors. When the units of analysis are specific debates, we call this a meso-level of analysis; when the units of analysis are individual actors, we speak of a micro-level of analysis. At the latter level, there is a great wealth of research questions that are still to be addressed. From the perspective of political psychology, we may ask how ideological preferences, dogmatism, and the level of stress experienced in a decision making situation may influence the discourse quality of individual actors. We may also simply ask whether the discourse quality of actors depends on their gender, their age, their social status, their religious denomination, and other such conventional variables (Rosenberg 2004; Searing et al. 2004).

Another interesting research field would be to aggregate the discourse quality to the macro-level of entire countries. At this macro-level, of course, the measurement properties of the discourse quality would become somewhat problematic. In an ideal world, we could take a random sample of all political debates in a country and weigh the individual debates according to their salience. As the senior author has shown elsewhere, such random and weighed investigations of political debates at the macro-level are virtually impossible to execute (Steiner and Dorff, 1988). But this does not mean that all research at the macro-level is impossible. In order to assess whether countries have different levels of discourse quality, we may investigate how some key issues are debated, for example in parliament and in the media. If some countries display a higher discourse quality for most such key issues, we may classify them with all the necessary caution in a higher category for discourse quality. If in this way we arrive at the classification of a fairly large number of countries, the discourse quality may become an important variable in comparative politics research. When our colleagues at Chapel Hill, Evelyne Huber and John Stephens, continue to study welfare policies at a cross-national level (see, for example, Huber and Stephens 2001), the explanatory power of their models could be increased if they added the discourse quality in a country as an independent variable.

Furthermore, we may submit some of our hypotheses to experimental tests, following the lead of Sulkin and Simon, whose research we reported in chapter 3. But we would not only investigate whether and how much the participants in experiments talk, but also at what discourse level this talk takes place. Of particular importance would be to find out through what kind of interventions the discourse quality can be increased (see Rosenberg, chapter 2). Such experimental research would be of great political relevance if undertaken in deeply divided societies. If, for example, in Kosovo we could bring together Serbs and Albanians to take part in such experiments, we might get some valuable information on how the two groups can learn to talk with each other in a deliberative way. This brings us back once more to consociational theory which gave us the impetus to undertake the current project. If we strive for democracy in deeply divided countries, we need not only the right kind of institutions but also the right kind of culture of talk among the various groups, both at the elite and at the citizen level.

Last but not least, we hope that empirical studies on deliberation will help to stimulate further philosophical work on the deliberative model (Chambers 2004; Dryzek 2004; Follesdal 2004; Goodin 2004; Fishkin and Luskin 2004). Political philosophers have to come to terms, for example, with our finding that the level of respect is lower in public than in non-public meetings. The prevailing view among philosophers of deliberation is that political decision making should be in the public eye as much as possible. At the same time, they postulate a high level of respect among political decision makers. The important philosophical question then is what the tradeoff should be between publicity and respect.

Appendix

Discourse Quality Index (DQI): instructions for coders

Each speech act is coded separately. The coding is done according to the seven categories explained below. Each coding decision must be justified in the comment section with supporting quotes and page or column numbers. So that the justifications can be easily found, use a separate paragraph for each coding decision and leave space between the individual paragraphs. Detailed and good justifications of the coding decisions are very important for the success of the project. These justifications allow the reader to understand why particular codes were chosen. Furthermore, detailed and good justifications of the coding decisions may allow the establishment of subcategories of the various codes in later stages of the project. For each speech, relevant and irrelevant parts have to be distinguished, and only the relevant parts should be coded. If a speech has no relevant parts, it is not coded at all. The relevant parts concern demands entering the debate. A demand is a proposal by an individual or a group on what decisions should or should not be made. Demands that are closely related to each other constitute an issue. If there are two or more issues, the debates on each issue need to be coded on separate coding schemes. If an actor makes two or more speeches in the same debate, each speech must be coded separately although the codes for the later speeches may be the same as the codes for the earlier speeches. When a speech is interrupted, these interruptions also count as speeches if they are relevant as defined above. A speech that is interrupted counts as a single speech; thus it is not a new speech that begins after the interruption. If an interruption does not contain a demand but friendly or unfriendly remarks towards other participants, still include such interruptions. Do not code them, however, but merely quote the remarks in the comments section.

170

Participation

Code 0: interruption of a speaker

This should only be used if a speaker explicitly says that he or she is disturbed by an interruption or if he or she is interrupted by a formal decision. It does not apply when the allocated speaking time is up.

Illustration: On June 25, 1998, the British House of Commons discusses social welfare. When John Swinney of the Scottish National Party speaks he is several times interrupted, which clearly annoys him. Finally he exclaims: "I shall not take any more interventions."

Code 1: normal participation is possible

This is probably the usual code in most parliamentary debates.

Level of justification for demands

A demand refers to what should or should not be done within the issue under debate. For its justification, we do not judge how good an argument for a demand is or whether we agree with it. We only judge to what extent a speech gives complete justifications for demands. Justifications are complete if they contain a conclusion on what should or should not be done, a reason for this conclusion and a linkage between conclusion and reason. Linkages are usually made with words such as "since," "because," "so," "thus," "therefore," and "for." Sometimes, linkages are not made explicit because the speaker expects that all listeners understand what the meaning of the linkage is. If such implicit linkages occur, the justification is still complete. But it must be beyond reasonable doubt for the coder that the meaning of the implicit linkage is well understood by the other participants in the debate.

Code 0: no justification

The speaker only says that X should or should not be done, that it is a wonderful or a terrible idea, etc. But no reason is given for why X should or should not be done.

Illustration: On December 2, 1998, aid to seaside towns is discussed in the British House of Commons. Labour MP Gordon Marsden supports such aid with a qualified justification (see below under qualified justification). Conservative MP Simon Burns interrupts Marsden in putting the rhetorical question: "As a Blackpool Member, would the hon. Gentleman agree that his plea for the Government to consider fully the town's problems has been more than adequately dealt with by his party, which has kicked Blackpool in the teeth by no longer holding its conference there." The implication of Burns's question is that no aid should be given to the seaside towns. But instead of giving a reason, he only taunts Marsden that the Labour Party is no longer holding its party conference in Blackpool, thus contributing to the problems of the town.

Code 1: inferior justification

Here, a reason Y is given why X should or should not be done. But no linkage is made between X and Y. If a conclusion is merely supported with illustrations, also give code 1. Justify in the comments section with quotes why you think that a linkage is missing or why the conclusion is only supported with illustrations.

Illustration: The debate on aid to seaside towns (see above) also offers an illustration of an inferior justification. Labour MP Shona McIsaac tries to justify why aid is necessary to the town of Cleethorpes in her constituency. Her reason is that "there are severe pockets of deprivation in the area," that "the deprivation is largely hidden," and "that hidden deprivation must be addressed." But it remains unclear how aid to the town of Cleethorpes would address the problem of deprivation, especially since it is hidden. Financial aid may easily bypass any hidden deprivation. Thus, the justification is incomplete.

Code 2: qualified justification

Here, a linkage is made why one should expect that X will contribute to Y. A single such complete justification already qualifies for code 2. Justify with quotes that a linkage is made.

Illustration: The debate on aid to seaside towns (see above) also offers an illustration of a qualified justification. Labour MP Gordon Marsden is supporting such aid. As a reason for this conclusion he argues that the hotels in the seaside towns need "revitalizing." The linkage between reason and conclusion is made in such a way that the money could be spent "to improve public transport links to seaside towns" and such improved links will help to revitalize the hotels in the seaside towns. Thus Mr Marsden gives a conclusion, a reason, and a linkage between conclusion and reason.

Code 3: sophisticated justification

Here at least two complete justifications are given, either for the same demand or for two different demands. Justify with quotes that two complete justifications are given.

Illustration: On December 5, 1997, special educational needs are debated in the British House of Commons. Estelle Morris, Parliamentary Under-Secretary for Education and Employment, presents a Green Paper by the Labour Government in which it is argued that more should be done to help children with special educational needs. She gives at least two complete justifications for this conclusion.

(1) "The Green Paper contains our proposals for the training of all teachers, particularly for Special Educational Needs coordinators and specialists. We acknowledge the role that they play and do something to improve their training and qualifications. They contribute a great deal to educating children with Special Educational Needs." Although Ms. Morris does not make explicit why a better training of teachers will help children with Special Educational Needs, the implicit linkage between reason and conclusion is so self-evident that it must have been clear to all participants what she meant the linkage to be.

(2) "The Green Paper emphasises the importance of co-operative working between the various agencies concerned with children's needs. We need to ensure that all local agencies – education, social services, and health, with the voluntary sector – work together in the interests of children with special needs. We shall never reach the position with Special Educational Needs where we do not have to use the skills of many professionals who are located in different areas of the system." Here again, Ms. Morris does not make explicit why more inter-agency cooperation will help children with special educational needs, but here too the implicit linkage is so strong that its meaning must have been clear to all participants.

Content of justification for demands

Codes 0, 2a, and 2b are not mutually exclusive and may all be given to a single speech. If code 1 is given, however, no other code is logically possible.

Code 0: explicit statement concerning constituency or group interests

The mentioning of a single constituency or group interest already qualifies for code 0. In the comments section give quotes for all constituency and group interests since it will be important to have available for further analyses the entire range of these interests in the individual speeches.

Illustration: On June 2, 1997, the British House of Commons debates an education bill whose main goal is to reduce class sizes in schools. The bill is introduced by David Blunkett, the Secretary of State for Education

and Employment. During his speech Labour MP Anne Campbell rises and
Blunkett yields to her for the following statement: "Is my right hon. Friend
aware how important the Bill is to my constituency, especially to parents at
Milton Road infant school, which had an excellent Ofsted report earlier this
year but now has to implement £25,000 of cuts imposed by the previous
Government?" Mrs. Campbell refers to the interests of her constituency and
to a special group within her constituency, and thus clearly qualifies for
code 0.

Code 1: neutral statement

No explicit reference to constituency and group interests or the common
good is made.

Code 2a: explicit statement of the common good
in utilitarian or collective terms

The common good in utilitarian terms means the best solution for the
highest number of people. The common good in collective terms means
the best solution for society as an abstract entity. Include also references not
made to the country but to a larger entity such as Europe or the world at large.
The mentioning of a single reference to the common good in utilitarian or
collective terms already qualifies for code 2a. Give quotes for all references
since it will be interesting to get the entire range of such references in the
individual speeches.

Illustration: On February 27, 1998, government priorities for women are
discussed in the British House of Commons. Harriet Harman, the Secretary
of State for Social Security and Minister for Women in the Labour government, refers to the best solution for the highest number of people, indeed
in a universal way for all families: "Child care must not be a poor service for
poor families but an excellent service for all families. It must be universal."

Code 2b: explicit statement of the common good in terms
of the difference principle

According to the philosopher John Rawls it is in the interest of the common
good if the least advantaged in a society are helped. This definition of the
common good goes by the term "difference principle." The least advantaged
in a society are, in particular, the groups that are poorest and the most
discriminated against. The difference principle may also refer, depending on
the context, to children and unborn generations. The difference principle
can also be expressed in terms of fairness and justice. If you choose code 2b,

it is important that you give all the corresponding quotes in the comments section.

Illustration: In the debate on priorities for women (above), Ms. Harman also refers to the most disadvantaged in society according to Rawls's difference principle: "The government's priority must be to help those who have the greatest difficulty in paying for it rather than spreading it evenly across the range."

Respect toward groups to be helped (empathy)

Code 0: no respect

There are only negative statements. A single negative statement already qualifies for code 0. Give quotes for all negative statements.

Illustration: On March 10, 1997, under the title public responsibility for social justice, the British House of Commons discusses increased aid to Scotland and Wales. Labour MP Brian Wilson of the Scottish constituency of Cunninghame North makes the following statement about nationalistically oriented Scots: "I wonder why we should be less concerned about people in England who are homeless than about those in Scotland and Wales. A proportionate number of people are homeless in England, many of whom are Scottish or Welsh in origin. Does that upset the primary nationalist argument that England is somehow a land flowing with milk and honey at Scotland's expense?" With the rhetorical question at the end Mr. Wilson implies that some Scots play in an undue way the nationalist card in order to get more aid.

Code 1: neutral

There are no negative statements but neither are there any positive ones.

Code 2: explicit respect

A single positive statement already qualifies for code 2. There may also be some negative statements but this does not change the code. Give quotes for all positive and negative statements.

Illustration: On June 25, 1998, the British House of Commons discusses social welfare and measures to help the most vulnerable in society. Labour MP Anne Begg shows explicit respect toward this group in stating that one should "make sure that vulnerable people get the benefits that they deserve."

Respect toward the demands of others

Since the critique of the demands of others often becomes an element of the justification of one's own position, the reaction to a demand by others may have to be coded not only under the current category but also with regard to level and content of justification.

The codes of this category are not applicable if there is only one demand on the agenda and the speaker supports this demand. In this case, we can automatically assume that the speaker respects the demand. Set N/A, not applicable.

Code 0: no respect

There are only negative statements toward the demands of others. Attacks against individuals and groups making demands also count as negative statements. A single negative statement already qualifies for code 0. Give quotes for all negative statements.

Illustration: On December 10, 1990, the British House of Commons discussed a bill to upgrade and modernize King's Cross Railway Station in London. Labour MP Tony Banks makes only negative statements concerning this demand: for example, "It is clear that past errors are vast, so can anyone view with any seriousness the opinions and calculations that British Rail is now making?"

Code 1: neutral

There are no negative statements but neither are there any positive statements.

Code 2: explicit respect

A single positive statement toward any demand by others already qualifies for code 2. The positive statement may refer to only one aspect of the demand. There may also be some negative statements but this does not change the code. Give quotes for all positive and negative statements.

Illustration: On December 5, 1997, special educational needs are discussed in the British House of Commons. Estelle Morris, Parliamentary Under-Secretary of State for Education and Employment, presents a Green Paper by the Labour government in which it is argued that more should be done to help children with special educational needs. Conservative MP Richard Ottaway, although making a critical remark about the policies of the Labour government, also utters the following positive statement: "I am pleased to hear that the Minister's commitment to special education needs is being developed through the Green Paper. I am also pleased at the tone of her speech."

Respect toward counterarguments

Counterarguments are arguments raised by political opponents that contradict one's own conclusion with regard to the demand. Since the critique of a counterargument often becomes an element of the justification of one's own position, the reaction to a counterargument may have to be coded not only under the current category but also with regard to level and content of justification. If there is not yet any counterargument on the table, code N/A. The speakers, however, may already anticipate a counterargument. In such cases do not code N/A but give an actual code. If there is more than one counterargument, the codes apply to the totality of the counterarguments.

Code 0: counterarguments are ignored

All counterarguments are ignored. They are not addressed at all in any way whatsoever.

Code 1: counterarguments are included but explicitly degraded

There are only negative statements toward counterarguments, although there may also be neutral statements. Attacks against individuals and groups making the counterarguments also count as negative statements. A single negative statement toward a single counterargument already qualifies for code 1. Give quotes for all negative statements.

Illustration: On December 16, 1997, the National Minimum Wage Bill is discussed in the British House of Commons. The Secretary of State for Trade and Industry, Margaret Beckett, introduces the bill on behalf of the Labour government. To counterarguments of the Conservative side, she states: "The underlying thrust of the policy of the previous government was to try to turn Britain into the sweatshop, certainly of Europe, if not the world." Turning to a specific member of the opposition, Mrs. Beckett exclaims: "I am indifferent to the rubbish that the right hon. Gentleman spouts." Since all reactions by Mrs. Beckett to counterarguments are of this negative vein, code 1 is justified.

Code 2: counterarguments are included – neutral

There are no negative statements toward counterarguments but neither are there any positive statements.

*Code 3: counterarguments are included and at least one
of them is explicitly valued*

A single positive statement toward any aspect of any counterargument already qualifies for code 3. There may also be some negative statements but this does not change the code. Give quotes for all positive and negative statements.

Illustration: On July 20, 1998, the Northern Ireland Bill is discussed in the British House of Commons. The Secretary of State for Northern Ireland, Mo Mowlam, introduces the bill on behalf of the Labour government. During her speech she is interrupted by Kevin McNamara. Although he is also a Labour member, he makes the following critical remark: "It would be very wrong if, in the transfer of powers, anyone in this House removed the right of Northern Ireland people to make their own decision on the matter." Mo Mowlam explicitly values this counterargument when she responds: "I hear what my hon. Friend says. From my preparation for the debate, I understand that the power is potentially a reserved one, even though – he is absolutely right – the 1967 Act does not apply. Given that it is a reserved power, the House will still have an opportunity to debate the matter."

Constructive politics

Code 0: positional politics

Speakers sit on their positions.

Code 1: alternative proposal

Use this code if a speaker makes a mediating proposal that does not fit the current agenda but belongs to another agenda. In such cases, the proposal is really not relevant for the current debate but may be taken up in a later debate.

Illustration: During the 1996 debate in the US House of Representatives on an increase in the minimum wage, Representative Campbell (Republican), who opposes the increase but advocates that the working poor may be helped in a better way, makes the following alternative proposal: "If you want to increase the earnings of those at the bottom of the income level, the way to do it is by an increase in the earned income tax credit." Under the earned income tax credit, working poor, under certain conditions, qualify for a cash payment from the government. To increase the earned income tax credit would certainly help the working poor. But within the current debate this proposal is not on the agenda. It may be taken up, however, on another occasion.

Code 2: mediating proposal

Use this code if a speaker makes a mediating proposal within the current agenda.

Illustration: On November 28, 1997, the British House of Commons debates the Wild Mammals (Hunting with Dogs) Bill whose goal is to outlaw the hunting of wild mammals with dogs. Labour MP Michael Foster expresses his strong wish to "vote to ban hunting with dogs," and he states that "during the general election campaign, at the many public meetings that I attended, I also expressed that view. Indeed, I was the only one of four candidates in Worcester who held this view." Yet, despite this strong view, he offers a mediating proposal in order to take account of a grievance of sheep farmers in Wales, who complain about too many foxes on their land. According to Foster, an exemption should be made "that dogs could be used to flush foxes out of cover, where they could be quickly and humanely shot."

References

Achen, Christopher H. 1982, *Interpreting and Using Regression*, Beverly Hills, CA: Sage Publications.

2001, "An Agenda for the New Political Methodology: Microfoundations and ART," paper presented at the Annual Meeting of the American Political Science Association, San Francisco.

Achen, Christopher H. and Snidal, Duncan 1989, "Rational Deterrence Theory and Comparative Case Studies," *World Politics* 41: 143–69.

Ackermann, Bruce and Fishkin, James S. 2002, "Deliberation Day," *Journal of Political Philosophy* 10: 129–52.

Aldrich, John H. and Rohde, David W. 2000, "The Republican Revolution and the House Appropriations Committee," *Journal of Politics* 62: 1–33.

Angell, Richard B. 1964, *Reasoning and Logic*, New York: Appleton-Century-Crofts.

Arnold, Felizitas and Koch, Barbara 2002, "Deliberative Demokratie. Wunsch oder Wirklichkeit? Eine vergleichende empirische Untersuchung der Debatten zur parlamentarischen Initiative 93.434, Schwangerschaftsabbruch. Revision des Strafgesetzbuches," master's thesis, Institute of Political Science, University of Bern.

Arrow, Kenneth J. 1973, "Rawls's Concept of Just Saving," *Swedish Journal of Economics* 75: 323–35.

Austen-Smith, David 1992, "Strategic Models of Talk in Political Decision-Making," *International Political Science Review* 13: 124–52.

1995, "Modeling Deliberative Democracy," working paper.

Austen-Smith, David and Feddersen, Timothy J. 2002, "Deliberation and Voting Rules," working paper.

Baccaro, Lucio 2001, "Aggregative and Deliberative Decision-Making Procedures: A Comparison of Two Southern Italian Factories," *Politics and Society* 29: 243–71.

Bächtiger, André 2004, "The Real World of Deliberation: A Comparative Study of its Favorable Conditions," Ph.D. dissertation, Institute of Political Science, University of Bern.

Baltes, Paul B., Staudinger, Ursula B., and Lindenberger, Ulman 1999, "Lifespan Psychology. Theory and Application to Intellectual Functioning," *Annual Review of Psychology* 50: 471–507.

Basu, Sammy 1999, "Dialogic Ethics and the Virtue of Humor," *Journal of Political Philosophy* 7: 378–403.

Benhabib, Seyla 1996, "Toward a Deliberative Model of Democratic Legitimacy," in Seyla Benhabib (ed.), *Democracy and Difference. Contesting the Boundaries of the Political*, Princeton: Princeton University Press, 67–94.

Beyme, Klaus von 1997, *Der Gesetzgeber. Der Bundestag als Entscheidungszentrum*, Opladen: Westdeutscher Verlag.

  1998, *The Legislator: German Parliament as a Centre of Political Decision-Making.* Aldershot: Ashgate.

Bobbio, Luigi 2002, "Smaltimento dei rifiuti e democrazia deliberativa," working paper, no. 1, Department of Political Studies, University of Turin.

Bogaards, Matthijs 2000, "The Uneasy Relationship between Empirical and Normative Types in Consociational Theory," *Journal of Theoretical Politics* 12: 395–423.

Bohman, James 1996, *Public Deliberation: Pluralism, Complexity and Democracy*, Cambridge, MA: Massachusetts Institute of Technology Press.

Bohman, James and Rehg, William 1997, "Introduction," in James Bohman and William Rehg (eds.), *Deliberative Democracy. Essays on Reason and Politics*, Cambridge, MA: Massachusetts Institute of Technology Press, ix.

Bowler, Shaun, Farrell, David M., and Katz, Richard S. (eds.) 1999, *Party Discipline and Parliamentary Government*, Columbus: Ohio State University Press.

Bryce, James 1921, *Modern Democracies*, 2 vols., New York: Macmillan.

Budge, Ian 2001, *Mapping Policy Preferences: Estimates for Parties, Electors, and Governments*, Oxford: Oxford University Press.

Burke, Edmund 1987, *Reflections on the Revolution in France*, New York: Macmillan.

Button, Mark and Mattson, Kevin 1999, "Deliberative Democracy in Practice: Challenges and Prospects for Civic Deliberation," *Polity* 31: 609–37.

Chambers, Simone 1995, "Discourse and Democratic Practices," in Stephen K. White (ed.), *The Cambridge Companion to Habermas*, Cambridge: Cambridge University Press.

1996, *Reasonable Democracy: Jürgen Habermas and the Politics of Discourse*, Ithaca: Cornell University Press.

1999, "Talking versus Voting: Legitimacy, Efficiency, and Deliberative Democracy," unpublished manuscript, University of Colorado.

2003, "Deliberative Democratic Theory," *Annual Review of Political Science* 6: 307–26.

2004, "Measuring Publicity's Effect: Reconciling Empirical Research and Normative Theory," paper presented at the Conference on Empirical Approaches to Deliberative Politics, European University Institute, Florence, May 21–22.

Checkel, Jeffrey T. 1999, "Norms, Institutions, and National Identity in Contemporary Europe," *International Studies Quarterly* 43: 43–83.

Chwe, Michael Suk-Young 1999, "Minority Voting Rights Can Maximize Majority Welfare," *American Political Science Review* 93: 85–96.

Cohen, Jacob A. 1960, "Coefficient of Agreement for Nominal Scales," *Educational and Psychological Measures* 20: 37–46.

1989, "Deliberation and Democratic Legitimacy," in Alan Hamlin and Philip Pettit (eds.), *The Good Polity: Normative Analysis of the State*, Oxford: Blackwell, 17–34.

Cohen, Joshua 1996, "Procedure and Substance in Deliberative Democracy," in Benhabib (ed.), 95–119.

Cox, Gary W. and McCubbins, Mathew D. 1993, *Legislative Leviathan: Party Government in the House*, Berkeley: University of California Press.

Czada, Roland 2000, "Konkordanz, Korporatismus und Politikverflechtung: Dimensionen der Verhandlungsdemokratie," in Everhard Holtmann und Helmut Voelzkow (eds.), *Zwischen Wettbewerbs- und Verhandlungsdemokratie*, Opladen, Wiesbaden: Westdeutscher Verlag, 23–49.

Daele, Wolfgang van den 2001, "Von moralischer Kommunikation zur Kommunikation über Moral," *Zeitschrift für Soziologie* 30: 4–22.

Dästner, Christian 1995, *Die Geschäftsordnung des Vermittlungsausschusses*, Berlin: Duncker und Humblot.

della Porta, Donatella 2003, "Democracy in Movement: Organizational Dilemma and Globalization from Below," paper presented at the Conference on Les Mouvements Alter/Anti-mondialisation, Paris.

2004, "Deliberation in Movement: Why and How to Study Deliberative Democracy and Social Movements," paper presented at the Conference on Empirical Approaches to Deliberative Politics, European University Institute, Florence, May 21–22.

Derrida, Jacques 1995, *On the Name*, trans. John P. Leavey, David Wood, Jr., and Ian McLeod, Stanford: Stanford University Press.

Deutsch, Morton 1985, *Distributive Justice: A Social-Psychological Perspective*, New Haven, CT: Yale University Press.

Diermeier, Daniel and Feddersen, Timothy J. 1998, "Cohesion in Legislatures and the Vote of Confidence Procedure," *American Political Science Review* 92: 611–38.

DiMaggio, Paul J. and Powell, Walter W. 1991, "Introduction," in Walter W. Powell and Paul J. DiMaggio (eds.), *The New Institutionalism in Organizational Analysis*, Chicago: University of Chicago Press, 1–38.

Döring, Herbert 1995, "Time as a Scarce Resource: Government Control of the Agenda," in Herbert Döring (ed.), *Parliaments and Majority Rule in Western Europe*, Frankfurt: Campus Verlag.

Dryzek, John S. 1990, *Discursive Democracy. Politics, Policy, and Political Science*, Cambridge: Cambridge University Press.

1992, "How Far Is It From Virginia and Rochester to Frankfurt? Public Choice as Critical Theory," *British Journal of Political Science* 22: 397–417.

2000, *Deliberative Democracy and Beyond*, Oxford: Oxford University Press.

2004, "Handle with Care: The Deadly Hermeneutics of Deliberative Instrumentation," paper presented at the Conference on Empirical Approaches to Deliberative Politics, European University Institute, Florence, May 21–22.

Dryzek, John S. and Braithwaite, Valerie 2000, "On the Prospects for Democratic Deliberation: Values Analysis Applied to Australian Politics," *Political Psychology* 21: 241–66.

Dunn, William N. 1981, *Public Policy Analysis*, Englewood Cliffs, NJ: Prentice-Hall.

Eckstein, Harry 1975, "Case Study and Theory in Political Science," in Fred I. Greenstein and Nelson W. Polsby (eds.), *Handbook of Political Science*, vol. 7: *Strategies of Inquiry*, Reading, MA: Addison-Wesley.

Ehrensperger, Elisabeth 2004, "Deliberation, Legitimacy, and Human Rights," paper presented at the Conference on Empirical Approaches to Deliberative Politics, European University Institute, Florence, May 21–22.

Elgström, Ole and Jönsson, Christer 2000, "Negotiation in the European Union: Bargaining or Problem-Solving?" *Journal of European Public Policy*, special issue: Negotiation and Policy-Making in the European Union – Processes, System and Order, 7: 684–704.

Elster, Jon 1998a, "Introduction," in Jon Elster (ed.), *Deliberative Democracy*, Cambridge: Cambridge University Press, 1–18.

1998b, "Deliberation and Constitution Making," in Elster (ed.), 97–122.

Feldman, Stanley, and Steenbergen, Marco R. 2001, "The Humanitarian Foundation of Public Support for Social Welfare," *American Journal of Political Science* 45: 658–77.

Fenno, Richard F. 1978, *Home Style: House Members in their Districts*, Boston: Little, Brown.

Fiorina, Morris P. 1981, *Retrospective Voting in American National Elections*, New Haven, CT: Yale University Press.

Fishkin, James S. 1991, *Democracy and Deliberation*, New Haven, CT: Yale University Press.

1997, *The Voice of the People*, New Haven, CT: Yale University Press.

Fishkin, James S. and Laslett, Peter (eds.) 2002a, "Special Issue: Debating Deliberative Democracy," *Journal of Political Philosophy* 10: 125–229.

2002b, "Introduction," in Fishkin and Laslett (eds.), pp. 125–6.

Fishkin, James S. and Luskin, Robert C. 2004, "Experimenting with a Democratic Deliberative Polling and Public Opinion," paper presented at the Conference on Empirical Approaches to Deliberative Politics, European University Institute, Florence, May 21–22.

Follesdal, Andreas 2004, "Looking for Deliberative Democracy," paper presented at the Conference on Empirical Approaches to Deliberative Politics, European University Institute, Florence, May 21–22.

Gabardi, Wayne 2001, "Contemporary Models of Democracy," *Polity* 33: 547–68.

Garner, Robert 1998, "Animal Welfare," in Philip Cowley (ed.), *Conscience and Parliament*, London: Frank Cass, 117–31.

George, Alexander L. and McKeown, Timothy J. 1985, "Case Studies and Theories of Organizational Decision Making," *Advances in Information Processing in Organizations* 2: 21–58.

Gerhards, Jürgen 1997, "Diskursive versus liberale Öffentlichkeit. Eine empirische Auseinandersetzung mit Jürgen Habermas," *Kölner Zeitschrift für Soziologie und Sozialpsychologie* 49: 1–34.

Goodin, Robert E. 1996, "Institutionalizing Public Interest," *American Political Science Review* 90: 331–43.

2004, "Sequencing Deliberative Moments," paper presented at the Conference on Empirical Approaches to Deliberative Politics, European University Institute, Florence, May 21–22.

Gutmann, Amy and Thompson, Dennis 1990, "Moral Conflict and Political Consensus," *Ethics* 101: 64–88.

1996, *Democracy and Disagreement*, Cambridge, MA: Belknap Press of Harvard University Press.

2000, "Why Deliberative Democracy Is Different," *Social Philosophy and Policy* 17: 161–80.

2002, "Deliberative Democracy Beyond Process," in Fishkin and Laslett (eds.), 153–74.

Habermas, Jürgen 1981, *Theorie des kommunikativen Handelns*, 2 vols., Frankfurt a.M.: Suhrkamp.

1983, *Moralbewußtsein und kommunikatives Handeln*, Frankfurt a.M.: Suhrkamp.

1984, *Vorstudien und Ergänzungen zur Theorie des kommunikativen Handelns*, Frankfurt a.M.: Suhrkamp.

1990, *Strukturwandel der Öffentlichkeit. Untersuchungen zu einer Kategorie der bürgerlichen Gesellschaft*, Frankfurt a.M.: Suhrkamp.

1991, *Erläuterungen zur Diskursethik*, Frankfurt a.M.: Suhrkamp.

1992, *Faktizität und Geltung: Beiträge zur Diskurstheorie des Rechts und des demokratischen Rechtsstaats*, Frankfurt a.M.: Suhrkamp.

1996a, *Between Facts and Norms. Contributions to a Discourse Theory of Law and Democracy*, trans. William Regh, Cambridge, MA: MIT Press.

1996b, *Die Einbeziehung des Anderen. Studien zur politischen Theorie*, Frankfurt a.M.: Suhrkamp.

Hall, Peter A. and Taylor, Rosemary C. R. 1996, "Political Science and the Three New Institutionalisms," *Political Studies* 44: 936–57.

Hammond, Thomas H. and Butler, Christopher K. 2003, "Some Complex Answers to the Simple Question 'Do Institutions Matter?': Policy Choice and Policy Change in Presidential and Parliamentary Systems," *Journal of Theoretical Politics* 15: 145–200.

Hasselsweiler, Ekkehart 1981, *Der Vermittlungsausschuss: Verfassungsgrundlagen und Staatspraxis*, Berlin: Duncker und Humblot.

Hauptmann, Emily 2001, "Can Less Be More? Leftist Deliberative Democrats' Critique of Participatory Democracy," *Polity* 33: 397–421.

Holsti, Ole R. 1969, *Content Analysis for the Social Sciences and Humanities*, Reading, MA: Addison-Wesley.

Holzinger, Katharina 2001, "Verhandeln statt Argumentieren oder Verhandeln durch Argumentieren? Eine empirische Analyse auf der Basis der Sprechakttheorie," *Politische Vierteljahresschrift* 42: 414–46.

Huber, Evelyne and Stephens, John D. 2001, *Development and Crisis of the Welfare State. Parties and Politics in Global Markets*, Chicago: University of Chicago Press.

Hug, Simon and Sciarini, Pascal 1995. "Switzerland – Still a Paradigmatic Case?" in Gerald Schneider, Patricia A. Weitsman, and Thomas Bernauer (eds.), *Towards a New Europe. Stops and Starts in Regional Integration*, Westport, CT and London: Praeger, 55–74.

Hug, Simon and Tsebelis, George 2002, "Veto Players and Referendums Around the World," *Journal of Theoretical Politics* 14: 465–516.

Huyse, Lucien 1971, *Pacificatie, passiviteit en verzuiling in the Belgische politiek*, Antwerp: Standaard Wetenschappelijke Uitgeverij.

Immergut, Ellen M. 1992, *Health Politics: Interests and Institutions in Western Europe*, Cambridge: Cambridge University Press.

Ismayr, Wolfgang 2001, *Der Deutsche Bundestag im politischen System der Bundesrepublik*, Leske und Budrich.

Janis, Irving L. 1982, *Groupthink: Psychological Studies of Policy Decisions and Fiascos*, 2nd edn, Boston: Houghton Mifflin.

Johnson, James 1998, "Arguing for Deliberation: Some Skeptical Considerations," in Jon Elster (ed.), *Deliberative Democracy*, Cambridge: Cambridge University Press.

Kaiser, André 1997, "Types of Democracy. From Classical to New Institutionalism," *Journal of Theoretical Politics* 9: 419–44.

Kameda, Tatsuya, Hulbert, Lorne, and Tindale, R. Scott 2002, "Procedural and Agenda Effects on Political Decisions by Small Groups," in V. C. Ottati, R. S. Tindale, J. Edwards, F. B. Bryant, L. Heath, D. C. O'Connell, Y. Suarez-Balcazar, and E. J. Posavac (eds.), *The Social Psychology of Politics*, New York: Kluwer Academic/Plenum Publishers, 215–40.

Kant, Immanuel 1975, *Werke in sechs Bänden*, ed. Wilhelm Weischedel, vol. VI: *Der Streit der Fakultäten*, Darmstadt: Wissenschaftliche Buchhandlung.

    1984, *Grundlegung der Metaphysik der Sitten*, in *Werkausgabe*, vol. VII, Frankfurt a.M.: Suhrkamp.

    1994, *Critik der practischen Vernunft*, reprint of the 1788 edition, London: Routledge.

Katz, Irwin, and Hass, R. Glenn 1988, "Racial Ambivalence and American Value Conflict: Correlational and Priming Studies of Dual Cognitive Structures," *Journal of Personality and Social Psychology* 55: 893–905.

Keohane, Robert O. 2001, "Governance in a Partially Globalized World. Presidential Address, American Political Science Association, 2000," *American Political Science Review* 95: 1–13.

Kies, Raphael and Jansen, Davy 2004, "Measuring Deliberative Potentialities on Online Forums," paper presented at the Conference on Empirical Approaches to Deliberative Politics, European University Institute, Florence, May 21–22.

Kitschelt, Herbert 1992, "The Formation of Party Systems in Eastern Central Europe," *Politics and Society*, 20: 7–50.

Koch, Barbara 2002, "Die Bedeutung des Standorts in der Diskursethik. Eine Auseinandersetzung mit dem Begriff 'Standort' von Hannah Arendt in bezug auf die Diskursethik von Jürgen Habermas," unpublished seminar paper, Institute of Political Science, University of Bern.

Kriesi, Hanspeter 1998, *Le système politique suisse*, Paris: Economica.

2001, "Die Rolle der Öffentlichkeit im politischen Entscheidungsprozess. Ein konzeptueller Rahmen für ein international vergleichendes Forschungsprojekt," Veröffentlichungsreihe der Arbeitsgruppe Politische Öffentlichkeit und Mobilisierung, Wissenschaftszentrums Berlin für Sozialforschung.

2004, "Argument-based Strategies in Direct-democratic Vote. The Swiss Experience," paper presented at the Conference on Empirical Approaches to Deliberative Politics, European University Institute, Florence, May 21–22.

Lamnek, Siegfried 1995, *Qualitative Sozialforschung*, vol. II: *Methoden und Techniken*, Weinheim: Psychologie Verlags-Union.

Landis, J. Richard and Koch, Gary G. 1977, "The Measurement of Observer Agreement for Categorical Data," *Biometrics* 33: 159–74.

Lascher, Edward L. 1996, "Assessing Legislative Deliberation: A Preface to Empirical Analysis," *Legislative Studies Quarterly* 21: 501–19.

Lehmbruch, Gerhard 1967, *Proporzdemokratie. Politisches System und Politische Kultur in der Schweiz und in Oesterreich*, Tübingen: Mohr.

2002, "Quasi-consociationalism in German Politics. Negotiated Democracy and the Legacy of the Westphalian Peace," in Steiner and Ertman (eds.), 175–94.

Lessing, Gotthold Ephraim 1853, *Lessings Werke in sechs Bänden*, vol. VI: *Anti-Goez*, Leipzig: Verlag von Gustav Fock.

Lewis-Beck, Michael 1988, *Economics and Elections: The Major Western Democracies*, Ann Arbor: University of Michigan Press.

Lhotta, Roland 2000, "Konsens und Konkurrenz in der konstitutionellen Oekonomie bikameraler Verhandlungsdemokratie: Der Vermittlungsausschuss als effiziente Institution politischer Deliberation," in Everhard Holtmann and Helmut Voelzkow (eds.), *Zwischen Wettbewerbs- und Verhandlungsdemokratie*, Opladen: Westdeutscher Verlag.

Lijphart, Arend 1968, *The Politics of Accommodation. Pluralism and Democracy in the Netherlands*, Berkeley: University of California Press.

1975, "The Comparable-Cases Strategy in Comparative Research," *Comparative Political Studies* 8: 158–77.

1984, *Democracies. Patterns of Majoritarian and Consensus Government in Twenty-One Countries*, New Haven, CT: Yale University Press.

1985, *Power-Sharing in South Africa*, Berkeley: Institute of International Studies, University of California Press.

1996, "The Puzzle of Indian Democracy: A Consociational Interpretation," *American Political Science Review* 90: 258–68.

1999, *Patterns of Democracy. Government Forms and Performance in Thirty-Six Countries*, New Haven, CT: Yale University Press.

Lind, Martin 2000, "Die Diskursethik von Jürgen Habermas: Eine Transformation der kantischen Moralphilosophie?" unpublished seminar paper, Institute of Political Science, University of Bern.

Linder, Wolf, 1999, *Schweizerische Demokratie: Institutionen – Prozesse – Perspektiven*, Bern, Stuttgart, and Vienna: Haupt.

Lipset, Seymour Martin and Rokkan, Stein (eds.) 1967, *Party Systems and Voter Alignments*, New York: Free Press.

Loomis, Burdett A. 1990, *Dear Colleagues: Civility and Deliberation in the U.S. Senate*, Washington, DC: Brookings Institution.

Lupia, Arthur 2002, "Deliberation Disconnected: What It Takes to Improve Civic Competence," *Law and Contemporary Problems* 65: 133–50.

Luskin, Robert C. and Fishkin, James S. 2002, "Deliberation and 'Better Citizens'," paper presented at the ECPR Joint Sessions, Turin, March 23–7.

Macedo, Stephen 1990, "The Politics of Justification," *Political Theory* 18: 280–304.

1999, "Introduction," in Stephen Macedo (ed.), *Deliberative Politics. Essays on "Democracy and Disagreement,"* Oxford: Oxford University Press, 3–14.

Manin, Bernard 1987, "On Legitimacy and Deliberation," *Political Theory* 15: 338–68.

March, James G. and Olson, Johan P. 1989, *Rediscovering Institutions. The Organizational Basis of Politics*, New York: Free Press.

1998, "The Institutional Dynamics of International Political Orders," *International Organization* 52: 729–57.

Mason, Andrew 1993, *Explaining Political Disagreement*, Cambridge: Cambridge University Press.

McGarry, John (ed.) 2001, *Northern Ireland and the Divided World*, Oxford: Oxford University Press.

McGraw, Kathleen M. 1991, "Managing Blame: An Experimental Test of the Effects of Political Accounts," *American Political Science Review* 85: 1133–57.

McKeown, Timothy J. 1999, "Case Studies and the Statistical Worldview: Review of King, Keohane, and Verba's Designing Social Inquiry: Scientific Inference in Qualitative Research," *International Organization* 53: 161–90.

Mendelberg, Tali 2002, "The Deliberative Citizen: Theory and Evidence," in Michael X. Delli Carpini, Leonie Huddy, and Robert Y. Shapiro (eds.), *Political Decision Making, Deliberation and Participation*, Amsterdam: Elsevier, 151–93.

Mill, John Stuart 1991, *Considerations on Representative Government*, Buffalo, NY: Promethus Books.

1998, *Utilitarianism*, Oxford: Oxford University Press.

Morris, Martin 2001, "Deliberation and Deconstruction: Two Views on the Space of a Post-National Democracy," *Canadian Journal of Political Science* 34: 763–90.

Mouffe, Chantal 1999, "Deliberative Democracy or Agonistic Pluralism?" *Social Research* 3: 745–58.

Müller, Jörg-Paul 1993, *Demokratische Gerechtigkeit. Eine Studie zur Legitimität rechtlicher und politischer Ordnung*, München: dtv.

1999, *Der politische Mensch – menschliche Politik. Demokratie und Menschenrechte im staatlichen und globalen Kontext*, Basel: Helbing und Lichtenhahn; Munich: C. H. Beck.

Nanz, Patrizia and Steffek, Jens 2004, "Assessing the Democratic Quality of Deliberation – Criteria and Research Strategies," paper presented at the Conference on Empirical Approaches to Deliberative Politics, European University Institute, Florence, May 21–22.

Neblo, Michael 2004, "On the Circulation of Communicative Power in Society: A Structural Taxonomy of Deliberation with Examples," paper presented at the Conference on Empirical Approaches to Deliberative Politics, European University, Florence, May 21–22.

Neidhart, Leonhard 1970, *Plebiszit und pluralitäre Demokratie*, Bern: Franke Verlag.

Niño, Carlos Santiago 1996, *The Constitution of Deliberative Democracy*, New Haven, CT: Yale University Press.

Noel, Sidney J. R. 1990, *Patrons, Clients, Brokers: Ontario Society and Politics 1791–1896*, Toronto: University of Toronto Press.

North, Douglas C. 1992, *Transaction Costs, Institutions, and Economic Performance*, San Francisco, CA: ICS Press.

Orlie, Melissa 1994, "Thoughtless Assertion and Political Deliberation," *American Political Science Review* 88: 684–95.

Ostrom, Elinor 1998, "A Behavioral Approach to the Rational Choice Theory of Collective Action," *American Political Science Review* 92: 1–22.

Pelletier, David, Kraak, Vivica, McCullum, Christine, Uusitalo, Ulla, and Rich, Robert 1999, "The Shaping of Collective Values through Deliberative Democracy: An Empirical Study from New York's North Country," *Policy Sciences* 32: 103–31.

Pellizzoni, Luigi 2002, "The Myth of the Best Argument: Power, Deliberation and Reason," *British Journal of Sociology* 52: 59–86.

Plato 1997, *Complete Works*, ed. John M. Cooper, Indianapolis and Cambridge: Hackett Publishing Company.

Posser, Diether 1992, "Aussenpolitik und Völkerrecht im Vermittlungs-ausschuss: drei Sitzungen im Jahre 1979," in Stefan Diekwisch und Torsten Wolfgram (eds.), *Recht und Pflicht: von der Freiheit eines Rechts-politiker*, Ronnenberg: Grütter, 86–90.

Post, Jerrold M. 1980, "The Seasons of a Leader's Life: Influences of the Life Cycle on Political Behavior," *Political Psychology* 2: 35–49.

Powell, Bingham G., Jr. and Whitten, Guy D. 1993, "A Cross-National Analy-sis of Economic Voting: Taking Account of the Political Context," *American Journal of Political Science* 37: 391–411.

Przeworski, Adam and Teune, Henry 1970, *The Logic of Comparative Social Enquiry*, New York: Wiley-Interscience.

Ragin, Charles C. 2000, *Fuzzy-Set Social Science*, Chicago: University of Chicago Press.

Rawls, John 1971, *A Theory of Justice*, Cambridge, MA: Belknap Press of Harvard University Press.

1985, "Justice as Fairness," *Philosophy and Public Affairs* 14: 223–51.

1996, *Political Liberalism*, New York: Columbia University Press.

Reynolds, Andrew 1999, *Electoral Systems and Democratization in Southern Africa*, Oxford: Oxford University Press.

2000, "Majoritarian or Power-Sharing Government," in Markus M. L. Crepaz, Thomas A. Koelble, and David Wilsford (eds.), *Democracy and Institutions. The Life Work of Arend Lijphart*, Ann Arbor: University of Michigan Press, 155–96.

(ed.) 2002, *The Architecture of Democracy. Constitutional Design, Conflict Management, and Democracy*, Oxford: Oxford University Press.

Risse, Thomas 2000, "Let's Argue! Communicative Action in World Politics," *International Organization* 54: 1–39.

Roberts, Nancy 1997, "Public Deliberation: An Alternative Approach to Crafting Policy and Setting Direction," *Public Administration* 57: 124–32.

Rosenberg, Shawn W. 2003, "Reason, Communicative Competence and Democratic Deliberation: Do Citizens Have the Capacities to Effec-tively Participate in Deliberative Decision-Making?" paper presented at the Annual Convention of the American Political Science Associa-tion, Philadelphia, August 27–31.

2004, "Examining Three Conceptions of Deliberative Democracy. A Field Experiment," paper presented at the Conference on Empirical Approaches to Deliberative Politics, European University Institute, Florence, May 21–22.

Rousseau, Jean-Jacques 1966, *Du contrat social*, Paris: Garnier-Flammarion.

Ryfe, David Michael 2002, "The Practice of Deliberative Democracy: A Study of 16 Deliberative Organizations," *Political Communication* 19: 359–77.

Saalfeld, Thomas 2000, "Members of Parliament and Governments in West-
    ern Europe: Agency Relations and Problems of Oversight," *European
    Journal of Political Research* 37: 353–76.
Sabatier, Paul 1998, "The Advocacy Coalition Framework: Revisions and
    Relevance for Europe," *Journal of European Public Policy* 5: 98–130.
Sanders, Lynn M. 1997, "Against Deliberation," *Political Theory* 25:
    347–75.
Scharpf, Fritz W. 1997, *Games Real Actors Play. Actor-Centered Institution-
    alism in Policy Research*, Boulder, CO: Westview Press.
Schimmelfennig, Frank 2001, "The Community Trap: Liberal Norms,
    Rhetorical Action, and the Eastern Enlargement of the European
    Union," *International Organization* 55: 47–80.
Schindler, Peter 1999, *Datenhandbuch zur Geschichte des deutschen
    Bundestages: 1949–1999,* Baden-Baden: Nomos.
Schmidt, Manfred G. 2003, *Political Institutions in the Federal Republic of
    Germany,* Oxford: Oxford University Press.
Schmidt, Volker H. 2000, *Bedingte Gerechtigkeit: soziologische Analysen und
    philosophische Theorien,* Frankfurt a.M.: Campus.
Scott, John T., Matland, Richard E., Michelbach, Philip A., and Bornstein,
    Brian H. 2001, "Just Deserts: An Experimental Study of Distributive
    Justice Norms," *American Journal of Political Science* 45: 749–67.
Searing, Donald D. 1994, *Westminster's World. Understanding Political Roles,*
    Cambridge, MA: Harvard University Press.
Searing, Donald D., Conover, Pamela Johnston, and Crew, Ivor 2004, "Study-
    ing 'Everyday Talk' in the Deliberative System. Does Democratic Dis-
    cussion Make Better Citizens?" paper presented at the Conference on
    Empirical Approaches to Deliberative Politics, European University
    Institute, Florence, May 21–22.
Sebeok, Thomas A. (ed.) 1986, *Encyclopedic Dictionary of Semiotics*, Berlin,
    New York, and Amsterdam: Mouton de Gruyter.
Shapiro, Daniel 1997, "Can Old-Age Social Insurance be Justified?" in Ellen
    Frankel Paul, Fred D. Miller, Jr., and Jeffrey Paul (eds.), *The Just Society,*
    Cambridge: Cambridge University Press, 116–44.
Shapiro, Ian 1999, "Enough of Deliberation. Politics is about Interests and
    Power," in Stephen Macedo (ed.), 28–38.
Siegel, Sidney 1956, *Nonparametric Statistics for the Behavioral Sciences,* New
    York: McGraw-Hill.
Smith, Adam 1991, *The Wealth of Nations*, New York: Alfred A. Knopf.
    2002, *The Theory of Moral Sentiments*, Cambridge: Cambridge University
    Press.
Spörndli, Markus 2004, "Diskurs und Entscheidung. Eine empirische Analy-
    se kommunikativen Handelns im deutschen Vermittlungsausschuss,"

Ph.D. dissertation, Institute of Political Science, University of Bern. Published 2004, Wiesbaden: VS Verlag für Sozialwissenschaften.

Steenbergen, Marco R., Bächtiger, André, and Steiner, Jürg 2004, "Toward a Political Psychology of Deliberation," paper presented at the Conference on Empirical Approaches to Deliberative Politics, European University Institute, Florence, May 21–22.

Steiner, Jürg 1970, *Gewaltlose Politik und kulturelle Vielfalt. Hypothesen entwickelt am Beispiel der Schweiz*, Bern: Paul Haupt.

1974, *Amicable Agreement Versus Majority Rule. Conflict Resolution in Switzerland*, Chapel Hill: University of North Carolina Press.

1998, *European Democracies*, 4th edn, New York: Longman.

Steiner, Jürg and Dorff, Robert H. 1988, "Analysis of Decision Cases," in Francis G. Castles, Franz Lehner, and Manfred G. Schmidt (eds.), *Managing Mixed Economies*, Berlin and New York: Walter de Gruyter.

Steiner, Jürg and Ertman, Thomas (eds.) 2002, *Consociationalism and Corporatism in Western Europe. Still the Politics of Accommodation?* Amsterdam: Boom Publishing (also published as special issue of *Acta Politica* 37, Spring/Summer 2002).

Stokes, Donald E. 1963, "Spatial Models of Party Competition," *American Political Science Review* 57: 368–77.

Strom, Kaare 2000, "Delegation and Accountability in Parliamentary Democracies," *European Journal of Political Research* 37: 261–89.

Sulkin, Tracy and Simon, Adam F. 2001, "Habermas in the Lab: A Study of Deliberation in an Experimental Setting," *Political Psychology* 22: 809–26.

Sunstein, Cass R. 1997, "Deliberation, Democracy, Disagreement," in Ron Bontekoe and Marietta Stepaniants (eds.), *Justice and Democracy: Cross-Cultural Perspectives*, Honolulu: University of Hawaii Press.

2002, "The Law of Group Polarization," in Fishkin and Laslett (eds.), 175–95.

Terchek, Ronald J. and Moore, David K. 2000, "Recovering the Political Aristotle: A Critical Response to Smith," *American Political Science Review* 94: 905–11.

Thelen, Kathleen and Steinmo, Sven 1992, "Historical Institutionalism in Comparative Politics," in Sven Steinmo, Kathleen Thelen, and Frank Longstreth, *Structuring Politics: Historical Institutionalism in Comparative Analysis*, Cambridge: Cambridge University Press.

Trechsel, Alexander H. and Sciarini, Pascal 1998, "Direct Democracy in Switzerland: Do Elites Matter?" *European Journal of Political Research* 33: 99–124.

Tsebelis, George 1995, "Decision Making in Political Systems: Veto Players in Presidentialism, Parliamentarism, Multicameralism and Multipartyism," *British Journal of Political Science* 25: 289–325.

2002, *Veto Players. How Political Institutions Work*, Princeton: Princeton University Press.

Tsebelis, George and Money, Jeannette 1997, *Bicameralism*, Cambridge: Cambridge University Press.

Ulbert, Cornelia, Risse, Thomas, and Müller, Harald 2004, "Arguing and Bargaining in Multilateral Negotiations," paper presented at the Conference on Empirical Approaches to Deliberative Politics, European University Institute, Florence, May 21–22.

Van Evera, Stephen 1997, *Guide to Methods for Students of Political Science*, Ithaca: Cornell University Press.

Varga, Christian 2001, "Grundlagen der Habermasschen Diskursethik," unpublished seminar paper, Institute of Political Science, University of Bern.

Voigt, Stefan 2001, "The Consequences of Popular Participation in Constitutional Choice – Towards a Comparative Analysis," paper presented at the Conference on Deliberation and Decision: Discourse Ethics Meets Constitutional Economists, Wittenberg Center for Global Ethics, September 24–26.

Walthier, Joseph B. and D'Addario, Keyle P. 2001, "The Impacts of Emotions on Message Interpretation in Computer-Mediated Communication," *Social Science Computer Review* 19: 324–47.

Wiesli, Reto and Linder, Wolf 2000, *Repräsentation, Artikulation und Durchsetzung kantonaler Interessen in Stände- und Nationalrat*, Institut für Politikwissenschaft, Universität Bern.

Young, Iris Marion 2001, "Activist Challenges to Deliberative Democracy," *Political Theory* 29: 670–90.

Index

Achen, Christopher H., 100, 153
Ackermann, Bruce, 22, 47
actor-centered approach, *see* institutionalism
Afghanistan, 167
agonistic confrontation, 39
Aldrich, John H., 101, 124
Althusius, Johannes, 79
Andeweg, Rudy, 11
anecdotal evidence, 1, 11, 13, 15, 42
Angell, Richard B., 21
Arendt, Hannah, 22
arguing, *see* deliberation
argument, force of the better, 2, 4, 5, 11, 13, 15, 17, 18, 23–5, 26, 28, 30, 40, 44, 48, 49, 50, 54, 56, 80, 88
Aristotle, 28, 87
Armingeon, Klaus, 80
Arnold, Felizitas, 72–3
Arrow, Kenneth J., 148
Austen-Smith, David, 8, 82, 91, 156
Australia, 44
Austria, 8–11, 61, 79, 86
authenticity, *see* truthfulness

Baccaro, Luico, 20, 45–6, 47
Baltes, Paul B., 154
bargaining, 1, 4–5, 11, 13–14, 15, 23–4, 49, 50, 52, 59, 77, 80, 88, 129, 167
    definition of, 23–4
Basu, Sammy, 40–1, 70

Belgium, 8–11, 79, 86
Benhabib, Seyla, 19
Beyme, Klaus von, 89, 140, 142, 144
Bobbio, Luigi, 51
Bogaards, Matthijs, 10, 12
Bohman, James, 26
Bosnia-Herzegovina, 15, 167
Bowler, Shaun, 102
Braithwaite, Valerie, 17, 42, 44
Bryce, James, 32
Budge, Ian, 104
Burke, Edmund, 87
Butler, Christopher K., 104
Button, Mark, 49

Canada, 47–9
Carver, Terrell, 39
case selection, 100–7, 143–4
categorical imperative, 30–1
Chambers, Simone, 19, 23, 26, 42, 47–9, 53, 91, 92, 169
cheap talk, 3, 8, 9, 91, 131, 148, 167
Checkel, Jeffrey T., 88
Chwe, Michael Suk-Young, 82
civil society, 37
civility, norms of, 87, 125, 129
civilizing effect, 88
cognitive development, 18, 20, 43, 76, 80, 162
Cohen, Jacob, 17, 19, 25, 26
Cohen, Joshua, 94